D0201278

BOOKS BY DONALD E. WESTLAKE

Crime Novels
The Mercenaries (also
   published as *The Cutie*) (1960)
Killing Time (1961)
361 (1962)
Killy (1963)
Pity Him Afterwards (1964)
The Comedy Is Finished (2012)

Comic Crime Novels
The Fugitive Pigeon (1965)
The Busy Body (1966)
The Spy in the Ointment (1966)
God Save the Mark (1967)
Who Stole Sassi Manoon? (1968)
Somebody Owes Me
   Money (1969)
Cops and Robbers (1972)
Help I Am Being Held
   Prisoner (1974)
Two Much (1975)
Dancing Aztecs (1976)
Enough (1977)
Castle in the Air (1980)
High Adventure (1985)
Trust Me on This (1988)
Baby, Would I Lie? (1994)
Smoke (1995)
Put a Lid On It (2002)

Dortmunder Novels
The Hot Rock (1970)
Bank Shot (1972)
Jimmy the Kid (1974)
Nobody's Perfect (1977)
Why Me (1983)
Good Behavior (1986)
Drowned Hopes (1990)
Don't Ask (1993)
What's the Worst That Could
   Happen? (1996)
Bad News (2001)
The Road to Ruin (2004)
Thieves' Dozen: Stories (2004)
Watch Your Back! (2005)
What's So Funny? (2007)
Get Real (2009)

Novels
Up Your Banners (1969)
Adios, Scheherazade (1970)
I Gave at the Office (1971)

Brothers Keepers (1975)
Kahawa (1981)
A Likely Story (1984)
Sacred Monster (1989)
Humans (1992)
The Ax (1997)
The Hook (2000)
Money for Nothing (2003)
Memory (2010)

Western
Gangway! (with Brian Garfield)
   (1973)

Juvenile
Philip (1967)

Short Stories
The Curious Facts Preceding
   My Execution and Other
   Fictions (1968)
Levine (1984)
Tomorrow's Crimes (1989)
A Good Story and Other Stories
   (1999)

Nonfiction
Under an English Heaven (1972)
The Getaway Car (2014)

Anthology
Once against the Law (coedited
   with William Tenn) (1968)
Murderous Schemes (coedited
   with J. Madison Davis) (1996)

Writing as Richard Stark

Parker Novels
The Hunter (1962)
The Man with the Getaway
   Face (1963)
The Outfit (1963)
The Mourner (1963)
The Score (1964)
The Jugger (1965)
The Seventh (1966)
The Handle (1966)
The Rare Coin Score (1967)
The Green Eagle Score (1967)
The Black Ice Score (1968)
The Sour Lemon Score (1969)

Deadly Edge (1971)
Slayground (1971)
Plunder Squad (1972)
Butcher's Moon (1974)
Comeback (1997)
Backflash (1998)
Flashfire (2000)
Firebreak (2001)
Breakout (2002)
Nobody Runs Forever (2004)
Ask the Parrot (2006)
Dirty Money (2008)

Grofield Novels
The Damsel (1967)
The Dame (1969)
The Blackbird (1969)
Lemons Never Lie (1971)

Writing as Tucker Coe
Kinds of Love, Kinds of Death
   (1966)
Murder among Children (1967)
Wax Apple (1970)
A Jade in Aries (1970)
Don't Lie to Me (1972)

Writing as Samuel Holt
One of Us Is Wrong (1986)
I Know a Trick Worth Two of
   That (1986)
What I Tell You Three Times Is
   False (1987)
The Fourth Dimension Is Death
   (1989)

**Writing as J. Morgan
   Cunningham**
Comfort Station (1973)

**Writing as Judson Jack
   Carmichael**
The Scared Stiff (2002)

Writing as Curt Clark
Anarchaos (1967)

Writing as Timothy J. Culver
Ex Officio (also published as
   Power Play) (1970)

THE GETAWAY CAR

Donald Westlake at home, with Max. Photo by permission of Abigail Westlake.

THE GETAWAY CAR

A DONALD WESTLAKE NONFICTION MISCELLANY

Edited by Levi Stahl

With a new Foreword
by Lawrence Block

THE UNIVERSITY OF CHICAGO PRESS

CHICAGO AND LONDON

The University of Chicago Press, Chicago 60637
The University of Chicago Press, Ltd., London
© 2014 by The University of Chicago
Foreword © 2014 by Lawrence Block
All rights reserved. Published 2014.
Printed in the United States of America

23 22 21 20 19 18 17 16 15 14   1 2 3 4 5

ISBN-13: 978-0-226-12181-9 (paper)
ISBN-13: 978-0-226-12195-6 (e-book)
DOI: 10.7208/chicago/9780226121956.001.0001

Most of Donald E. Westlake's writings in this volume are
published by permission of Abigail Westlake. For additional
credits, please see page 215.

Library of Congress Cataloging-in-Publication Data

Westlake, Donald E., author.
   [Works. Selections. 2014]
   The getaway car : a Donald Westlake nonfiction miscellany /
edited by Levi Stahl ; with a new foreword by Lawrence Block.
      pages ; cm
   Summary: "Collection of published and unpublished gems: a
memoir about learning to write, an imaginary interview between
Westlake's various identities, essays on writing, introductions,
and letters to writers like Stephen King and Brian Garfield. A true
miscellany, this includes a piece by Abigail Westlake, a recipe for
'May's Famous Tuna Casserole' and a 'Midnight snack.'"—From
the publisher.
   Includes index.
   ISBN 978-0-226-12181-9 (pbk. : alk. paper) —
ISBN 978-0-226-12195-6 (e-book)
   I. Stahl, Levi, editor.   II. Block, Lawrence, writer of
foreword.   III. Title.
   PS3573.E9A6 2014
   813'.54—dc23
                                        2014003017

♾ This paper meets the requirements of ANSI/NISO Z39.48-1992
(Permanence of Paper).

No matter where he was headed,
Don always drove like he was
behind the wheel of the getaway car.

ABBY ADAMS WESTLAKE

CONTENTS

FOREWORD

Sometime in the early spring of 1959 I plucked a book from a shelf in Yellow Springs, Ohio, and paid thirty-five cents for it. The title was *All My Lovers*, by Alan Marshall, and I bought it because I noted that it had been published by Midwood. Back in August I had sat up late in my parents' house in Buffalo writing a book for Midwood, and I'd since returned to Antioch College, where I was assiduously neglecting my studies while writing a couple more books for the same publisher, all of them examples of what we've since learned to call Midcentury Erotica.

And now I'd actually found a Midwood title offered for sale. I took it home and read it, and realized right away that Alan Marshall, whoever he might be, was pretty good. I kept reading and encountered a scene I still recall. A principal character was a cad who had, in the manner of his tribe, behaved badly with a young woman from *el barrio*. Her brothers responded by paying him a visit and beating the crap out of him. And then they left, and I'll quote the scene's closing words from memory: "They did not take anything. They were not thieves."

Damn. This guy Marshall was good.

He was, as you've probably worked out on your own, Donald E. Westlake, whom I was yet to meet. He, however, had already met me, when I turned up in New York during Christmas vacation and dropped in at the Scott Meredith office. That was where I had worked from August 1957 to May 1958, and it was where Don was working that December. I had a brief conversation with Henry Morrison, my agent, and Don will share his recollection of the moment later in this volume.

So he met me, but it was one-sided; his was just a face in the background. Come summer, I'd finished the year at Antioch and taken a room at the Hotel Rio on West 47th Street; I planned to spend the summer writing more Midcentury Erotica before returning to Yellow Springs for a final year. (Shows what I knew. The school had other ideas, and while I was at the Rio, they sent me a letter, informing me that they felt I'd be happier elsewhere. Boy, were they ever right.)

One of the Rio's charms (and they were thin on the ground) was its proximity to the Scott Meredith offices, then at Fifth Avenue and 47th Street. I was a frequent visitor—to drop off a manuscript, to sign a contract, to pick up a check—and at one such visit I met Don. The workday was ending, and we introduced ourselves, and he suggested we go get a beer.

Why not?

One beer led to another, and we wound up at the Westlake apartment on West 46th between Ninth and Tenth. That's a desirable address nowadays, which just shows what a difference half a century can make. Don was living there with his wife, Nedra, and their infant son, Sean. (Don was given to introducing Nedra as "the first Mrs. Westlake," which turned out to be unintentionally prophetic.) I stayed for dinner, and we talked far into the night. As we were apt to do for the next fifty years.

On three occasions, back in the Midcentury Erotica days, we collaborated, and the resultant books (*A Girl Called Honey*, *So Willing*, and *Sin Hellcat*) were as much fun as I've ever had at a typewriter. They bore a joint byline ("by Sheldon Lord and Alan Marshall"), and the first carried a dedication: "To Don Westlake and Larry Block," it read, "who introduced us."

Indeed.

Speaking of introductions—

Once, four or five years before Don's death, I spotted a hand-lettered sign on the wall over his desk. NO MORE INTRODUCTIONS, it proclaimed. That struck me as bizarre. Here was this wonderfully personable fellow, always a genial and eager host; what made him resolve at this late date to quit introducing his guests to one another?

What he meant, I soon learned, was that he'd resolved to stop responding favorably to requests that he write an introduction to someone's new collection, or a review of someone's book, or indeed any of the occasional pieces that one is constantly being invited to turn out.

Pieces, in fact, which make up a substantial portion of this present volume. Don enjoyed this sort of writing, and as you'll soon see, he was superb at it, but what made him forswear the pursuit was the amount of time and energy it took. He had books to write, and that's where he wanted to focus his efforts.

Well, I get the point. I receive a fair number of similar requests myself— one such has me writing the words you're now reading—and it sometimes strikes me that I could put my time to more productive use. But, see, I wouldn't; I'd spend those hours playing computer solitaire, or posting inanities on Facebook, or hopscotching my way through Wikipedia.

So what the hell.

As for Don's labor in this varietal vineyard, I'm grateful for it; to it we owe this book's existence. I'd read most of these pieces, but read them again as preparation for this foreword. (And that's another way introductions drain one's batteries. You don't just have to write a thousand words. First, you have to read fifty or a hundred times as many words of the material you've agreed to introduce. In this instance it was a pleasure. That, alas, is not always the case.) It has been my delight to count as friends a couple of people who've never written a bad sentence, a clumsy paragraph, or a dull page. Evan Hunter was one. Donald E. Westlake was another.

Levi Stahl has done a superb job of sifting through Don's miscellaneous effort, separating the best of the wheat from the rest of the wheat—

Don didn't do chaff—and organizing and notating the result. If I'm to take issue with anything, it's with a word he uses.

Jokes.

In his introduction, Levi describes these selections as being replete with jokes, and says Don found it almost impossible to write a page without putting in a joke. Now I read the entire book, and I can't recall a single joke.

A joke is something a comic tells. A joke generally starts with a guy walking into a bar. Or two guys, or even three.

This is a joke: A Frenchman, a German, and a Jew walk into a bar. The Frenchman says, "I am tired and thirsty. I must have wine!" The German says, "I am tired and thirsty. I must have beer!" The Jew says, "I am tired and thirsty. I must have diabetes." There. That's a joke, and as far as I can tell, it's the only one you'll find in this book.

What you will find, however, and I suspect you'll find it on every page, is wit. Don was a wonderfully witty man, a fellow of infinite jest, and he took pains to make what he wrote amusing. Wit enlivened his conversation, even as it brightened his writing, fiction and nonfiction alike. In his fiction, his goal was to tell a story; in his other writing, he strove to relate an incident or convey information or make a point. In either case, it was second nature for him to do so with wit and humor.

The Getaway Car. It's an inspired title, and Abby's epigraph is dead accurate. While aspects of their author found their way into every one of his characters, when Don settled himself behind the wheel (and *settled* may not be *le mot juste* here), he became Stan Murch, ace wheelman of the Dortmunder gang. Like another of his characters, Don's ideal car was one that would get you from point A to point B in zero seconds.

When I met him, Don's New York State driver's license had been suspended; this happens when you've drawn enough speeding tickets, and he was always good at that. He wouldn't have wanted a car anyway on West 46th Street, but that changed when he moved out to Canarsie. And the day came when the three-year suspension was up, and his license was restored.

Whereupon he bought a car, and applied for insurance. And was astonished when the insurance company gave him a safe driver discount because he hadn't had an accident or a speeding ticket in the past three years.

There's a word for that sort of thing. *Westlakean.*

An interviewer once asked John O'Hara if he missed the old days of the Algonquin Round Table.

"No," he said. "When Benchley died, the party was over."

I know what he meant.

Lawrence Block
Greenwich Village

EDITOR'S INTRODUCTION

If this is the first book by Donald E. Westlake you've ever held in your hands, stop right here. Put it down and walk away . . . straight to the crime section of your bookstore, where I'd suggest you start with *The Hunter*, the first book in his classic series about Parker, the heister's heister; or *The Hot Rock*, the first misadventure of hapless thief John Dortmunder and his crew; or *The Ax*, Westlake's painfully acute dissection-through-crime of contemporary economic pain; or the brilliantly funny stand-alone *Somebody Owes Me Money*, whose opening line—"I bet none of it would have happened if I wasn't so eloquent"—tells you all you need to know about the voice of its put-upon cabbie narrator. When you've run through those, and the couple dozen more they'll lead you to, we'll gladly welcome you back here.

This is a book for fans. And there are a lot of us. For nearly fifty years, Donald Westlake turned out novels and short stories that ran the gamut of crime fiction, from the hardest of hard-boiled to the most madcap comedy. Westlake's books may vary wildly in topic, theme, and approach, but when you open one, you know instantly that you're in good hands. They share a discernible ethos: a belief in clear, declarative sentences, an appreciation for efficiency and precision, and a fundamental confidence that things that can go wrong will do so, spectacularly. Different genres add different spins—the serious crime novels display a fascination with our darker sides, ruthlessness, and the ease with which we (often unwillingly) identify with bad guys, while the comedies rest on the assumption that almost anything is funny when looked at from the right angle, and that, as Robert Burns reminds us, there's nothing more ridiculous than people and their plans—but a Donald Westlake book is always instantly recognizable as the work of his hand.

If you read a lot of Westlake, it's hard not to build a picture of the man himself, but it's all assembled by inference. Unlike crime writers like John D. MacDonald or Raymond Chandler, Westlake doesn't pepper his books with statements of opinion that can be attributed, directly or indirectly, to himself as the author. From the Parker novels alone, we infer that he appreciates hard work and craftsmanship, and abhors sloppiness and laziness; from the Dortmunder books, we learn that he knows better than to take himself, or anyone, too seriously. But that doesn't answer a lot of the questions that fans can't help but ask. What did he think about his work? How did he conceive of and understand crime fiction, his own and that of others? What writers did he learn from, imitate, or cherish, and why?

That's where this book comes in. By bringing together a careful selection of Westlake's nonfiction writing across a variety of venues, formats, and genres—including a number of pieces that are published here for the first time—*The Getaway Car* offers the closest look we've had yet at the mind of Donald E. Westlake. Outside of his one foray into book-length nonfiction (*Under an English Heaven*, the odd but charming history of a quixotic 1969 invasion of Anguilla by the British "in which nobody was killed but many people were embarrassed"), Westlake didn't write all that much nonfiction, considering how many decades he put in at the typewriter. He wrote just enough, in fact, that it was tempting to try to make this collection complete. And a legitimate argument could have been made for that approach: while not everything Westlake wrote was substantial, what I found when I dug into his archives was that there was *something* that fans would enjoy in almost every piece. Even the two dozen or so straightforward book reviews he wrote for outlets like the *New York Times* and *Washington Post*, though often dealing with forgettable writers and books, almost always included an observation, a joke, or a moment of analysis that makes them worth reading. If you find yourself wanting more when you've finished this collection, a trip to your local library to seek those out will definitely repay your time.

Ultimately, however, I opted for selectiveness, and in choosing the contents of this collection I've tried to keep the focus on the man, his work, and his chosen genre. You'll find pieces that delve into the whats, hows, and whys of crime fiction; analyses and appreciations of his mentors, models, and contemporaries; essays and letters that reveal what he thought of his own work and the process of creating it; and fragments from an unpublished autobiography that, along with some of the interviews, and a few more personal essays, give us our first real glimpse into the early life and experiences of Donald Westlake off the page. Most of the pieces are presented complete, with headnotes that supply context and point out where material has been cut. Typographical errors, meanwhile, have been silently corrected (though they were few and far between—the man was as meticulous about his typing as he was about everything else).

Threaded through the whole are, of course, jokes. As I went through Westlake's files, two conclusions were inescapable: first, that the labor of a working writer never stops, and, second, that Donald Westlake almost never typed up a whole sheet of paper—be it a business letter or a note to a fan—without finding room for at least one joke. (I'll admit to including a couple of letters solely for their jokes.) As Westlake himself put it in an appreciation of movie director Stephen Frears, "If we aren't going to enjoy ourselves, why do it?" That's not a bad way to go through life.

In a letter to a Boston University librarian in 1965, early in his career, Westlake wrote, "If I were a sculptor, I might be used to the idea of permanence, but as it is the thought leaves me rattled." Sculptor or not, he's achieved permanence, and I hope this collection won't leave his ghost too rattled. Enjoy.

ONE MY SECOND LIFE

Fragments from an Autobiography

Around the time of his seventieth birthday, Donald Westlake took a stab at writing an autobiography. According to his widow, he never quite felt that it was ready for publication—but when I got a chance to read the draft in his files, I found that it included a number of memories and anecdotes of Westlake's childhood and early experiences with writing that seemed well worth sharing.—Ed.

I was born in Brooklyn, New York, on July 12, 1933, and I couldn't digest milk. Not mother's milk, nor cow's milk, nor goat's milk, nor anybody's milk. Nor could I digest any of the baby formulas then available. Everything they fed me at the hospital ran right through me, leaving mere traces of nutrients behind. On the fourth day, the doctors told my parents to prepare for the worst: "He'll be dead by his eighth day." Just another squirming little bundle of muscle and heat that didn't make it.

Then, on the fifth day, the doctors learned about an experimental baby formula, based on soybeans, nearing the end of its trials in a hospital in Manhattan. There was nothing else to try, so phone calls were made, the formula was shipped from Manhattan to Brooklyn, and for the first time in my young life I found something I could tolerate.

If I'd been born three months earlier, I was dead in eight days. If I'd been born in Baltimore or Boston, much less some small town somewhere, or anywhere else in the world, I was dead in eight days. Only a surprise ending saved my life.

By the eighth day, instead of snuffing out, I was putting on my baby fat. On the ninth day, my second life began.

My first conscious memory dates from when I was three years old, and it connects directly with the central obsession of my entire life: story. From the time I could understand language, I loved story. Tell me a story. Both my father and my mother would read stories to me, and those times were the peak of my existence.

Unfortunately, I never got enough story to satisfy my addiction. This was the Depression, and both my parents worked. My mother, who was a clerk-typist, often brought typing work home in the evenings, and my father, who was a loyal member of the Veterans of Foreign Wars, eventually becoming regional commander in the New York–New England area around Albany, was often out in the evenings on VFW affairs. I simply wasn't getting enough story.

My toys then included a set of wooden square blocks with letters on them and, with their help, my mother had taught me the alphabet, so I knew what the letters looked like, and I knew what they were supposed to sound like. But when I saw words on a piece of paper I just could not make sense out of them. How was I supposed to guess that "help," for instance, began with the letter "aitch"?

I was three when I finally broke the code, and that's my first coherent memory. We lived in Yonkers, then, the last time we lived in a one-family house, our later homes in Albany always being the upstairs flat in a two-family house. On this particular day in Yonkers, I was on the living room floor, to the left of where the somewhat cramped staircase went up to a landing then turned left above the kitchen door. I was on all fours, hunkered on top of the Yonkers newspaper, which was a large paper like the *New York Times* rather than a smaller tabloid like the *New York Daily News*, so I could get all four limbs completely on it. There was a photo—black and white in 1936 of course—at the top of the page, showing a group of men on a stage or platform of some sort, outdoors. It was winter, and they were all in heavy coats and what looked like military officer caps. There was a suggestion of the military about the group, though I suppose that's a conclusion I'm drawing later.

I looked at the picture, and I looked at the caption under it, and the first word was "The." I knew "T," I knew "he," I knew "e," but I could not for the life of me figure out "The." I stared at the picture, I stared at that word, and then, as usual, I gave up and went on to the next word, which was "police."

Police. I tried saying it out loud, forming my mouth around it. "Pee-oh-el-*eye*-cee-ee. Pee-oh-el-*eye*-cee-ee."

No. I couldn't get it. I stared at the picture some more, and then the word, and all at once it was there. Police.

That's when I learned the secret, broke the code. They don't use the whole letter, the "pee" or the "el," they just use a kernel of it, "puh" or "ll." Some, like the "ee," they don't really use at all. But once you understand that central fact, the sheer wastefulness of letter-sounds, that they are both kernel *and* husk, it's a snap. Police!

The next word just poured into my brain. "De-part-ment." And now, back at that treacherous, nasty, secretive stub of a word that started the whole thing: "*The*! The, you son of a bitch, *The*!" (I don't remember what three-year-olds say instead of "son of a bitch," but whatever it is I'm sure I said it.)

Yes, the first word I ever read was "police"; sorry about that. Sometimes reality really is banal.

*   *   *

I first started making up my own stories when I was about eight, during those summer months when my bedtime was long before sundown. I wasn't permitted to read. I wasn't permitted to do anything but lie in my bed in my room and, presumably, sleep.

But daylight filtered through the drawn window shade and the sounds of the activities of the adults came through my just-ajar door and in through my open window, because of course there was no air-conditioning and nobody particularly wanted to roast me alive in there. So, bored, awake, distracted by the sounds and lights of life, I started to tell myself stories, hoping to keep the sagas going until sleep should find me.

The stories I made up were jumbles of the stories I'd been taking in from all sources, at first pretty much limited to the exciting parts, though I soon realized, if I was going to keep myself interested in one of these stories, I'd have to do more than just have cars going off cliffs and planes crash-landing into jungles. To keep my stories moving, and to make them worth my time, I was going to have to add two elements: people, and reasons. Why is he in the car? Why is it going off the cliff?

I resented having to do this boring detail work, but the story wouldn't emerge without it, and figuring out all that housekeeping did at least pass the time, so that often I'd barely have set my stage and introduced my cast when unconsciousness would conquer all. And often, the next night, I would have little or no memory of what I'd worked out toward the end the night before, and I'd have to start all over.

There did come a time, though, when I perfected my own private serial, and that story took me through the long evenings for quite a while. I think I was ten, maybe a little older. A couple of the movie serials I'd seen at the Delaware Theater had included sequences on PT boats and other small war boats well-mounted with machine guns.

That was my vehicle. Somewhere in some island-filled ocean, the Pacific, I think, a crew of half a dozen of us had adventures on that boat that went on for months. If, on a particular evening, I didn't remember how last night's episode had ended—or, rather, where it had stopped, since this story was without an ending—I'd simply go back to the part I last remembered, and invent anew.

This boat saga did many things for me, in addition to helping me while away the idle hours confined to bed though wide awake. It taught me continuity, for one thing, continuity of character and setting. It taught me that every event had to be followed by another event, so we'd better be sure we only provide events that can generate some further occurrence.

There was the time, for instance, when I had our boat hit by a torpedo and sunk, so that we were all bobbing in the vasty ocean, clinging to bits of wreckage. But that event didn't really work, because there was no possible subsequent event except drowning and a watery grave. So I had to go back and make the torpedo score a near miss, so that the next event became the search for the enemy submarine, which I believe had fled up a river in a nearby island. So I was also learning how to rewrite.

*   *   *

It was inevitable that, after playing air guitar for a couple years, I'd feel ready to move on to the real thing. My mother often brought typing work home to do in the evening, on her big, industrial-strength L. C. Smith typewriter, a big black shiny monster that actually did sound like a machine gun when she used it and like a slow popcorn machine under my own fingers. Fairly early on I learned how to peck out words on that machine. I didn't know the touch system yet, or any other system, but it did the job.

When I first started to try to write stories on paper, I operated from a misunderstanding that, in retrospect, only helped me. In books and magazines and newspapers, columns of print were always smooth and straight on both sides, but the typewriter didn't want to do that. I could produce straight left margins, that was easy, but my right margins looked like mountain ranges lying on their sides.

I decided, if ever I was going to be taken seriously as a storyteller, I'd better correct those right margins, and the only way I could think to do it was synonyms. I arbitrarily decided that a line of my writing would be sixty spaces long. If a line was too long or too short, I'd go back and change some of the words. Is "enter" too short? Come in. A house can *be* a home, if that's what fits.

This was, of course, an exercise in futility, but it was also an exercise in working with language. No matter what it is I want to say, I learned, it *can* be said in lines sixty spaces long. I must say I'm pleased to know I don't have to labor under that restriction, but the practice and the discipline were good for me.

*   *   *

Which brings me, I suppose reluctantly, to what it is I was writing. The first story I tried to put on paper, hunt and peck, sixty spaces to the line, was set at a baseball game and all I remember is, the catcher had a pistol concealed in his mitt. God knows why. I think I didn't know why.

*   *   *

My sophomore year at Champlain College, one of the guys in my dormitory was always talking about burglary. He came from Brooklyn, apparently from an environment where it was considered a good thing to be thought of as living on the wrong side of the law (though you didn't actually have to *be* on the wrong side of the law, just give the impression), and his way to maintain his credibility was to describe the burglaries he could perform on campus, the laxity of the security, the easiness of the job, the profits to be made.

I had a conversation with this guy at an unfortunate moment. My beer truck job had ended earlier in the fall, and I was pretty well scraping bottom. In about a week, I'd go back to Albany for the two-week Christmas break and my job with the brotherhood, but when I returned to Champlain College the larder would be empty, with the bills for the spring semester dead ahead.

I had no idea what I was going to do, and that's when I had the conversation with this fellow, who said the chemistry lab was just ripe for plucking, we could go in there that very night and rip off a couple microscopes. Who knows what they were worth? Hundreds! "Let's do it," I said.

We did it. It was as easy as he'd said it would be. I thought about nothing but how the money from this microscope would make it possible for me to come back to school next semester. I put it in my luggage and brought it home to Albany and pawned it in one of the many pawnshops then down along S. Pearl Street.

I got twenty-five dollars; not enough. Would I steal more microscopes, at twenty-five bucks a pop? The idea made me very queasy.

Still, I had my latest wages from the New York Central, so with that, and the twenty-five dollars, I went back to school. I spent the first morning in class and then, in an early afternoon class, word came that I was wanted in the provost's office. Blindly, it didn't even occur to me what this might be about.

Probably in deference to the school, the two cops were in plainclothes, but they showed their badges and thanked the provost and we went away. They were polite but aloof. I asked no questions, and they offered no small talk.

At the state police headquarters in town, they walked me down a hall where, in a side room, I glimpsed my partner in crime, seated hunched desperately forward, looking considerably less macho than before. At the end of the hall I was shown into the nice office of the head of CID, who said to me, "Do you want to tell me about it?"

If he wants to know if I want to tell him about it, he already knows all about it. I immediately told everything, and was taken away to be booked and placed in a cell in the Plattsburgh jail, with my co-bandit in another cell, and a couple of other desperadoes—mainly alcoholics—to fill out the roster.

This part is not that easy to talk about. The next day, my father drove up to Plattsburgh, and the nadir of my life came when we met in the visitors' room at the Plattsburgh jail. He took some of the blame on himself, for being unable to support me, which made me feel worse, and which I absolutely rejected, then and now. We all do the best we can, and sometimes the best we can do is make a mistake.

I spent four nights and five days in that jail, and hated it, even more than you might expect. Every instant was intolerable. I hate being here now; I hate being here now; I hate being here *now*.

Years later, when I was writing novels about criminals, and when at least some of the criminals were still literate, I'd occasionally get a fan letter from somebody doing time, and in a few instances, when I replied, I gave an edited version of my own jail time so I could ask the question: How can you live in an intolerable state for years? I couldn't stand one single second of it for a mere five days; how do you do it year after year?

The answer I got was always the same, with minor variations. Yes, what I described was what they, too, had gone through, the absolute unbearable horror, but I'd quit the experience too early. Some time in the second week, they told me, your brain flips over and *this* becomes the reality. This becomes where you live now. And how, I wonder, do you come back from *that* damage?

As usual, my father could come through for someone else, in this case me. Through political friends, or VFW friends, or somewhere, he reached out to the state legislator from that district, who was of course a lawyer, and hired him to represent me. The family had to borrow money from everybody they knew, but they got me represented by the local state legislator, who was, among other things, known to be a friend and supporter of Champlain College.

In our time in jail together, my former classmate remained a basket case, weeping, tossing and turning on his cot, once crushing a whole apple in his bare hand, ever bemoaning the loss of his dream of a medical career. We had no conversations, compared no notes, made no plans, melded in no way.

Which was just as well. From this point on, everything I learned about my fellow thief made things worse. First, it turned out he already knew a fence in Plattsburgh, which he hadn't mentioned to me, so he'd simply turned his microscope over to that guy, who at that time of year transported stolen goods to New York City for resale concealed in truckloads of Christmas trees. (I know; is nothing sacred?)

This fence, returning from the city a day early, found his wife in bed with a husband not her own. The fence beat this trespasser badly enough to put him in the hospital. However, deciding this had been an insufficient response, he then snuck into the hospital to beat the other guy up all over again, in his hospital bed, until the cops pulled him off and stuck him in the same jail where I was soon to find myself. He stayed there until the day school reopened. First thing in the morning, my partner was picked up on campus, and once he was delivered to the CID the outraged fence was released from jail without charges. My partner was interviewed in the morning, and they came for me in the afternoon. I guess they hadn't invented *omerta* yet.

Once my father got the guy with clout to be my lawyer, the other guy's family wanted him, too, and insisted when we demurred. I think they already knew their son was in more trouble than I was, because in the basement of the family home in Brooklyn several items were found bearing the oval bronze plaque marked ACUNY [Associated Colleges of Upper New York—Ed.].

Bail was of course impossible, so I had to stay there until they decided what to do with me. On the fifth day, the other guy and I were brought to court, where the judge accepted a sealed indictment against each of us. This meant, if I was not indicted for any additional crime over a period of time to be determined by the judge, the indictment would be quashed and not exist as part of my record. I would never have been arrested, never indicted. This was an outcome that left me weak with relief.

* * *

By 1958, I'd graduated from painting ceilings to an actual job, as a petty conman in a crowded office on Fifth Avenue at 47th Street. I'd answered an ad in the *Times* for an "associate editor at a literary agency" and wound up at an employment office, where I had to undergo a little written test.

First I was handed a short story called "Rattlesnake Cave." Then I was told to read it and to write a letter to the author as though I were the agent. I had three choices: I could accept the story and tell the author where I expected to sell it; I could point out flaws in the story and suggest I'd like to see it again after a rewrite; or I could reject it, with reasons.

The story had been written by a professional writer, Lester Del Rey, deliberately to be full of unacceptable elements. It was framed, a story within a story, encumbered by an unnecessary narrator. It was full of dialect. The peril in the story turned out to be a fake, what is known in the trade as a paper tiger. And several more things like that. In its way, it was a masterful piece of work.

In taking this test I didn't want to be so harsh as to reject the story outright, but I knew better than to say it could be published anywhere. I expressed willingness to see it in revised form, and then pointed out several of the ways in which it was hopeless.

This turned out to be the way to go. If you rejected the story or asked for revisions, and if you showed an understanding of the market and a feel for story and an ability of your own to put words together, you'd be offered the job. I was offered it and I took it.

The job was with the Scott Meredith Literary Agency, which was both a successful legitimate agency, with clients ranging from tough-guy paperback novelists through Norman Mailer and P. G. Wodehouse, and also a successful con game, in which advertisements in writers' magazines offered a careful consideration and potential representation for any amateur who sent in a short story with five dollars.

By golly, I'd done that myself, back when I was sixteen! I'd sent one of my stories and five of my dollars to Scott Meredith and got back a letter that treated my story judiciously, pointed out a few flaws, and urged me to send in more stories (and money). Somehow, instinctively, I'd known with that first whiff that this wasn't an outfit I wanted to deal with any further, but now here I was on the other side of the looking glass. From now on, I would be the guy who *wrote* those letters.

It was piecework. We got a dollar a short story and five dollars a novel (out of Scott's twenty-five), and we wrote the letters to a formula that meant you never had to give any of these tales more time than they deserved.

What a lot of bad stories the amateurs dreamed up. One of the things I learned in the six months I worked for Scott was just how many ways there were to do it wrong.

At the time I went to work there, the other in-house fee reader was a sardonic soul from the other South—Florida—named Hal Dresner, who showed me the ropes and said of our boss, Henry Morrison, who was Scott's assistant, "If Henry ever asks you if you know anything about, and mentions some kind of story, say yes. You'll get an assignment."

Okay, I said, and a couple of weeks later Henry said, "Do you know anything about confession stories?" "Oddly enough, yes," I said. "Another guy and I did content analysis on confession magazines in a sociology course in college, and when we wrote to Macfadden Publishing for information they sent us a bunch of the magazines and their own survey of the readership."

This was more information than Henry needed. He said, "You write three one-paragraph story descriptions, they pick the one they want, you write it at three thousand words for fifty dollars."

Done. Back home, I pulled out the content analysis and simply repeated the three most common stories we'd found in the magazines, and that was the first time the publisher accepted all three outlines. I did the three stories over the weekend.

In the next few months, I mined the content analysis for further inspiration, and one morning during this time Henry said, "Do you know anything about sex novels?" "Sure," I said, though I didn't. "Give me two chapters and an outline," he said. "They pay a flat six hundred dollars."

I waited till after lunch, by which time I figured Henry would be used to the idea I had the assignment, and then I went to him and said, "When I was a kid, in the drugstore there were these little paperback books, staple-bound like *TV Guide*, with titles like *Impatient Virgin*, and the girl almost does it all the way through and finally does do it at the end. Is that what you're talking about?" "No," he said in disgust, and handed me three paperbacks.

These books, which had a brief existence in the late '50s and early '60s, just before the sexual revolution made them look like hoopskirts, were actual stories, with a dozen or so sex scenes viewed gauzily through a kind of mist. I used to call them euphemism novels, and would say it's easy to get to fifty thousand words when you can't call anything by its rightful name. This stuff was trash, of course, like the confession stories, but useful trash, honing narrative skills, teaching how to shape a story. They were like the workout before the big game, a useful limbering of the muscles.

In April, I got six hundred dollars for my first sex novel. My wife was seven months pregnant, I had no other money and no prospects except the promise of another six hundred dollars if I wrote another of those books.

So I quit my job. I haven't had a job since.

TWO DONALD E. WESTLAKE, A.K.A . . .

HEARING VOICES IN MY HEAD: TUCKER COE, TIMOTHY J. CULVER, RICHARD STARK AND DONALD E. WESTLAKE

Originally published in 1977 in *Murder Ink*, a grab-bag anthology edited by Dilys Winn, "Hearing Voices in My Head" brings together a handful of Westlake's pen names for a contentious roundtable discussion. Tucker Coe was the name he used for his five Mitch Tobin novels, Timothy J. Culver helmed a 1970 thriller titled *Ex Officio*, and of course Richard Stark was the name behind the Parker series.—Ed.

Recently gathered with a moderator inside a Japanese-made cassette recorder to discuss the state of their art were Donald E. Westlake, Richard Stark, Tucker Coe and Timothy J. Culver.

MODERATOR: The mystery story, detective thriller, *roman policier*, call it what you will, has been a basic influence in the history of fiction since the days of Greece and Rome. While Edgar Allan Poe is the acknowledged father of the modern detective story, it is still true that *Oedipus Rex* is a seminal mystery tale. Today's novelists of crime, passion, suspense, can with pride count Shakespeare, Dostoevsky and the Brothers Grimm among their family tree. Tucker Coe, what do *you* think of all this?

TUCKER COE: Sounds terrific.

MODERATOR: Ah. Yes. I see. Well, umm . . . Richard Stark. As an—

RICHARD STARK: Present.

MODERATOR: Yes. As an innovator in the crime field, suspense story, call it what you will, what would you say is the outlook for the mystery tale? You have been—

RICHARD STARK: Well, I think—

MODERATOR: —an innovator, of course, in that you created Parker, a professional thief who never gets caught. Also, he is not merely a thinly disguised battler for the underdog, as were Robin Hood or The Saint or The Green Hornet. Parker's reaction to the underdog would probably have been to kick it. Having yourself altered the thriller or mystery form, what would you say are the portents for tomorrow?

RICHARD STARK: Well, I suppose—

MODERATOR: People have declared the detective novel, the murder story itself, dead, murdered by repetition, staleness, a using up of all the potentials of the form, replaced by who knows what public fancies, whether for Comedy, History, Pastoral, Pastoral-Comical, Historical-Pastor—

RICHARD STARK: Say, wait a minute.

MODERATOR: Or, let us say, the Western, Science Fiction, the Family Saga. Nevertheless, the crime/suspense/mystery/thriller story, the tale of ratiocination, call it what you will, has continued to flourish, much like the Grand Old Lady of the Theater, the Broadway Stage, which so often has—

RICHARD STARK: Listen.

MODERATOR: —been reported dead. But, if we may borrow a phrase, Watchman, what of the night? What do *you* think tomorrow will bring to the thriller, the detective—

RICHARD STARK: *I* think it's—

MODERATOR: —story, the *roman noir*, the 'tec tale, call it what you—

RICHARD STARK: Listen, you. Either I get to *answer* that question or I'll damage you.

MODERATOR: —will, the essential—Eh? Oh, yes. Certainly.

CHAPTER TWO

RICHARD STARK: Right. Now. Uhh—What was the question?

MODERATOR: Well, the gist of the—

RICHARD STARK: Not you. Tim?

TIMOTHY J. CULVER: Future of the mystery.

RICHARD STARK: Right. There isn't any.

MODERATOR: There isn't any?

RICHARD STARK: The detective story died about thirty years ago, but that's okay. Poetry died *hundreds* of years ago and there're still poets. By "die," by "dead," I mean as a hot center of public interest. In the Thirties you could have honest-to-God *detective* stories, on the bestseller lists. Ellery Queen, for instance. The detective story was hot when science was new, with gaslight and then electricity, telephones, automobiles, everything starting up, the whole *world* seeming to get solved all at once, in one life span. World War II shifted the emphasis from gaining knowledge to what you'd do with the knowledge, which is kill people. So the big postwar detective was Mike Hammer, who couldn't *deduce* his way up a flight of stairs, and the emphasis shifted from whodunit to who's-gonna-get-it. The Mike Hammer thing leads into all these paperback hobnail vigilantes with their *Thesaurus* names: the Inflictor, the Chastiser, the Flaggelator. Deduction, the solving of a mystery—they don't even put in a token appearance anymore.

MODERATOR: But does that mean you yourself have given up the mystery field, thriller field, whatever label you may choose?

RICHARD STARK: Grrrrrrrrr.

MODERATOR: Sorry. But no new Parker novel has been published since 1974. *Have* you given up writing crime novels, thrillers, or—um.

RICHARD STARK: Parker is a Depression character, Dillinger mythologized into a machine. During the affluent days of the Sixties he was an interesting fantasy, but now that money's getting tight again his relationship with banks is suddenly both to the point and old-fashioned. He hasn't yet figured out how to operate in a world where heisting *is* one of the more rational responses to the situation.

MODERATOR: Tucker Coe, do you agree?

TUCKER COE: Well, yes and no, I suppose. In a way. Looking at all sides of the issue, *without* becoming overly involved in a too personal way, if we could avoid that, insofar as it's ever really possible to avoid personal involvement in a discussion of one's own work, I suppose the simple answer is that for *me* the detective story was ultimately too restricting. Others, of course, might find possibilities I missed. I'm sure they will, and the problem was as much in me as in the choice of character and genre.

MODERATOR: Would you care to amplify that, to give us further insights into—

RICHARD STARK: Watch it. Go ahead, Tuck.

TUCKER COE: Thanks. The problem for me was that Mitch Tobin wasn't a static character. For him to remain miserable and guilt-racked forever would have changed him into a self-pitying whiner. My problem was, once Mitch Tobin reaches that new stability and becomes functional in the world again, he's merely one more private eye with an unhappy past. Not to name names but don't we have *enough* slogging private eyes with unhappy pasts?

MODERATOR: But surely the detective story has been used as a vehicle for exploring character. Nedra Tyre, for instance. Patricia Highsmith, Raymond Chandler.

RICHARD STARK: His sentences were too fat.

MODERATOR: But wasn't he interested in character?

RICHARD STARK: He was interested in literature. That's the worst thing that can happen to a writer.

TIMOTHY J. CULVER: I couldn't agree more. And let me say, I speak from a different perspective from everybody else here. These guys all write what *they* want to write, I write what *other people* want me to write. I'm a hack, I'm making a living, I'm using whatever craft I've learned to turn out decently professional work that I'm not personally involved with. In my opinion, the best writers are always people who don't care about anything except telling you what's in their heads, *without boring you*. Passion, plus craft. The Continental Op didn't have to have a miserable home life or a lot of character schticks because Hammett could fill him up with his own reality.

MODERATOR: But mystery novelists are nevertheless commercial writers, aren't they? Mr. Culver, I don't entirely follow the distinction you're making.

TIMOTHY J. CULVER: The difference between a hack and a writer is that the hack puts down on paper things he doesn't believe. Dick Stark mentioned Mike Hammer. Now, Mickey Spillane wasn't a hack, not then at least, and that's because he really *believed* all that paranoid crap. But the thousand imitators didn't believe it. You know, one time I was talking to a professor at the University of Pennsylvania, and he had to leave the party early to go work on an article for one of the scholarly journals. I asked him what it was about, and he said it didn't matter, just some piece of crap. "But I have to keep turning them out if I want tenure," he said. "It's pretty much publish or perish in this business." "It's about the same in mine," I told him.

MODERATOR: Frankly, Mr. Culver, you sound to me like a cynic.

TIMOTHY J. CULVER: I act based on my opinion of the world, so I am a realist.

MODERATOR: Donald E. Westlake, from your vantage point, would you say that Mr. Culver seems to be a realist?

DONALD E. WESTLAKE: Sure he is. A realist is somebody who thinks the world is simple enough to be understood. It isn't.

TIMOTHY J. CULVER: I understand it well enough to get by.

DONALD E. WESTLAKE: Meaning you can tie your own shoelaces. Terrific.

MODERATOR: Gentlemen, gentlemen. Um, Mr. Westlake, you your-self began with the traditional detective novels, did you not?

DONALD E. WESTLAKE: The first story I ever wrote was about a pro-fessional killer knocking off a Mob boss. I thought it would be nice to make the setting a fancy office, as though the Mob boss were a lawyer or a doctor. I was eleven years old, the story was about two hundred words long, and all that happened was this guy walked in, stepped around the bodyguards, shot the Mob boss at his desk, and then walked out again. But the point was the long detailed description of the office. I was in love with what I suppose was my first discovery as a writer:

that there was something marvelous in a contrast between setting and action. A mismatch between What and Where could create interest all by itself. Of course, now I realize it was comedy that had taught me all that—the fart in church, for instance, a favorite among children—but I never thought comedy was what I was good at. All through school, I was never the funniest kid, I was always the funniest kid's best friend. I was a terrific audience.

MODERATOR: And yet, now you are known primarily as the author of comic caper novels, comedy thrillers, what Anthony Boucher termed the comedy of peril, call it what you will—

DONALD E. WESTLAKE: Taradiddle.

MODERATOR: I beg your pardon?

DONALD E. WESTLAKE: You want me to call these books what I will, and that's what I call them. Taradiddles. Tortile taradiddles.

MODERATOR: Tortile . . .

DONALD E. WESTLAKE: Taradiddles.

MODERATOR: Yes. Well, these, um, things . . . You are primarily known for them, so what led you from ordinary detective stories to these, hm?

DONALD E. WESTLAKE: I couldn't take them seriously any more. I did five books, and started a sixth, and it kept wanting to be funny. As Dick Stark pointed out, there isn't much money in writing mystery novels, so I wasn't risking a lot if I went ahead and wrote it funny. At that time, there weren't any comic mysteries around, so I couldn't prejudge the reception. Craig Rice had been the last comic detective novelist. But ideas and feelings float in the air, and later on it turned out that simultaneously a guy named John Godey, who later became famous for *The Taking of Pelham 1-2-3*, was writing a comic mystery novel called *A Thrill a Minute with Jack Albany*. It constantly happens: writers who don't know one another come up with the same shift in emphasis or the same new subject matter at the same time. We all swim in the same culture, of course.

MODERATOR: Would you say you were influenced by Craig Rice?

DONALD E. WESTLAKE: No, I wouldn't. *She* was influenced by

Thorne Smith, who was magnificent, but every time I try to borrow from Thorne Smith the material dies in my hands. It's difficult to be truly whimsical without being arch. I can't do it.

MODERATOR: And P. G. Wodehouse?

DONALD E. WESTLAKE: He couldn't do it, either. That's a minority opinion, of course.

MODERATOR: Would you care to talk about who *has* influenced your work?

DONALD E. WESTLAKE: Not until they're in the public domain.

MODERATOR: I suppose you've been asked where you get your ideas?

DONALD E. WESTLAKE: Never. Who would ask a schmuck question like that?

MODERATOR: I see. Yes. To return to this first, um, tortile—?

DONALD E. WESTLAKE: *The Dead Nephew.*

MODERATOR: Really? My fact sheet says *The Fugitive Pigeon.*

DONALD E. WESTLAKE: Your fact sheet is on the money. I haven't always been lucky with titles. At the time, I was persuaded to change from the original, but now, sixteen years later, I'd rather be the author of *The Dead Nephew* than *The Fugitive Pigeon.*

MODERATOR: Why?

DONALD E. WESTLAKE: It's funnier and it's meaner, and therefore more to the point.

MODERATOR: To *return* to the point, you wrote this first tortile tara-diddle because you—

DONALD E. WESTLAKE: Nicely done.

MODERATOR: —couldn't—thank you—take the mystery novel seriously anymore. Does that mean you agree with Richard Stark about the gloomy future of the crime story, the thriller, the detective novel, call it what you will?

DONALD E. WESTLAKE: Depends on what you call it.

MODERATOR: I beg your pardon?

DONALD E. WESTLAKE: I have a friend, Robert Ludlum, who writes—

TIMOTHY J. CULVER: Name-dropper.

DONALD E. WESTLAKE: —books, and very good books, too, which are full of suspense, mysteries to be solved, murders, detection, crime, chases, *all* the elements of the mystery story. If they were called mysteries or detective stories, if they were placed on the publisher's "Mystery List," they would sell a fraction of what they do. The best-seller list is crammed with sheep in wolves' clothing. Sidney Sheldon, Frederick Forsyth, Jack Higgins under all his many names.

TIMOTHY J. CULVER: You should talk.

DONALD E. WESTLAKE: Tim, you *are* a pest.

TIMOTHY J. CULVER: But indispensable.

DONALD E. WESTLAKE: Like the Sanitation Department. You take the garbage.

MODERATOR: Gentlemen, gentlemen. If mystery novels appear on the best-seller list under another category name, would you be willing to reveal that name?

DONALD E. WESTLAKE: "Blockbuster." You see an ad for a book, it says the book is a blockbuster, that means it's a category crime novel— usually forty thousand words too fat—breaking for the big money.

MODERATOR: Then why aren't *all* mystery novels simply called blockbusters?

DONALD E. WESTLAKE: Because they have to be Fifties mystery novels, full of Kirk Douglas–type characters. If you write Thirties mystery novels, whodunits with puzzles and clever murderers (never killers) and cleverer detectives, or if you write Forties private eye novels—"A mean man walks down these lone streets"—you can't possibly get out of the ghetto.

MODERATOR: What about Ross Macdonald?

DONALD E. WESTLAKE: The former editor of the *New York Times Book Review* has admitted in print that that was the result of a conspiracy to see if he really *could* boost an author he liked onto the best-seller list. Since he claimed that was the only time such a conspiracy occurred, to his knowledge, Macdonald is a fluke.

MODERATOR: Do you have an opinion about his work?

DONALD E. WESTLAKE: He must have terrific carbon paper.

MODERATOR: You mentioned Thirties, Forties and Fifties crime novels. What about the Sixties?

DONALD E. WESTLAKE: The Sixties crime novel was joky (as opposed to funny), smart-alecky, full of drugs, and self-consciously parading its cast of blacks and homosexuals. The only Sixties mysteries with any merit at all were written in the Fifties by Chester Himes. On the other hand, the Sixties Western was even worse: Remember *Dirty Dingus Magee*?

RICHARD STARK: Okay, this has gone on long enough. Everybody on your feet.

MODERATOR: Good God, he's got a gun!

RICHARD STARK: Empty your pockets onto the table. Come on, snap it up.

TIMOTHY J. CULVER: You can't mean this, Dick. We're your friends.

RICHARD STARK: No book published since '74. How do you think I live? Give me everything you've got.

DONALD E. WESTLAKE: Will you take a check?

RICHARD STARK: *Beat the Devil*, 1954, Robert Morley to Humphrey Bogart. They ought to ask *me* where you get your ideas. You, Tucker Coe, on your feet.

MODERATOR: He's not moving, he—

RICHARD STARK: Get him up. You, Moderator.

MODERATOR: He's dead!

TIMOTHY J. CULVER: This water glass—yes, just as I thought. A rare undetectable South American poison. Tucker Coe has been murdered.

DONALD E. WESTLAKE: I didn't do it!

MODERATOR: Wait a minute. If the poison is undetectable, how do you know that's how he was killed?

TIMOTHY J. CULVER: There isn't a mark on the body, the glass contains a colorless, odorless liquid, and none of us has left the room. Isn't the conclusion obvious?

RICHARD STARK: Let's not forget me over here with my gun. Cough up your money and valuables.

MODERATOR: I can't believe this is happening.

RICHARD STARK: Hey, Culver, *this* is all you got?

TIMOTHY J. CULVER: Realists don't travel with a lot of cash.

RICHARD STARK: You, Moderator, get me the stuff out of Coe's pockets.

MODERATOR: You want me to rob a corpse?

RICHARD STARK: Rob one or be one, the choice is yours. That's better.

TIMOTHY J. CULVER: We'll see about—

MODERATOR: They're struggling! Look out!

RICHARD STARK: You asked for—

MODERATOR: You shot him! Timothy J. Culver is dead!

RICHARD STARK: No mystery about *that* body.

DONALD E. WESTLAKE: I didn't kill Tucker Coe!

RICHARD STARK: Anybody else feel like a hero? No? All right; don't move from this room for thirty minutes.

MODERATOR: Good God! He's getting away!

DONALD E. WESTLAKE: I want to make one thing clear. I didn't kill Tucker Coe.

MODERATOR: We don't dare leave. We have to stay in the room with these two bodies. What can we *do* for the next half-hour?

DONALD E. WESTLAKE: We could play Twenty Questions. I'm thinking of something that's part vegetable and part mineral.

MODERATOR: Oh, shut up.

LIVING WITH A MYSTERY WRITER, BY ABBY ADAMS

Abby Adams Westlake wrote this in 1977 to accompany "Hearing Voices in My Head" in *Murder Ink.*—Ed.

Living with one man is difficult enough; living with a group can be nerve-wracking. I have lived with the consortium which calls itself Donald Westlake for five years now, and I still can't always be sure, when I get up in the morning, which of the mob I'll have my coffee with.

Donald E. Westlake is the most fun, and happily we see more of him than any of the others. He is a very funny person, not jolly exactly, but witty; he loves to laugh and to make other people laugh. His taste in humor is catholic, embracing brows low, middle and high, from *Volpone* to Laurel and Hardy. (His cuff links, the only ones I've ever seen him wear, depict Stan and Ollie, one on each wrist.) He's a clown at times; coming home from the theater recently with a number of children (more about them later), he engaged in a skipping contest (which he won—he's very competitive, a Stark characteristic spilling over) with several of the younger kids, causing the eldest girl acute embarrassment.

Westlake has in common with many of his characters a simplicity and naivete about life that is disarming, especially if you don't know about the Stark and Coe personae lurking in the background. Looking for an American Express office, he walked through the red-light district of Amsterdam without once noticing the "Walletjes"—plate-glass windows set at eye level in the seventeenth-century canal houses, behind each of which sits a lightly clad hooker, under a red light just in case the message has not been put across. I had to take him back and point them out: "There's one, Don, isn't she pretty? And here's another one."

Like his character Dortmunder, Westlake is unpretentious, unmoved by style or fashion. He dresses simply, wearing the same clothes year after year, wearing hush puppies until they literally fall off his feet. I cut his hair, but he does his own mending and sews on his own buttons. (Mine, too.) Also like Dortmunder he takes a great deal of pride in his work (with, thank God, more success), but is not otherwise vain.

Behind the wheel of a car he is Murch. One of the four publications he subscribes to is *Car and Driver*. (The others are *Horizon*, the *New Yorker* and the *Manchester Guardian*; what is one to make of all *that*?) He drives passionately, never failing to take an advantage. We once drove across the United States and were passed only three times: twice by policemen and once by a battered old pickup truck full of cowboys that whizzed past us at ninety on a road in Wyoming that I still shudder at the memory of. (We were doing seventy-five.)

Like Harry Künt, the hero of *Help, I Am Being Held Prisoner*, Westlake will do almost anything for a laugh. Fortunately, he does not share Künt's proclivity for practical joking or I would no longer share his bed. Like Brother Benedict of *Brothers Keepers*, he really is happiest leading a quiet life and being able to get on with his own work in peace. However, his life, like a Westlake plot, seldom quiets down for more than five minutes. ("I'm sick of working one day in a row," he sometimes says.) Like many of his heroes, he brings this on himself, partly out of restlessness and partly out of a desire to make things happen around him. For instance, all these children.

Westlake has four, by various spouses, and I have three. Not satisfied with the status quo—his four scattered with their mothers from Binghamton, New York, to Los Angeles, California ("I have branches in all principal cities," he is wont to say) and mine living with me in New York City—he ups and gathers everybody, with all their typewriters, baseball cards, Legos, musical instruments, movie books, and stuffed animals, and brings us all to *London* for a year. Then, not content with London, he rents buses and takes this traveling circus all over Great Britain, including Scotland in January (snow) and Cornwall and Wales in February (rain). Still not content, he drives us through the Continent in April for a sort of Grand Tour: Holland, Belgium, Germany, Luxemburg and France in three weeks. Because, like Brother Benedict again, he is obsessed with Travel.

Also, like every Westlake hero, Donald E. Westlake is sex-crazed, but I'm not going to talk about that.

Tucker Coe is the gloomy one, almost worse to have around the house than Richard Stark. We see Tucker Coe when things go wrong. The bills can't be paid because the inefficient worlds of publishing and show business have failed to come up with the money to pay them. Children are rude, noisy, dishonest, lazy, loutish and, above all, ungrateful; suddenly you wonder what you ever saw in them. Ex-wives are mean and grasping. Cars break down, houses betray you, plants refuse to live, and it rains on the picnic. Coe's character Mitch Tobin builds a brick wall in his backyard when he's feeling sorry for himself; Coe has never actually built a wall, but he has built enough bookcases to fill the 42nd Street library, for himself and his friends. Also, when the Tucker Coe mood is upon him, he will do crossword puzzles, jigsaw puzzles (even ones he has done before), fix broken electrical things—in fact, do almost anything except work at his typewriter or talk with other human beings.

Timothy Culver is the professional—hack, if you prefer. He will write anything for anybody and doesn't care how much he's paid, just as long as the typewriter keys keep flying. If he doesn't have any actual work to do, he will write letters; and if you've ever received one, you'll know they're just as well-written as his books. Well-typed, too. Part of his professionalism is that he produces copy so clean you could simply photostat the pages and put them between boards and have a book with fewer misprintings than most actual volumes.

His desk is as organized as a professional carpenter's workshop. No matter where it is (currently, it's a long white dressing table at one end of the living room here in London), it must be set up according to the same unbending pattern. Two typewriters (Smith Corona Silent-Super manual) sit on the desk with a lamp and a telephone and a radio, and a number of black ball-point pens for corrections (seldom needed!). On a shelf just above the desk, five manuscript boxes hold three kinds of paper (white bond first sheets, white second sheets and yellow work sheets) plus originals and carbon of whatever he's currently working on. (Frequently one of these boxes also holds a sleeping cat.) Also on this shelf are reference books (*Thesaurus*, *Bartlett's*, *1000 Names for Baby*, etc.) and cups containing small necessities such as tape, rubber bands (I don't know *what* he uses them for) and paper clips. Above this shelf is a bulletin board displaying various things that Timothy Culver likes to look at when he's trying to think of the next sentence. Currently, among others, there are: a newspaper photo showing Nelson

Rockefeller giving someone the finger; two postcards from the Louvre, one obscene; a photo of me in our garden in Hope, New Jersey; a Christmas card from his Los Angeles divorce attorney showing himself and his wife in their Bicentennial costumes; and a small hand-lettered sign that says "weird villain." This last is an invariable part of his desk bulletin board: "weird" and "villain" are the two words he most frequently misspells. There used to be a third—"liaison"—but since I taught him how to pronounce it (not *lay*-ee-son but lee-*ay*-son) he no longer has trouble with it.

The arrangement of the various objects on and around The Desk is sacred, and should it be disturbed, nice easygoing professional Timothy Culver turns forthwith into Richard Stark. Children tremble, women weep and the cat hides under the bed. Whereas Tucker Coe is morose and self-pitying, Stark has no pity for anyone. Stark is capable of not talking to anyone for days, or, worse yet, of not talking to one particular person for days while still seeming cheerful and friendly with everyone else. Stark could turn Old Faithful into ice cubes. Do you know how Parker, when things aren't going well, can sit alone in a dark room for hours or days without moving? Stark doesn't do this—that would be too unnerving—but he can play solitaire for hours on end. He plays very fast, turns over the cards one at a time, and goes through the deck just once. He never cheats and doesn't seem to care if the game never comes out. It is not possible to be in the same room with him while he's doing this without being driven completely up the wall.

Stark is very competitive and does whatever he does with the full expectation of winning. He is loyal and honest in his dealings with people and completely unforgiving when they are not the same. Stark is a loner, a cat who walks by himself. He's not influenced by other people, doesn't join clubs or groups, and judges himself according to his own standards. Not the easiest man to live with, but fortunately I seldom have to. About the best you can say for Stark is that he can be trusted to take messages for Westlake and the others which he will deliver the next time they come in.

The question that now comes to mind is: What next? Or should I say, Who next? A half-completed novel now resides on The Desk, title known (but secret), author still unchristened. I feel a certain suspense as I await the birth of this creature; yet whoever he turns out to be I know he will probably be difficult to get along with, but not boring.

WRITERS ON WRITING: A PSEUDONYM RETURNS FROM AN ALTER-EGO TRIP, WITH NEW TALES TO TELL

This was originally published in the *New York Times Book Review* on January 29, 2001, following the publication of *Flashfire*, the nineteenth Parker novel.—Ed.

I've just completed another few months being Richard Stark, and a very pleasant time it was. Richard Stark is the name I write under when I'm not writing under the name Donald Westlake, which is the name I was born with, and these days it is doubly pleasant for me to visit with Stark, because for twenty-three years he wouldn't answer my calls.

The relationship between a writer and his pseudonym is a complex one, and never more so than when the alter ego refuses to appear. I became Richard Stark in the first place, forty years ago, for both of the usual reasons. As a young writer, effervescent with ideas, I was turning out far too much work to ship to the publishers under just one name. Also, being a writer who worked in a variety of styles, I thought it a good idea to offer brand-name definition. Westlake does this, Stark does that.

For twelve years, from 1962 to 1974, Stark did a whole bunch of that, being sixteen novels about a coldblooded thief named Parker and four novels about an associate of Parker's named Grofield. By the late sixties, Stark was better known and better paid than Westlake, which felt a little odd. But after all, we were both me, so there was no reason for jealousy. In 1967 the first Stark novel was made into one of the seminal

American movies, *Point Blank*, with Lee Marvin (remade recently as *Payback* with Mel Gibson), and half a dozen other Stark novels were also filmed, including one in France directed by Jean-Luc Godard.

But then, in 1974, Richard Stark just up and disappeared. He did a fade. Periodically, in the ensuing years, I tried to summon that persona, to write like him, to be him for just a while, but every single time I failed. What appeared on the paper was stiff, full of lumps, a poor imitation, a pastiche. Though successful, though well liked and well paid, Richard Stark had simply downed tools. For, I thought, ever.

It seems strange to say that for those years I could no longer write like myself, since Richard Stark had always been, naturally, me. But he was gone, and when I say he was gone, I mean his voice was gone, erased clean out of my head.

Which leads to the question I am most frequently asked about Richard Stark when I'm at a book signing or on an author panel somewhere. Are you, people want to know, a different person, with different attitudes and character traits, when you're writing as Richard Stark? Are you sometimes Dr. Jekyll, sometimes Mr. Hyde? (My wife is asked this question about me, too, and her answer is to roll her eyes.)

The real answer, of course, is no. I'm not schizophrenic, I know who's sitting at that desk. But the other answer is, if we really want to get down to it, well, yes.

In the most basic way, writers are defined not by the stories they tell, or their politics, or their gender, or their race, but by the words they use. Writing begins with language, and it is in that initial choosing, as one sifts through the wayward lushness of our wonderful mongrel English, that choice of vocabulary and grammar and tone, the selection on the palette, that determines who's sitting at that desk. Language creates the writer's attitude toward the particular story he's decided to tell. But more than that, language is a part of the creation of the characters in the story, in the setting and in the sense of movement. Stark and Westlake use language very differently. To some extent they're mirror images. Westlake is allusive, indirect, referential, a bit rococo. Stark strips his sentences down to the necessary information.

In *Flashfire*, the Richard Stark novel just recently published, he writes, "Parker looked at the money, and it wasn't enough." In one of his own novels a few years ago, Donald Westlake wrote, "John Dortmunder and a failed enterprise always recognized one another." Dortmunder, Westlake's recurring character, proposes a Christmas toast this way, "God help us, every one." Parker answers the phone, "Yes."

For years, it was enjoyable and productive to go back and forth between the two voices. Letting the one guy sleep while the other guy stretched helped me avoid staleness, sameness, the rut of the familiar, kept me from being both bored and, I hope, boring.

I missed Stark during his truancy. But finally after fifteen years I did come to the reluctant conclusion that he was as gone as last year's snow. Then an odd thing happened.

I had taken the job of writing the film adaptation of Jim Thompson's *Grifters*, and the director, Stephen Frears, insisted he wanted Richard Stark to write—and sign—the screenplay. He didn't want Westlake, with his grins and winks, his peering around corners. He wanted Stark, blunt-fingered and dogged and with no taste for romantic claptrap.

I demurred, saying I was perfectly capable of writing the screenplay myself, and in any case Stark didn't seem to exist anymore. But it remained a bone of contention between us until I finally pointed out that Richard Stark wasn't a member of the Writer's Guild, and I wasn't about to let him scab. In that case, although Stephen might grumble, he was prepared to accept the second-best, so I went ahead and wrote the script.

Or did I? Thompson was very much more like Stark than like Westlake, and so was the script. And it was immediately after *The Grifters* that I began to think about and noodle with a new story about Parker. I didn't believe in it, but I went to it anyway, went away from it, went back to it, and all at once there it was. Richard Stark was back.

I sensibly enough called that book *Comeback*, and it was followed by *Backflash* and now *Flashfire*. (The Stark book he and I just completed, to be published next year, is called *Firebreak*. A subtle pattern begins to emerge.)

DONALD E. WESTLAKE, A.K.A. . . .

So was Stephen Frears right after all? Did that screenwriting job wake Stark from his slumbers? Did he actually write that script, with me merely as the union-card-carrying front? I don't really know how I could answer that, one way or the other, for absolutely sure.

Such confusion is rare, however. For instance, this piece is clearly, uh, written by, uh . . .

THREE SO TELL ME ABOUT THIS JOB WE'RE GONNA PULL

On Genre

THE HARDBOILED DICKS

This essay was first delivered as a talk at the Smithsonian Institution on May 13, 1982.—Ed.

The hardboiled dicks. The term *hardboiled*, to mean an unsentimental person, began as World War I slang, and its first reference was to the tough drill sergeants who pounded all those citizens into citizen-soldiers. Wartime slang tends to follow the citizen-soldier home when the battle is done. Somebody who was hardboiled then became any person who wasn't sympathetic to *your* problem.

The term *dick*, in this context—and I shall consider no other context—is a little older. It came from Canada, it came from the underworld, and it's merely an arbitrary shortening of the word *detective*. A French-Canadian slurring of an English word is possible, but by no means sure. Anyway, *dick* came across the border from Canada with the cases of hooch when Prohibition started in 1919. So here we have these two words, but they haven't yet been put together.

It has been said that, in Europe and America, the First World War utterly changed the social fabric, and that in some ways we're all still living through the aftershocks. Certainly the prewar *assurance*, the belief that everyone was in his appropriate place in the smoothly running machine of society, came to an end. Doubt, alienation, and then what I'm going to call *atomation* took place. The idea that a person is not locked into a specific place and role in the stately dance of civilization, but that we are all loose, unjoined atoms. In America, there were only four months between the end of the war and the beginning of Prohibition, which I think has to be listed as the most stupid social experiment since the Children's Crusade. In addition to organizing crime, in addition to giving criminal gangs a vast new source of wealth, in addition to making the corruption of policemen and politicians and other authority figures absolutely inevitable, Prohibition did something even worse. It put us all over on the criminal's side, doing business with him, agreeing with his rejection of the law, and encouraging him to remain rich and unrepentant.

The detective story started as a puzzle. Poe and all that. In France in the later nineteenth century, Émile Gaboriau invented the detective called Monsieur Lecoq and used his detective and the puzzles to comment on and describe the aftershocks of *his* century's great trauma, the French Revolution and the dispersal of the aristocracy. He had a knack, by the way, for absolutely wonderful titles. *Other People's Money. The Widow LeRouge. Within an Inch of His Life.*

In England a little later, Conan Doyle used the puzzle for its own sake, as Poe had, and as many other practitioners did, and as they could do because there were no *large* puzzles. In the orderly, self-confident, measured prewar world, the only possible enigmas were small ones.

Since the First World War and Prohibition combined to create the atmosphere in which the puzzle would be transmogrified into something new that would reflect the new reality, I think it's nice that the phrase for that new thing should itself combine words from the war and the bootleggers. Hardboiled dicks. Tough guys who were interested in a very rough kind of immediate justice having to do with this particular case at this particular moment, because there *are* no reliable long-term social truths or social contracts. The determination to turn the puzzle story on its head shows very clearly in its changed treatment of class, of persons in different social strata. In the previous form—previous in origin but by no means dead, then or now, very much still with us—the detectives and the victims alike tend to be from the upper classes, or at least not below the professional middle class—I mean, no tradesmen—while the murderer could be of any class at all. Frequently, however, he would turn out to be jumped-up, to belong actually to a less exalted class than the one to which he'd been pretending. I mention only Lord Peter Wimsey and Philo Vance. The puzzles tended to be rather more like crossword puzzles, in that the solution might hinge on esoteric knowledge, of bell-ringing or Chinese vases or Turkish cigarette ash.

But on come the hardboiled dicks, and everything goes out the window. Puzzle solutions require knowledge no more esoteric than that people are sometimes greedy, people are sometimes jealous, people are sometimes afraid. The hardboiled dick himself was middle-class at best, more probably working-class in his background, never claiming much more than a high school education, and the only thing he will ever offer as special knowledge is that he knows where the bodies are buried. He's an insider, in other words, in this new doubt-ridden, topsy-turvy, unsentimental world. As for the upper classes, who are popularly thought of as having caused the war and profited from it— much of which turned out to be true, by the way—they don't even come off well in these stories. When they appear at all, they are made fun of and despised, they are gullible patsies for con men and professional gamblers, their daughters are dumb enough to run away to Mexico with ex-cons. They are even, at times, the murderer, and their motivations are as human and messy as anybody's.

The social viewpoint that had created this new genre was very strong within the stories. The first writers tended to be veterans of the recent war, middle-class men themselves with some physical labor in their background, and they weren't the sort of people who would think Prohibition was a good idea. They had known some violence, they were a bit alienated from normal society—as any writer who makes his living with his pen inevitably is—and they had formed social opinions. All of that is in the stories. Gangsters can be trusted up to a point. The upper classes are silly fops. Politicians are crooked and hate the hero, except for that rare honest politico who likes the hero but worries about him. Women and Ford cars are nice to have, but things can suddenly go wrong with both. Intuitive street-smart *brains* are good, but brains and a gun are better.

The new genre, the detective stories about the hardboiled dicks, began in magazines, in the pulps, initially with a magazine called *Black Mask*. Starting his life in short stories, the hardboiled dick had one more quality in addition to his social and historic qualities: he was terse. It was not necessarily a *new* use of language—Mark Twain could be pretty terse, to name just one—but combining the elements of terseness and the puzzle and social attitudes and topical reality created something that had never been seen before.

Black Mask was one of a bunch of magazines publishing the older sort of puzzle, but in which the new sort was uncertainly being born. The first hardboiled dick seems to have been—I'm weaseling out here, because the history of the early pulps is very uncertain—but anyway, he seems to have been a fellow named Race Williams, created by a writer named Carroll John Daly. Daly wasn't a particularly good writer, and he did tend to apologize to the reader for his character's uncouth behavior, but by his first appearance in *Black Mask* magazine he had the genre and the tone down pat. An opening sentence of a Race Williams story: "I dropped to one knee and fired twice." Okay? Another opening sentence: "I didn't like his face and I told him so."

Dashiell Hammett, a vet with tuberculosis—what they called in those unsentimental days a lunger—had also been a private detective with the Pinkertons. He started writing while recuperating from TB, and *Black Mask* was his natural home. He improved on Carroll John Daly in several ways: first, he didn't try so hard to be a tough guy, and second, he didn't apologize. He also added irony to the genre, which kept it nicely oiled; without irony, the hardboiled dick would be too brittle and unbending to survive. Here's the opening sentence of a Hammett *Black Mask* story called "The Gatewood Caper," in which the irony, the social and class attitudes, and the lack of sentiment all stand out in very nice relief:

> Harvey Gatewood had issued orders that I was to be admitted as soon as I arrived, so it took me only a little less than fifteen minutes to thread my way past the door-keepers, office boys, and secretaries who filled up most of the space between the Gatewood Lumber Corporation's front door and the president's private office.

Compare this, complete with its class-consciousness, with a typical Race Williams entrance:

> I just lifted my foot and let the door have it. Then I walked into the hall. The butler was sailing ungracefully across the highly polished wood until he struck a small rug and continued on that. Rough? Of course it was rough. But if you're going to force your way into a place, let it be deter-mined. Let them be damned thankful that you didn't shoot your way in.

You can see that the toughness is a little forced, a little over-stated, and then apologized for. And the descriptions are minimal. All we know about the hall is that the floor is highly polished wood, with a small rug, and we only know those facts because they are part of the butler's recession. If I knew just *one* unnecessary thing—the color or style or provenance of that small rug, for instance—I would believe Race Williams a little more than I do now.

Race Williams wasn't merely the first of the hardboiled dicks, he was also the original of a type that still continues in the genre. Here's another example of Williams's braggadocio:

> The papers are always either roasting me for shooting down some minor criminals or praising me for gunning out the big shots. But when you're hunting the top guy, you have to kick aside—or shoot aside—the gunmen he hires. You can't make hamburger without grinding up a little meat.

The defensiveness, the awareness of publicity, the pride in being trigger-happy; could this be Mike Hammer's father?

But that takes us out of sequence. We're in the middle twenties now, and a new kind of story is being formed, spontaneously generated by several different writers out of their common experiences of the last decade. And when Captain Joseph M. Shaw—he was a captain in the war, and he retained the title—when Captain Shaw took over the editorship of *Black Mask*, beginning with the November 1926 issue, he became the first editor anywhere to make this new genre the *subject* of a magazine. He himself was anything but terse and tough in his writing, but he recognized vitality when he saw it. In his words, written some twenty years later:

> We had recently returned from the five-year sojourn abroad during and following the First World War. Happening upon a sporting magazine, to which we had haphazardly contributed in years past, we were curious enough to investigate the remarkable change that had taken place in its format and appearance.

You see the style. Skipping ahead, he says:

> In friendly conversation we were asked to edit another magazine in the same group: *Black Mask*, a detective story magazine. Before that, we had never seen a copy, had never even heard of the magazine.

That didn't stop him. I'm skipping ahead again:

> We meditated on the possibility of creating a new type of detective story differing from that accredited to the Chaldeans and employed more recently by Gaboriau, Poe, Conan Doyle.

I love that reference to the Chaldeans. Waltzing onward, Captain Shaw says he studied the work of the writers already contributing to the magazine and discovered Dashiell Hammett: "He told his stories with a new kind of compulsion and authenticity." With Hammett leading the way, a whole corps of writers developed who were devoted to—and quite good at—the hardboiled story.

Most of those Hammett contemporaries are as forgotten now as Carroll John Daly, and in some cases that's a pity. Lester Dent, for instance, was such a master of brevity, of delivering whole worlds of information in the unexpected word inside a sentence, that his work has an almost ballet-like simplicity and smoothness. Here's the opening of a story called "Sail," introducing his hardboiled hero, Oscar Sail,

> The fish shook its tail as the knife cut off its head. Red ran out of the two parts and the fluid spread enough to cover the wet red marks where two human hands had failed to hold to the dock edge.
>
> Oscar Sail wet the palm of his own left hand in the puddle.
>
> The small policeman kept coming out on the dock, tramping in the rear edge of glare from his flashlight.
>
> Sail split the fish belly, shook it over the edge of the yacht dock and there were some splashes below in the water. The stuff from the fish made the red stain in the water a little larger.

There's talent and cleverness in this writing, and something more. These people are working with a new toy, a brand-new toy. They're having *fun*. A writer named Forrest Rosaire, in a *Black Mask* story called "The Devil Suit," tried playing with the toy in the present tense. At a time when Damon Runyon had made the present tense his own—and had used it to create a kind of artificial smart-alecky chamber music, Rosaire had the nerve to make it colloquial and hardboiled and glib. The story begins:

> This is one night up in LA when Steve Parker and I are driving home after a little game with the boys. Out on Los Feliz Boulevard Steve sees the sign of Barr's Cafe and pulls up to the curb, saying, "How's for a steak?"

A little later, there's a brawl in front of the cafe, and the energy and enjoyment in the writing are like watching kids play basketball. Listen:

I guess it would have been better to swing him around with the left hand and sock him with the right, because with the conversation he starts a left that I have to back quick to get away from. There's one of these single wire railings around the lawn, and I back neatly into it, do a back flipflop, and come down on the base of my neck. The boy dives on me like he dived on the dog. I get hold of the inside of his coat, rip the pocket out, then feel something like a star-shell explode under my left eye. Next thing I have is the box, which I throw at random; the guy is standing over me now and I see him lift his foot back to kick me in the middle of the face. I see him lift his foot back, I repeat; after that, as Shakespeare says, is silence.

Nothing remains the same—as my waistline keeps reminding me. The vitality of a new genre is partly caused by that very newness. As time goes on, the novelty must inevitably fade, and at that point the genre itself must either fade or find some other kind of vitality, nourishment from a different source. I would like to suggest that in popular fiction, when a new genre moves out of its youth, the vitality necessary to its survival comes in fact from ritual, and, further, that ritual is a kind of poison which inevitably will kill it. Like those poisons which give the human face an appearance of ruddy health while doing their quiet work within the body. Or, more appropriately, like those substances, such as strychnine, which in controlled doses are useful to a body waning in vitality, but which in overdosages or prolonged use inevitably produce death.

Marshall McLuhan, who said a lot of foolish things, sometimes said interesting things as well, and one thing he said was that it is impossible to describe an environment if you are in it. Environments can only be described from the outside. My own corollary from that would be that we might be able to describe our own environment by inference, if we study similar environments. Coming back to Earth, I would like to spend a moment comparing the hardboiled detective story with the Western. Both forms, of course, are ways of trying to describe a specific world to people who are only slightly familiar with, but fascinated with, that world. The Western described the frontier to the stay-at-homes. The hardboiled detective story described the wreck of society to those who were living on the parts yet afloat. In contrast, the puzzle story is an affirmation of the existence and axioms of an agreed-upon shared social structure, and so is less like the hardboiled story than the Western is.

The Western began as exaggerated reportage. The penny dreadfuls, the hyped-up exploits of people like Buffalo Bill and Wyatt Earp, were lies and nonsense and tall stories, but the point is that they were lies told by people who *knew the truth*. The first writers in the genre had been there, out West, out on the frontier among the pioneers, and they had behind them a reality upon which to build when telling the lies they knew would please an audience back East. They might invent gun battles, Indian raids, grizzly bear attacks, some of them even went so far as to invent non-existent animals, but the spirit behind the stories—and the terrain on which the stories were played—were real and alive and vibrant in the writers' minds. There was a half-conscious truth beneath the lies, and a part of that truth was the writers' love for the places and the people they were writing about. They even loved the lies, as being a part of the scene—the lies were part of the truth.

As time went on, though, and as the reality of the West itself changed, that early relationship between the writer and his material had to change. New writers came along who had never walked that ground but who nevertheless wrote the stories. Clarence E. Mulford, writer of the Hopalong Cassidy stories, lived his life in New England and was over fifty the first time he traveled west of the Hudson River. These writers, who hadn't been there, who hadn't lived the truth, had nothing to go by but their predecessor's stories. Their invention could not springboard from the rocks and dust and trails and trees of the actual terrain, but had to develop out of previous fiction. Which is what leads to ritual. In order to be sure not to stray too far from the acceptable—that is, not the real, but what was *perceived* as real—in order to stay within what the readership would believe, the writers had to tell them things that had already been believed before.

For instance, in the historical Old West, not every adult male owned a sidearm, a revolver, but among those who did, fewer than one in ten also owned a holster, hanging down there on the right hip. Most men who owned a revolver, if they wanted it with them, carried it either in a pocket or stuck into their belt. But the ritual required not only that all men own revolvers and that all men own holsters, but that all men had practiced at getting the one out of the other *very fast*.

Years after the period of the Old West, an ancient survivor of seven barroom shootouts—not much in ritual terms, but a lot in real life—described how he'd done it. He did own a holster, and when he saw that shooting was about to start, he'd reach down and pull the trigger. The bullet would go into the floor, of course, but the main point was the noise. While his opponent tried to figure out whether he'd just been killed or not, this guy would in leisurely fashion draw his revolver and shoot him dead.

But that sort of reality will never overtake the ritual. And what happens is that the genre becomes increasingly predictable and routinized, until you can never be sure if you've read *this* one already or not. In another example, several years ago there was a paperback fad for gothic romance, and an editor in the field told me one day about a book he was publishing—one of the four gothics from his house that month—that he was truly excited about because it was a bold breakthrough. "The girl isn't a governess," he said. "She's the *cook!*"

There was no strength in those gothic romances beyond the ritual, so they soon withered and died. The Western had strength, and survived, and endured, and from time to time the very ritual itself leads to art. I think of Jack Schaefer's novel *Shane*.

From exaggerated reality to ritualized refried fiction to the possibility of art; that's the Western. How does that illuminate the hardboiled detective?

In the first place, both the Western and the hardboiled detective story are involved with the same ritual subject: the chivalrous man in an unchivalrous world. That wasn't exactly what either the penny dreadfuls or the early *Black Mask* were about, but it became what the rituals were in aid of. And this, of course, takes us directly to Raymond Chandler.

Hammett was the premier practitioner of the first wave, those who had been there and knew the reality that was their raw material. A decade later, in 1936, Chandler began writing for *Black Mask*: a bookish, English-educated sort of mama's boy whose raw material was not the truth but the first decade of the fiction.

This is not to denigrate Chandler, or at least not to denigrate him very much. The fact is, as time went on, the world continued to change, the first wave of writers were themselves further from their origins, the First World War was buried in the rumbling rumors of the next war to come, Prohibition was ended and replaced by a Depression, and even the social attitudes underwent a further shift; with the Depression, people needed one another more, and needed to believe in commonality rather than isolated individuality. With all these changes, and the passage of time, most of the first-wave writers, including Hammett, simply ran out of steam.

One of the strangest sequences in fiction occurs in Hammett's last novel, *The Thin Man*. Nick and Nora Charles are in a speakeasy called the Pigiron Club, talking with the owner, Studsy, a thug named Morelli, and a few other people. Then we have this:

> An immensely fat blond man—so blond he was nearly albino—who had been sitting at Miriam's table came over and said to me in a thin, tremulous voice: "So you're the party who put it to little Art Nunhei—"
>
> Morelli hit the fat man in his fat belly, as hard as he could without getting up. Studsy, suddenly on his feet, leaned over Morelli and smashed a big fist into the fat man's face. I noticed, foolishly, that he still led with his right. Hunchbacked Pete came up behind the fat man and banged his empty tray down with full force on the fat man's head. The fat man fell back, upsetting three people and a table. Both bar-tenders were with us by then. One of them hit the fat man with a blackjack as he tried to get up, knocking him forward on hands and knees, the other put a hand down inside the fat man's collar in back, twisting the collar to choke him. With Morelli's help they got the fat man to his feet and hustled him out.

Pete looked after them and sucked a tooth. "That goddamned Sparrow," he explained to me, "you can't take no chances on him when he's drinking."

Studsy was at the next table, the one that had been upset, helping people pick up themselves and their possessions. "That's bad," he was saying, "bad for business, but where you going to draw the line? I ain't running a dive, but I ain't trying to run a young ladies' seminary neither."

Dorothy was pale, frightened; Nora wide-eyed and amazed. "It's a madhouse," she said. "What'd they do that for?"

"You know as much about it as I do," I told her.

And that's the truth. The fat man called Sparrow will never reappear in the book. This sequence doesn't come out of anything, and it doesn't lead to anything. Its only reason for existing at all is to show that Nick doesn't know what's going on anymore, he's become a visitor to the scene he used to live in. And when I say Nick, I mean Hammett.

Hammett was a major writer, for a lot of reasons, one of them being that the texture in his writing comes so very much from himself. Writing inside an action genre, where subtleties of character and milieu are not primary considerations, he nevertheless was, word by word and sentence by sentence, subtle and many-layered, both allusive and elusive, delicate and aloof among all the smashing fists and crashing guns. He put himself in his writing, and that makes *The Thin Man* a very strange read, in that singular way that *The Tempest* is strange; inside the story, the writer can be seen, preparing his departure.

A little before the Sparrow sequence, Nick arrives at one of the parties that dot the book, parties he much prefers to the crime-solving he's supposed to be involved with. The host and hostess are described far beyond their importance to the story, and then there's a bit of dialogue:

Halsey Edge was a tall scrawny man of fifty-something with a pinched yellow face and no hair at all. He called himself "a ghoul by profession and inclination"—his only joke, if that is what it was—by which he meant he was an archaeologist, and he was very proud of his collection of battle-axes. He was not so bad once you had resigned yourself to the fact that you were in for occasional cataloguings of his armory—stone axes, copper axes, bronze axes, double-bladed axes, faceted axes, polygonal axes, scalloped axes, hammer axes, adze axes, Mesopotamian axes, Hungarian axes, Nordic axes, and all of them looking pretty moth-eaten. It was his wife we objected to. Her name was Leda, but he called her Tip. She was very small and her hair, eyes, and skin, though naturally of different shades, were all muddy. She seldom sat—she perched on things—and liked to cock her head a little to one side. Nora had a theory that once when Edge opened an antique grave, Tip ran out of it, and Margot Innes always spoke of her as the gnome, pronouncing all the letters. She once told me that she did not think any literature of twenty years ago would live, because it had no psychiatry in it. They lived in a pleasant old three-story house on the edge of Greenwich Village and their liquor was excellent.

A dozen or more people were there when we arrived. Tip introduced us to the ones we did not know and then backed me into a corner. "Why didn't you tell me that those people I met at your place Christmas were mixed up in a murder mystery?" she asked, tilting her head to the left until her ear was practically resting on her shoulder.

"I don't know that they are. Besides, what's one murder mystery nowadays."

The *nowadays*, by the way, is also strange in that book. It was published in January 1934, nearly a year after the end of Prohibition, but it contains speakeasies and seems to exist within the Prohibition era. At the same time, it is very aware of the Depression, and contains characters who are much more sophisticated than those in the hardboiled stories of the twenties.

You notice also the passing reference to literature that will or will not last. *The Thin Man* is a very sad book, made even sadder by how bravely and smilingly the narrator *hides* his sadness. Hammett is not leaving the hardboiled detective story. The genre is leaving him.

Enter ritual, to save the form. Chandler took the tough-guy lingo and smoothed it into a kind of narrative poetry, all baroque images and *Weltanschauung*. Stylistically, his antecedents are not the *Black Mask* writers; the clouds he comes out of are Milton's. "Him there they found squat like a toad, close at the ear of Eve," was written by Milton, not Chandler. In fact, *Paradise Lost* is a very Raymond Chandler sort of title, isn't it?

The English like Chandler better than Hammett because they can understand him more. The ritual is firmly in control. In Hammett, in *The Dain Curse*, there's a question about some money a character has, and we get this:

> Rhino said, "Ain't nobody's business where I got my money, I got it. I got—" He put his cigar on the edge of the table, picked up the money, wet a thumb as big as a heel on a tongue like a bath-mat, and counted his roll bill by bill down on the table. "Twenty—thirty—eighty—hundred—hundred and ten—two hundred and ten—three hundred and ten—three hundred and thirty—three hundred and thirty-five—four hundred and thirty-five—five hundred and thirty-five—five hundred and eighty-five—six hundred and five—six hundred and ten—six hundred and twenty—seven hundred and twenty—seven hundred and seventy—eight hundred and forty—nine hundred and forty—nine hundred and sixty—nine hundred and ninety-five—ten hundred and fifteen—ten hundred and twenty—eleven hundred and twenty—eleven hundred and seventy. Anybody wants to know what I got, that's what I got—eleven hundred and seventy dollars. Anybody want to know where I get it, maybe I tell them, maybe I don't. Just depend on how I feel about it."

Now, what the hell is that all about? Chandler would never have done a thing like that. He was always too correct.

One thing more about *The Dain Curse*. It was originally published as three separate novelettes in *Black Mask*, each with its own murders and solution, and the subsequent stitching together is craftsmanship of a very high order, even though the book winds up rather too plot-heavy. Several years ago, a movie producer approached me to write a screenplay of *The Dain Curse* and I re-read it for the first time in several years, making notes on how a lot of that underbrush could be cleared away and simplified, to make something movie-sized. When I got to the end, I discovered that the one character I had definitely eliminated as extraneous was the murderer. There was also no way to turn that book into a movie, which I told the producer, suggesting he make a movie out of a Hammett story called "The Gutting of Couffignal" instead. He did even better; he got out of the movie business and didn't make any picture at all. And *The Dain Curse* was finally done as a miniseries on television, where there was length enough to get it all in. And I thought it was a nice touch that they didn't cast a hero who looked like Hammett's descriptions of The Continental Op, they cast someone who looked like Hammett. Tall, thin, white-haired. James Coburn, in clothing to emphasize the similarity. Of *course* Hammett was the Op, laconic and fatalistic and sure-footed.

After Hammett and the first-wave writers, Chandler and the second-wave writers also *were* their characters, but not in the same way. Reality was replaced by fiction, experience replaced by ritual, storytelling replaced by literature. Self-consciousness, which we see setting in in the later Hammett, was there from the beginning with Chandler.

Chandler also brought in another new element, a smothered, unacknowledged homosexuality. Story forms on male preserves—the Western again, sea stories, war stories, God knows prison stories—are always open to this potential, and the tougher, the more overtly he-man, the genre is, the more the tension inevitably is created by this addition of homosexuality. In Chandler, it created a dark chiaroscuro that furnishes much of the fascination of his stories, particularly the novels. The world in which Philip Marlowe moves seems more than usually murky, with dark and unexplained patches, with an overriding sense of solitude and sadness unrelated to the plots. The social attitudes of the first wave of the writers—their belief in social disconnectedness, of general untrustworthiness relieved by isolated examples of comradeship—become both more mysterious and more poignant when given a homosexual coloring.

About the closest this homosexual content ever came to the surface in Chandler's work is in the first five chapters of *The Long Goodbye*. Marlowe's relationship with Terry Lennox, from the moment he picks Lennox up—literally and figuratively—in front of a bar and restaurant called "The Dancers," is inexplicable in any other way. If this is not a homosexual relationship, what on earth *is* it?

I am not suggesting that Chandler was or was not homosexual, only that a homosexual content was one of the elements—along with literariness and world-weariness—that gave his hardboiled stories their texture and fascination, and make them still alive today, more than forty years after they began.

The Second World War was not good for the private eye. The wandering daughters of bullying rich men seemed less important than before, but what could a detective, no matter how hardboiled, do against the Third Reich? Spies and innocent bystanders were heroes appropriate to the moment—that is, from reality, professional soldiers and citizen-soldiers—and the private eye had to mark time until the war was over.

The third wave of hardboiled writers hit the beach in 1947. Kenneth Millar started then, and did three novels under his own name before inventing Lew Archer and Ross Macdonald in 1949. So did Donald Hamilton, several years before he would invent Matt Helm. And so did the writer whose first book, published in 1947, began like this:

> I shook the rain from my hat and walked into the room. Nobody said a word. They stepped back politely and I could feel their eyes on me.

Mickey Spillane. *I, the Jury*. An unexpectedly quiet entrance, but within a couple of pages Mike Hammer is making a speech to his murdered friend:

> "Jack, you're dead now. You can't hear me any more. Maybe you can. I hope so. I want you to hear what I'm about to say. You've known me for a long time, Jack. My word is good just as long as I live. I'm going to get the louse that killed you. He won't sit in the chair. He won't hang. He will die

exactly as you did, with a .45 slug in the gut, just a little below the belly button. No matter who it is, Jack, I'll get the one. Remember, no matter who it is, I promise."

Spillane took the plot of *The Maltese Falcon*, the brooding darkness of Chandler, the overstated tough talk of the second-rate hardboiled writers, wedded them all to the anxious, impatient overcharged postwar atmosphere, and came up with a winner.

World War I had left people tired and alienated. World War II left them hopped-up, incomplete, wanting the party not to be over, but at the same time feeling lost and nostalgic for their prewar lives. The war had gone on too long, had been too brutal, had changed too many things. *Nobody* could go home again. Twenty years earlier, Hammett's Continental Op had said, "Emotions are nuisances during business hours," but for these new writers the emotions were all too strong, too insistent. Some, like Spillane, let the emotions pour out like diseased honey, giving a pulpy stickiness to their work. Some, like a lot of writers with *Donald* in their name—Ross Macdonald, John D. MacDonald, Donald Hamilton—permitted emotion to leach through a stiff-upper-lip impersonal facade. In either case, the ritual had been roughed up by the war, had become something stronger and harsher than it had been.

One exception to this—and it was an exception that people loved for quite a while—was Richard S. Prather, whose Shell Scott was a private eye gone bonkers. All the other guys were glooming and brooding and not really having much fun in life, but Shell Scott *loved* the ritual, *loved* being a private eye, *loved* being a pulp fiction character. He started chuckling and winking and mooning at us in 1951, and here's the start of *The Wailing Frail* from 1956:

She yanked the door open with a crash and said, "Gran —" but then she stopped and stared at me. She was nude as a noodle.

I stared right back at her.

"Oh!" she squealed. "*You're* not Grandma!"

"No," I said. "I'm Shell Scott, and you're not Grandma, either."

She slammed the door in my face.

Yep, I thought, this is the right house.

What I think is my favorite opening for a private eye story comes from a 1953 Shell Scott short called "The Sleeper Caper." Here it is:

> You take a plane from the States and head south; a few hours later and up more than seven thousand feet, where the air is thin and clear, you land at Mexico City and take a cab to the Hipodromo de las Americas, where the horses run sideways, backwards, and occasionally around the seven-furlong track, and you go out to the paddock area after the fourth race.
>
> You see a big, young, husky, unhandsome character with a Mexico City tan, short, prematurely white hair sticking up in the air like the head of a clipped whiskbroom, and his arms around the waists of two lovely young gals who look like Latin screen stars, and you say, "Geez, look at the slob with the two tomatoes."
>
> That's me. I am the slob with the two tomatoes, and the hell with you.
>
> Five days ago I'd left Los Angeles . . .

Different as they were in other ways, Prather and Spillane were alike in being a complete political turnaround from the original *Black Mask* writers of the twenties, almost all of whom had been to the left of the political spectrum, favoring unions, disapproving of mine owners and other rich people, believing America had a good system which at times was corrupted by greedy people for personal gain. Mike Hammer and Shell Scott are much more to the right, their attitudes clearly influenced by the war. The true enemy is frequently foreign in one way or another, and anybody who disagrees with the *status quo*, who wants to offer any change, is suspect. Their only objection to things-as-they-are, in fact, is that they find the criminal justice system too lenient, and frequently feel there's nothing for them to do but hand out justice—or something—themselves.

This is a long way from the origins of the genre. The private eyes of the twenties weren't vigilantes, because they weren't devoted to a cause. Hammer and Scott and so on, in the fifties and sixties, were devoted to a cause.

History is an elephant; mess with her and you could get stepped on. The Vietnam War made the opinions of Hammer and Scott seem boorish and irrelevant; their popularity slipped and has not recovered.

If Hammett was the major figure in the first wave of hardboiled writers, and Chandler the same in the second, it's been generally agreed that Ross Macdonald was the shining light in the third, and if so, he's also an excellent example of the dangers inherent in ritual. Somewhere in the midpoint of his career, Macdonald began to write a novel in which the mystery was centered on a person's parentage and the revelation of a twenty- or thirty-year-old secret was at the core of the solution to the puzzle.

Macdonald wrote that book over and over again for about twenty years. It didn't matter what anybody said. We could plead and beg, we could threaten, we could weep, we could hold our breath and stamp our feet on the floor, he didn't care—he just went on writing that goddam book. You talk about hardboiled!

Macdonald also became increasingly mannered, till finally he was nothing but mannerisms. The tortured similes, the brooding introspection, the jaundiced view of society—nobody ever has *any* fun in a Ross Macdonald book.

Here are a few bits almost at random from just one novel, *Black Money*, of 1966.

His front teeth glared at me like a pair of chisels.

Under his carefully tailored Ivy League suit he wore a layer of fat like easily penetrable armor.

She was handsome and dark, with the slightly imperious look of the only woman in a big house.

Like Jane Eyre? Here's a paragraph; not so much an extended metaphor as an extended groping about:

> The college was in what had recently been the country. On the scalped hills around it were a few remnants of the orange groves which had once furred them with green. The trees on the campus itself were mostly palms, and looked as if they had been brought in and planted full grown. The students gave a similar impression. [Unlike most colleges, where the students look as though they were born and raised there.—Westlake]
>
> One of them, a youth with a beard which made him look like a tall Toulouse-Lautrec . . .

Just one more.

> He had a long nose, slightly curved, which appeared both self-assertive and inquisitive.

I hope my nose is looking disbelieving.

From time to time, a very few writers have tried to avoid the ritual and use some sort of reality instead as the framework for their writing, and I think by far the best of these mutants is Joe Gores, who arrived late in the third wave. From the late sixties on, Joe Gores took the private eye form and, in place of *either* some earlier reality or the standardized conventions, he wrote stories and novels reflecting his own career as a private detective in *our* world, rather than the world of the twenties or the forties. His novels and stories about the Dan Kearny Agency are at the same time firmly within the genre and yet *alive*, and his non-series novel *Interface* (1974) stretches the genre about as far as anybody has done.

However, in addition to turning out some excellent and readable work, Joe Gores has inadvertently also proved again the proposition that, once a genre is dependent on ritual, it will not return to reality. The body that lives on strychnine cannot live without strychnine.

The third wave broke on the rock of Vietnam. War is never good for the private eye, and the Vietnam War was worse. It trivialized everything. Nothing was sure anymore, nothing was true, don't trust anybody over thirty or under thirty or thirty. The finest bit of hardboiled dialogue in the entire era was said by Eugene McCarthy at Chicago in 1968 when his presidential bid failed: "Six months on the road for nothing." Frank Sinatra turned out to be the movie cop of the time, in *The Detective* and *Tony Rome*, and brutality turned out to be the entire message.

Except for television. The real world never never *never* impinges on the entertainment side of television, so fully realized private eyes continued to perform their pulp kabuki all over the tube. Mannix and Cannon and all those fellows, of whom the best was by a long shot Rockford. Rockford didn't try to break out of the rituals, but used them in a very knowing and able way. His relationships with society, with the police, with his clients, with women, were all very much in the tradition, and yet Rockford was an individual, a human being you could believe in rather than a cardboard figure in a trench coat.

A few months ago, a friend told me about an actor who stars as a private eye in a current show based in Hawaii, who had to return to Los Angeles for eye treatments. In order to film him against all that Hawaiian sun, they had to shine so much light on this poor fellow that it's burning his eyes, risking his sight. You want a metaphor for what's happened to the private eye? There's too much light on him. He can't see anymore.

Postwar times seem to generate new private eye waves, and I understand there's one going on now, but I admit I don't know much about it. I know that several people are writing exact replicas of private eye novels. I know that there is an organization called the Private Eye Writers of America, and that it has about seventy-five members, and that every member has published at least one book or story about a private eye. I think about these things, and I try to inhale, and I don't sense any air here. The next to the last stage of the Western was the hermetically sealed story about gunfighters and ranchers and schoolmistresses, none of it reflecting any reality anywhere, some of it joky about its artificiality, like *Vera Cruz*. The last stage of the Western was Sergio Leone, the spaghetti Western, *The Good, the Bad, and the Ugly*, pictures made exclusively in close-up because a long shot would have shown the characters standing on a barren airless moon.

A while ago the Mystery Writers of America joined up with a couple of overseas organizations to have a big meeting in Stockholm. The writers came from every continent. Private eye novels are being written, and published, and read, in Kenya and Zimbabwe, in Japan, in Russia. What are these books? What truth do they connect to? The brevity of the early *Black Mask* days is long gone. The relevance of those days is gone. The vitality of novelty is gone. The reflection of an underlying truth is gone. I'm not really sure *what's* left.

Except the books and stories that started it all. Hammett reads as smoothly and honestly today as he ever did. His contemporaries are just as lively, and not very much dated. Chandler retains his strength and his complexity. The early work of the Donalds—Ross, John D. and Hamilton—is still good and real and very evocative of that postwar time. Mike Hammer and Shell Scott are still, in their very different ways, as loonily readable as ever.

The private eye novel may have become very strait-jacketed by ritual, but it's certainly not dead. The hardboiled dicks are still viable, and may yet produce a *Shane*. It came close with Joe Gore's *Interface*. In the meantime, I look forward with mixed feelings to the first spaghetti private eye.

INTRODUCTION TO *MURDEROUS SCHEMES*

Westlake wrote this introduction for *Murderous Schemes: An Anthology of Classic Detective Stories,* which he coedited with J. Madison Davis for Oxford University Press in 1996.—Ed.

The major flaw with the genre under consideration is that no one knows quite what to call it. Many people call it the "mystery story," though that doesn't take into account all those stories firmly within the genre which are *not* mysteries, such as heist novels, in which we follow the crooks before, during, and after a crime, usually a robbery: *The Asphalt Jungle*, for instance. "Mystery story" also leaves out all those murder stories in which the identity of the murderer is known to the reader/audience from the beginning: the *Columbo* series on television, as one example, or C. S. Forester's *Payment Deferred*, or the charmingly self-referential "The Man Who Read John Dickson Carr."

"Crime story" certainly covers the possibilities, but somehow in terms of this genre the phrase "crime story" has lost its generality and has come to mean almost exclusively stories about professional criminals, leaving out all those wife murderers and greedy heirs. The British, and briefly also the Americans, tried to call our genre the "thriller," but that never quite took, sounding more like fantasy or horror before settling where the "thriller" resides today, as a definition of a story combining spies with technology, meaning in most cases a story more than usually devoid of thrills.

"Suspense" is also used sometimes as a name for the genre, but suspense is not a kind of story, it's an element in *all* story, it's the element that creates the desire to know what happens next, which is to say, the desire to be told the story. Suspense is the nicotine of storytelling, the drug that brings us back. Suspense began when Eve reached for that apple, which was a long, long time ago. We can't co-opt the word for one single genre, as though to say there's no suspense in it when the rustler cuts through the barbed wire or the paratrooper jumps out of the airplane over the combat zone.

My own preference for a name for this genre is "detective story," even though I personally have almost never written about detectives, and in fact most of my characters, when confronted by a detective, do their level best to blend in with the wallpaper. But I like the term "detective story," and will use it from here on in this essay, mostly because it is a term of disparagement.

Well, yes, it is. I can no longer count the times I have been at a cock-tail party and heard someone say, "I never have any time for serious/good/real novels any more. When I want to unwind, I just go to bed with a detective story." That is the context in which the phrase "detective story" is now used, and right now, at this exact moment when you are reading this sentence, the phrase "detective story" is being spoken in exactly that same familiar, easy, disparaging way at least forty times somewhere on the planet.

Who are these speakers? They are intelligent, they are educated, they are usually in the professions (though sometimes in the arts). They are precisely the people any writer would be delighted to count among his readership, and I *am* delighted, and I am willing to accept the barb that comes with it.

Because I know what they really mean, and they don't. Consider: When it comes time for them to unwind, do they unwind by fooling with the Etch-a-Sketch? No. Do they unwind by watching *I Love Lucy* reruns on cable television? No. They don't even unwind with western stories or biographies. Every reader I've ever heard speak in this fashion unwinds with "detective stories."

What they are seeming to say, these people, when they assure us they "just" read detective stories, is that they unwind by insulting their own intelligence. Their brains and educations and wide-ranging intellects, they would like us to know, better fit them for better books, the serious, praiseworthy novels they would certainly be reading if they hadn't tired themselves out at the office.

The mistake is that too many people are confused about what reading fiction is *for*. They believe you're supposed to read novels to be improved, to be present at the clash of great ideas, to be challenged by new and profound ways to look at life. And then it turns out, they're too tired.

Oh, they buy the books, the serious award winners, described by publisher and critic alike as important, ground-breaking, even deeply disturbing. They pay their dues. But when the moment comes, once again they fail. Just for now, just as a stopgap, sheepishly they slink off, inadvertently to read fiction for the right reason: Because it's fun. Just for now, they'll read detective stories.

What are these detective stories, that so enthrall people who should be spending their time on more worthy pursuits? What is this drug anyway?

The purpose of this anthology, assembled and annotated with J. Madison Davis, is to answer that question by showing it has many answers, that the sundry schemes and proliferating variations have been the norm in detective stories from the beginning. Whether examining psychological coercion in the category I Confess! or exploring the undeniable attraction of evil in Come Into My Parlor, the detective story is protean, adapting itself to the manifold purposes of its practitioners, so that to define it is a slippery prospect at best.

Which is why we have chosen something better than definition. We have chosen to describe the detective story in terms of its categories, and to let the categories themselves spread as they will. And when we do that, we see that nitty-gritty realism belongs in the detective story, and formal puzzles do, and comedy does (I'm happy to say), and social commentary, and regional realism, and just about anything you can think of in fiction of any kind at all. About the only constant in every detective story is crime; they all contain some sort of crime.

Why is that? Why is the element of crime so useful to the storyteller and such a magnet to the reader? I'd like to try to answer that by borrowing from the classical description of theater: One character on a stage is a speech, two characters an argument, three characters drama. The variant I would propose begins with society. When you have only society, you have predictability and order; life in an anthill. When you have society and the individual, you have conflict, because the greater good of society is never exactly the same as the greater good of any one individual within it. When you have society and a crime, you have a rent in the fabric, a distortion away from predictability and order; but to no effect, it's merely disordered. When you have all three, society and the individual and a crime, you have all the multiple possibilities of drama, plus all the multiple possibilities of free will; that is, life.

Society and crime are in unending opposition, but the individual is in a shifting relationship to the other two, depending on how *this* individual feels about *this* crime in *this* society.

That's why there are detective stories about cops, but also detective stories about robbers; detective stories in which virtue is triumphant, and detective stories in which virtue is trampled in the dust; detective stories hinged on professional expertise, and detective stories hinged on amateur brilliance; detective stories in which we root for the hero, and detective stories in which we root for the villain.

Because the reach of the detective story is so long, and its field so wide, there is I think a natural tendency to want to categorize it, to make some order out of this protean disorder. Critics speak of police procedurals and private eyes and so on, though acknowledging that all these cousins live inside the same large tent (to borrow, only this once, an image from the political world). In this anthology, we look beyond the typical organization of stories by subgenre and delve into a variety of recurring plot devices. This unique and innovative arrangement shows how various writers throughout the ages have shaped the basic story structures. But in doing so we have also demonstrated the impossibility of doing so, because the detective story just doesn't fit into neat pigeonholes.

Take the very first category in this volume, The Locked Room. The four stories collected under that heading could not be more unalike, while they certainly all fit the category, to demonstrate how even an apparently simple and constricting discipline can permit great latitude. But then move on, and the very first story in the section entitled Only One Among You, "The Secret Garden," while it certainly belongs in that category, is also a locked room mystery! And very different from the preceding four.

But that isn't all. In The Caper, the third category, "The Impossible Theft" is both a caper and a locked room story. In the next section, The Armchair Detective, "The Blue Geranium" is certainly an armchair detective story, but it is also—no surprise—a locked room story.

The variants flow into one another, feed one another, feed the underlying concept of story. But in this process, when we first sort the stories into category, and then see how they are not fully confined by those neat labels, we come to an understanding of the entire field of the detective story in a way we could not have done if we'd merely left it all an unexamined jumble.

When we see the relationships between the stories, and between the categories, when we see how the best writers have made personal use of the traditional schemes and the limitless variations, and when we see at the same time how free this field of the detective story leaves its practitioners to explore their own imaginative concerns, we can understand why the detective story has not only attracted so many readers for so long but has also been such a magnet to the best writers. Beginning from that basic triumvirate, society and the individual and a crime, writers of every stamp, attracted to different categories within the field, have been exploring the schemes and variations, measuring the possibilities, expanding the territory of the detective story, since . . .

Well, there's some dispute about that. There are those who will tell you the story of Cain and Abel is the first murder mystery, and we can only nod and agree, while saying that doesn't help us much. The modern detective story essentially began with Edgar Allan Poe, who invented most of it, including the first consulting detective, C. Auguste Dupin, out of whom was bred Sherlock Holmes and then, by eccentric fits and starts, various progeny leading at last to today's private eye.

Poe started others of our plots spinning as well. Tales told by brooding murderers (today mostly of the bran-enriched serial kind) come slouching out of Poe's "The Imp of the Perverse," and Indiana Jones is a direct descendent of William LeGrand in "The Gold Bug." The Poe story in this volume, "'Thou Art the Man,'" introduces both the amateur detective and the unjustly accused innocent who must struggle to clear himself.

Since Poe, the detective story has, like a tree, grown tall and fruitful, with many branches sprouting from those original roots, but with all of them holding to the original recipe: a heightened mixture of intellect and emotion, wedded to the triumvirate of society/individual/crime. Some of Poe's offspring he himself might have trouble recognizing, but the lineage is clear.

In the century and a half since Poe started it all, the detective story has gone through greater and lesser phases of semi-respectability (never full respectability, thank God), and has attracted writers gifted with every degree of talent and art from the idiosyncratic genius of a Damon Runyon or a Chester Himes (both represented in these pages) to cookie-cutter hacks who couldn't rise above formula with the aid of a hydraulic lift (none of them represented herein).

The hacks have always outnumbered the geniuses, but that's true everywhere, and the entire community of writers, from the most brilliantly original to the most ploddingly imitative, do all feed the genre, help to keep it alive, to reassure the reader that, whenever there's unwinding to be done, there will always be another new detective story, unread, unsavored, unsolved, very near to hand.

And these readers, after all, are still intelligent and discriminating, even when all they want is "just" a detective story. As they read, they can tell the good from the better, and the better from the best. Then, as time, the great winnower, moves on, the also-rans fall away and the geniuses remain, to segue into literary history, and become objects of study and interpretation.

But a dangerous trend has become evident within the last two decades. The scholars have grown less patient, less content to wait for a detective story writer to be safely tucked away on the inactive shelf before they turn their serious eyes on him. This very volume might be considered a part of this trend: if so, I apologize to my fellow entertainers. The last thing we want is for our readers to think of us as more than "just" detective story writers. If they thought there was any meat in that stew, they'd flee at once. They don't want to be harassed. They want to unwind.

On the other hand, where would they flee? If driven from the detective story by perceived seriousness, where could the unwinders go? Not to eco-politics-riddled science fiction. Not to biography, which reverses the satisfying pattern of the detective story; where the detective story begins (often) with a death, a biography by its very nature ends with one. Hardly bedside reading, that.

Even the movies aren't safely frivolous any more.

No, I'm sorry, we're still, if not the only, the best game in town. For the intelligent, educated reader who, despite his or her best efforts to remain serious and responsible twenty-four hours a day, nevertheless inadvertently reads fiction for the right reason (because it's fun), the detective story still is, as Goldilocks said about Baby Bear's porridge, "*just* right."

The tales in this book are all detective stories, just detective stories, some of the best work by some of the best writers in the field. Welcome aboard. Enjoy. It is, after all, better to be read than dead.

INTRODUCTION TO *THE BEST AMERICAN MYSTERY STORIES, 2000*

This essay served as Westlake's introduction to that year's installment of the annual series edited by his friend, poker buddy, and sometime publisher Otto Penzler.—Ed.

The durability of the short story is astonishing, all in all. It does not these days make any reputations, nor are the financial rewards particularly lush. Today's slick magazines pay for a short story exactly what the slick magazines of the twenties paid for a short story; not adjusted dollars, real dollars. F. Scott Fitzgerald got the same pay from the magazines as today's writers in similar venues, but in his day that was enough to keep him in Paris, whereas today the same income is enough to keep you on the farm.

Today's digest-size magazines also pay just what their uncles, the pulps, used to pay. Up and down the market, this is the one and only example in the entire American economy of a durable and successful resistance to inflation.

Then why does the short story continue to endure? Given the way our world works, the modest financial return very strongly implies a modest readership; if the millions were clamoring for short stories as though they were Barbie dolls, the price would go up.

Still, there they are. The slicks do still publish short stories, though nowhere near as many as they used to. The digest-size magazines toddle along, far fewer than the pulps of yesteryear but still alive and in good health. University publications produce a hefty number of short stories every year, but that's probably because their content providers are in the main academicians, and it's a given that the writer of short stories will be keeping his day job.

So it must be love that keeps the form alive, the writer's love for the work. It has been said that jazz and the short story are the two American contributions to the world of art, and they do seem to have at least this one thing in common: both are engaged in by the practitioner primarily for the love of doing it.

There's another link as well between the short story and jazz. Both are exemplified by the extended riff on a clean and simple motif. What the novel is to the symphony, the short story is to jazz. Like the best jazz solos, what the best short stories have to offer is a sense of vibrant imagination at work within a tightly controlled setting. That's what turns the writers on, and that's what maintains for the form a strong and knowledgeable readership. There is a joy in watching economy of gesture when performed by a real pro, whatever the art.

The short story evolved from several sources. The medieval *conte*, the tale meant to amuse the idlers at court (and the wanna-be idlers), and which more often than not involved a young wife and her lover putting one over on her much older husband, is one source. The traveler's tale, such as those in Chaucer and Boccaccio, twists of fate and reversals of fortune, morality lessons in which the irony is mostly delivered by the hand of God, is another. The joke, particularly the shaggy dog story, of ancient lineage, is a third.

All of these sources came into the American psyche through the campfire yarns, the tall tales and frontier reports by which the early settlers tried to describe to themselves this new world they were blundering through. When these rowdy chronicles became tamed for print, by Mark Twain and Ambrose Bierce and many others, the American short story had begun.

What the short story shares with its forebears, and what it does not share with novels or movies or television plays (except in the early days of live television from New York), is a singularity of focus, of character and effect. Though a story might cover years, as does Barbara D'Amato's lovely "Motel 66" in this volume, or hundreds of miles, as does David Edgerly Gates's somberly beautiful "Compass Rose," its movement is nevertheless within the confines of the Aristotelian dictum that a drama consists of the playing out of one action. The short story is not a place for digression.

Which leads me to a second vein of short story writing that's been popular now for some forty years or more, but which needn't hold our attention for long, because you'll find none of them in here (though some of them are very good indeed). This kind of story establishes a mood or an attitude or a situation and stops when the establishing is done. These stories are more closely allied to painting than to narrative and can be very strong, emotionally, though a certain limpness is always a danger.

These other stories are frequently called slices of life, and from a narrative point of view they don't have endings, which is why I could find none of them to include here. A story in the mystery or crime or detective genre (I've *never* known an inclusive enough term for this particular corner of the literary world) by definition has to have an ending. One way or another, the story of the type you'll find in this volume begins with a problem and cannot end until that problem has been dealt with, though not necessarily solved. These stories slice life too, but lengthwise. While it is true that one cross-section of a river, shore to shore, will imply everything upstream and everything downstream, it is also true that as a general rule the river itself is more interesting.

Given the constrictions of length and subject matter—there must, after all, be a crime somewhere in the story—it's still astonishing to me just how broad a range the mystery short story can cover. For instance, the American South has always been fruitful ground for stories of every length and kind, and here we have Thomas H. McNeely's harrowing "Sheep," Dennis Lehane's gothic "Running Out of Dog," Tom Franklin's gritty "Grit," and Shel Silverstein's rollicking "The Guilty Party." All are clearly and evocatively set in that part of America, all are steeped in the flavor of the region, but could any four stories be more unalike?

(It's a sad reminder also that, Shel Silverstein having died last year, long before his time, this is probably the last effusion we're likely to see from that wonderfully fertile and varied mind, but at least he certainly did go out on a roisterous high note.)

I am encouraged also when I see that the field is in no way stuck in yesteryear, though the traditions of fairness, cleverness, and excellence remain intact. Within those traditions, we find much that couldn't be more new. Here we have a story told to a video camera, a story that makes bizarre use of the latest telephone equipment, and a new way of seeing—look out for it—in the ICU.

The venues where these stories first appeared remain, as always, as broad a spectrum of American periodical publishing as you're likely to find anywhere. Here we have the major mainstream magazines *Playboy* and the *Atlantic Monthly*, and here we also have the more specialized *Oxford American* and *Chattahoochie Review*. Plus we have selections from three fine anthologies. And of course we have the faithfuls, *Alfred Hitchcock's Mystery Magazine* and *Ellery Queen's Mystery Magazine*, principally the latter.

For nearly sixty years, *Ellery Queen* has been the polestar of the mystery short story, finding and publishing the newest writers, the latest expansions of the genre, everything that keeps the field exciting and fresh. *Ellery Queen's* Department of First Stories, the first published work by a brand-new writer, has been a staple of the magazine forever, and an amazing number of those stories have made it onto best-of-the-year lists. I'm happy to say we have one this year, "Jumping with Jim," by Geary Danihy, that I think is one of the best debuts ever, told with such assurance and skill that I had to keep looking back at the first page; yes, this is the Department of First Stories. Long may it continue.

CHAPTER THREE

It's been a long time since the mystery story was no more than a puzzle acted out by marionettes for the amusement of the cloistered Victorian mind. In the stories of this volume there are surprises galore, but they are surprises of character, of motivation, of story, not merely surprises of mechanical puzzle-playing. Although it is certainly possible for some writer somewhere to come up with a new and richer variant on, say, the locked-room story, there's no tired smoke-and-mirrors exercise of that former sort to be found here. Every one of our writers has more serious fish to fry.

And many show their awareness that they are writing at the end of the millennium, that, in a way, everything that was published in 1999, in any genre, served as a kind of summing-up. Even our Department of First Stories entry begins by contrasting past with present, the current narrator with Joseph Conrad's Lord Jim. At the other extreme, Robert Girardi's "The Defenestration of Aba Sid" and half a dozen other stories all draw a picture, clear and concise, of just where America found itself at the end of the twentieth century.

I suppose that must inevitably lead me into a discussion of the future of the mystery short story. Our genre began with the publication, in April 1841, of "The Murders in the Rue Morgue" by Edgar Allan Poe, so it is now entering its third century and its 159th year, so wouldn't I like to say where I expect it will travel next? "Whither," and all that?

Well, no. I'm terrible at predictions, always have been. I don't even know what *I'm* going to do next, so I'm not likely to be a particularly reliable oracle when it comes to the fate of an entire genre of popular fiction. Come to think of it, it's probably my inability to guess what's going to happen next that makes me such a fan of the mystery short story in the first place.

More a fan than a practitioner, I'm afraid. I've done a few short stories myself, enough to inform my admiration when I see the thing done well, but I admit I find it hard. In the novel I feel more at home, I can stretch and wander and take my time. In the short story, I can't be self-indulgent, I can't explain at length, I can't distract the reader with subplots or amusing but ultimately irrelevant characters and settings.

All of which, of course, is the point. A good short story is a jewel in miniature, as concise and carefully wrought as a fine watch, but at the same time alive. Like the stories herein.

DON'T CALL US, WE'LL CALL YOU

In 1960, Westlake submitted an essay to *Xero*, a science fiction fanzine edited by Pat and Dick Lupoff. It was one of the most spectacular acts of bridge burning in the history of publishing. Additions in brackets are my own.—Ed.

About a year ago, Henry Morrison asked Randy Garrett and me to speak at an ESFA [Eastern Science Fiction Association] meeting over in Jersey. The last echoes of the science fiction boom had faded away, the alarming dimensions of the resulting crater were becoming increasingly noticeable, and the people at ESFA thought it would be interesting to know what a couple of writers in the field intended to do next. Garrett was there as the old pro; I, as the recent entry into professional science fiction writing. Despite the disparity of our standings in the field, we both wound up by giving precisely the same answer: "I am a professional writer. My entire income comes from writing. If science fiction can't support me, I'll write in some other field."

That was a year ago. Today, I am a full-time mystery writer, working on my fifth mystery novel. (The first had already been published at the time of the ESFA meeting). And the last time I saw Randy Garrett (a week ago) he was working on a biography for decent money.

Isaac Asimov is writing good science fact these days. Lester del Rey is writing bad science fact. [Ray] Bradbury and all the little Bradburys ([Richard] Matheson, [Charles] Beaumont, et al.) are writing bad big-time fantasy for television and *Playboy*. Arthur C. Clarke is writing popular science fact. [Robert] Sheckley is writing paperback mysteries. Judith Merrill is anthologizing. [Lyon Sprague] De Camp and a lot of others aren't doing much of anything. God knows what [Algis] Budrys is doing. The list of living ex–science fiction writers approaches infinity.

The field can't support us. It can't support even the big boys, the established names, and it sure as hell can't support anybody new. But what's worse, it can't even interest us.

It's time for credentials, before going into this thing any deeper. If I'm going to talk as a professional writer who isn't doing anything in science fiction and who claims that he might have done something worthwhile if it were worth his while to do so, I ought to show my identity card. Therefore:

Science Fiction. I have sold thirteen stories, two of which have not yet been published and none of which are any damn good. I have sold to *Universe, Original, Future, Super, Analog, Amazing, If,* and *Galaxy*. A fourteenth story was sold to *Fantastic Universe*, which proceeded to drop dead before they could publish it. Both John Campbell and Cele Goldsmith have asked me to write sequels to novelettes of mine they had bought (I haven't written either, and won't). In a desk drawer I have twenty-odd thousand words of a science fiction novel, which is good, but which I'm not going to finish because it isn't worth my while.

Avalon pays three hundred and fifty dollars for a book, and I wouldn't support such piracy either by writing for them or buying their wares. John Campbell isn't the hero, so it can't be serialized in *Analog*. If finished, it would run a lot longer than forty-five thousand words, so that leaves out Ace. There's no gratuitous sex, so that excludes Galaxy/Beacon (or would if they were still being published). It isn't a silly satire about a world controlled by advertising agencies or insurance companies or the A&P, so it can't be serialized in *Galaxy Magazine*. It's in sensible English, so *Amazing* is out. It isn't about the horrors of Atomic War, so no mainstream hardcover house would look twice at it. I'd like to write it anyway for my own amusement (you know, like a real writer-type), but unpublished manuscripts unfortunately have a low enjoyment quota, at least for me. So the hell with it.

I have three other stories sitting around the house and all I have to do is rewrite them the way the various editors want, and they are sold. To hell with them too.

Mystery. I have sold twenty-five short stories, a couple of which are pretty good. They've appeared in *Manhunt*, *Mystery Digest*, *Alfred Hitchcock's Mystery Magazine*, *Guilty*, *Tightrope*, *77 Sunset Strip* (a one-shot, though they didn't mean it that way), *Ed McBain's Mystery Book*, and *The Saint*. One was reprinted in *Best Detective Stories of 1959*, four more are shortly to be anthologized here and there, and one is maybe (at the time of this writing, I'm not sure yet) going to be bought for television.

I have sold three mystery novels to Random House, a fourth (aimed paperback) is currently being considered by Dell, and the fifth is in the writing. The first, *The Mercenaries*, won a second-place Edgar from the Mystery Writers of America for best first novel of the year. Anthony Boucher called the second, in the *Times*, "a considerable novel," giving it a very long and very pleasant review.

I am not sitting around bragging. I'm simply trying to make something clear: I can write. I can write well. I am capable of first-class work. But the only thing I've ever written in science fiction that I am at all proud of is a novel I'll never finish because there is economically, stylistically, and philosophically no place for it.

Do you know what I'm talking about? *I cannot sell good science fiction.* All right, the field can't support me, so what? I don't spend all my time writing mysteries. I could still, it would be financially feasible for me to, write an occasional science fiction story, five or six a year, or maybe cut the budget a little and write a novel. But it doesn't *interest* me, the requirements of the field are such that I couldn't write anything that would interest *me*, so how could I presume to interest *you*? All the *ex*– science fiction writers could still write in the field part-time, but they don't. I guess it doesn't interest them either.

In *Xero 4* a letter-writer bitched about the *deus ex psionica* ending of *Out Like a Light*, the second Kenneth Malone serial by Randy Garrett and Larry Harris, in *Analog*. I know Randy and Larry, so let me tell you something: They had a relatively good ending for that story, one that would have satisfied your letter-writer's conditions for believability. John Campbell made them rewrite the ending, to make Kenneth Malone a psuperman, a John Campbell hero. Sixty thousand words at three cents a word is eighteen hundred dollars. Plus the virtually inevitable "An Lab" bonus (serial chapters always place first or second, or almost always) of three to six hundred dollars.

Randy and Larry disliked Campbell's ending, but couldn't talk him out of it. Had they decided not to prostitute themselves on a bed of gold (the letter-writer's phrase), they would have been throwing away not only the time they'd spent on the serial, but also nine to twelve hundred dollars in real money for *each* of them. At that point, I'd have rewritten the damn thing, too, and the hell with integrity. But I'm not ever going to get to that point; I'm not writing the stuff anymore.

Now let me tell you a very sad and very funny story. A while back, Randy Garrett was staying at my place. We worked in the same room, and we were both writing stories aimed at *Analog*. Enjoying ourselves in the process, we both included private jokes for the other guy's benefit, and one thing I did was make a minor character, an Air Force Colonel who showed up in the last three pages of the story, the spitting image of John Campbell, betting Randy that Campbell would never notice it. I described the guy as looking like Campbell, talking like Campbell, and thinking like Campbell.

We brought our respective stories in at the same time, handed them to the great man, and both went back the next week because he wanted revisions on both stories. I forget what he wanted Randy to change in his story, but I'll never in the world forget what he wanted done with mine: He wanted me to make the Colonel the lead character. I did it. Eighteen thousand words. Four hundred and fifty dollars.

(P.S. That's the story he wanted a sequel to. He really liked that Colonel.)

(P.P.S. It was a better story the first time, when it was only fourteen thousand words. If I was going to rewrite, I wanted more money, so I padded four thousand unnecessary words into it. It makes for duller reading, but frankly, my dear, I don't give a damn.)

More recently, when Frederik Pohl took over *Galaxy*, my agent suggested that I aim a story at him, as he was in a mood to build an inventory of his own. So I researched. I read the introductions to all the

Pohl-edited *Star Fiction* series, and I reread the first and last sentence of every Frederik Pohl story I had around the house (which was a lot, since I have all but six issues of *Galaxy* up till this year, when I stopped buying it), and then I wrote a Frederik Pohl story, "The Spy in the Elevator."

A Pohl title and a Pohl story, and a very silly insipid story it was, but by that time I was getting cynical. Pohl bought it. It was my next-to-last science fiction story. It would have been the last, but a few months later my agent got me an assignment from Cele Goldsmith to do a cover story for *Amazing*. I'd never tried to match a story to a pre-drawn cover before, so I took the assignment, figuring I ought to get some enjoyment out of the thing. And there I stopped. So far as I can see now, I'll never write another word of science fiction again. (After this article, assuming the editors at least have sense enough to read the fanzines for the temper of the readership, which judging from their competence otherwise isn't necessarily true, I don't suppose anything of mine would be too welcome on their desks anyway. I've never burned a bridge with more joy.)

Campbell is an egomaniac. [Robert P.] Mills of *F&SF* is a journeyman incompetent. Cele Goldsmith is a third-grade teacher and I think she wonders what in the world she's doing over at *Amazing*. (Know I do.) As for Pohl, who can tell? *Galaxy* is still heavily laden with [H. L.] Gold's inventory, and when Pohl edited *Star* he had the advantages of no deadline and a better pay rate than anybody else in the field, so it's difficult to say what *Galaxy* will look like next year, except that Kingsley Amis will probably like it.

I will not end with a panacea. I have none. A lot of professional science fiction writers have moved on to other fields in the last few years, and a lot more haven't bothered to take their place. You may have wondered why, and since I'm one of them I thought I'd tell you, speaking only for myself. I don't know whether I speak for any of the others or not, but I suspect so. (The guy who beat me out for the first-place Edgar, by the way, was Jack Vance, another escapee.)

I don't know why science fiction is so lousy. I suspect there are a lot of reasons. But I can at least hint at one reason which has special refer-ence to *you*. At the ESFA meeting I mentioned earlier, Sam Moskowitz mentioned a story from *Weird Tales*, some time in the thirties. All the members had read it, and remembered it. A little later, Randy Garrett mentioned a story from the previous month's *Analog*. Two members present had read it.

The letters page in issue 8 of *Xero* was filled with impassioned responses—including one from Frederik Pohl and another from Avram Davidson, who would go on to be recognized as one of the genre's late masters. Westlake replied in issue 9.—Ed.

Sorry to have taken so long to answer. Frankly, I wasn't sure whether I should answer or not. My agent advised me to stop, and since he has done more for me in my writing career than almost anyone else I can think of, and since he is a knowledgeable man in this business, his advice carried a lot of weight. On the other hand, you people had been kind enough to send along *Xero 8*, which did contain comments and questions which shouldn't be left up in the air. So this letter will be the last chapter on the subject and I'll try to make it inoffensive. The people I offend, it seems, don't tell *me* about it; they call my agent.

Point number one: I have never tried to imitate anyone's writing *style*, Frederik Pohl's or anybody else's, and I hardly think I could even if I tried. I have tried, however, to aim at editorial interests. In Mr. Pohl's case, I had to go on the stories he had written rather than the stories he had bought, for obvious reasons. (By the time he wrote the letter which appeared in *Xero 8*, he still had two stories in inventory that Gold had bought.) If the implication that I was doing a pastiche was contained in my article, it was unintentional. The point of my "phoney inside stuff" was that I was aiming at the market *and nothing more*. In other words, the story I had written had no merits other than as an example of aiming at a particular market. And so, a lousy story.

Which brings me to Avram Davidson's suggestion that I'm not a science fiction writer at all, but wandered into the field by accident.

This idea had never occurred to me before, but now that it has been suggested, I must admit it might be true. I gave up Perry Mason for science fiction when I was fourteen, and read science fiction voluminously for the next six years, before the Air Force took me at twenty. In 1958, when I started the drive to become a self-supporting writer, it was to science fiction that I returned, compiling a library of about five hundred magazines, being *Galaxy* and *F&SF* complete, *Astounding* back to 1948, and a batch of secondary magazines, and it was only after having waded through all this that I decided to branch out into the mystery field and see what I could do there. My first sale, in 1953, when I was nineteen, was to *Universe Science Fiction*. My sales in 1958 and 1959 were about half and half, mystery and science fiction. All of this might sound like the beginnings of a career as a science fiction writer, but obviously the appearances are deceiving.

Let's pursue Avram Davidson's idea. The first stories I sold in both the mystery and science fiction fields were nothing spectacular—the mysteries to *Hitchcock* were the drab droll dreck used as ballast in that magazine, the science fiction was summed up by Mr. Pohl's comments on "Spy"—but gradually I think I improved. In mysteries anyway. As my "slanting for the market" became less conscious and worrisome, I could concentrate more on the story itself, and so the stories began to have more meat on their bones. I imagine that this is normal development of a writer in any field; first conscious agitating, "aiming" at the market, gradual mastery of the conventions and taboos and interests and typings in that market, and so gradual freeing of the concentration for the story itself.

This process happened to me in the mystery field, but it didn't happen in science fiction. I never got beyond stage one. When the chance came to send a story to *Galaxy* with guaranteed sympathetic attention, I honestly didn't know what to do with it. If I muffed it, I come close to closing a market. I was still in stage one; *slant* the story. That was in 1961, and I still hadn't found a firm footing in the field.

On those few occasions when I thought I'd taken a small step forward, I was immediately returned to Start, either by a No Sale or a slant-oriented revision. The Campbell story about the Colonel is a fine instance. (It was in the May issue of *Analog*, to answer the questions.) In the original the Colonel showed up at the end of the story. There was no secret organization of psupermen in the Air Force. The point of view never deviated from Jeremy. It was a story about a *person*. God knows it was no masterpiece, but it was a *story*. (In this connection, Harry Warner Jr.'s idea that the Colonel was a "real, living characterization" just ain't so. *Analog* is full of Secret Societies with Strange Powers, and the Colonel under one name or another, runs them all. You will find this same character in spy stories. He's the chief of Counter-Intelligence, the hero phones him in Washington every once in a while, and his name is Mac.) At any rate, I for one am more interested in a *person*, who suddenly and shatteringly learns he is a teleport, who doesn't want to be a teleport, and who more than half suspects he's lost his mind, who struggles through the problems thus created—aggravated by the fact that he can neither control nor repeat the initial teleportation— and works things out to some sort of solution or compromise with the world, than I am in all the Secret Societies and Mystical Powers in the Orient. But the writing and rewriting of the story kept me vigorously marching in place, back there at stage one.

So you see, Mr. Davidson may be right. I had read more science fiction than mystery. I was more interested in science fiction, and had sold my first story to a science fiction magazine. But it was in the mystery field that I could adapt myself to the requirements of the market and then go on to stories—and books—that fulfilled for me *more* than the simple requirements of the market. In science fiction, once I had fulfilled the requirements of the market, I never had any elbow room left. Using that Colonel story again, once that man and his Secret Society took over the story, it became impossible to do anything with Jeremy, my teleportee. Instead of his taking his own risks, fighting his own way through to triumph and defeat, the story became a Mystical Inner Circle affair. Jeremy still struggled, but he was no longer his own man. His every move was planned and anticipated by the Secret Society, and the whole story became the recounting of an initiation into the club. All it lacked was a badge with a decoder on the back, for spelling out Ralston. Phooey.

Could I have fulfilled the market requirements with that story, and still have written a story interesting to *me*? No. Is that a flaw in my writing ability? Maybe. I have not thought so, but maybe it is. If so, it's a flaw that seems to bother me only in science fiction.

Point number three: At a certain risk, I must point out that at least one sentence in Frederik Pohl's letter is balderdash. This is the crack about "other markets" having "lower standards" than the science fiction magazines. He must be referring to those non–science fiction editors so obtuse as to buy stories and/or books from me. Among these editors are Lee Wright, a senior editor at Random House, generally accepted as being the top mystery editor in the United States, and possibly in the world. Bucklin Moon of Pocket Books, who is no slouch. The good people at T.V. Boardman in England, Gallimard in France, Mondadori in Italy, and so on and so on, who have bought various foreign rights to my books. Hans Stefan Santesson, William Manners, and Ed McBain, who have bought short stories from me in the mystery field. The people at Dell, who have bought reprint rights to my mystery novels. If in Frederik Pohl's world these people have "lower standards" than the six science fiction magazines which have not yet joined their sisters in silence, then either Mr. Pohl or myself is living in a parallel universe.

Point number four (and last): My article, in twenty-five hundred ill-chosen words, attempted to say one thing: *science fiction is neither an artistic nor a commercial field*. Avram Davidson suggested I was in the wrong pew. L. Sprague de Camp objected to my cavalier ignoring of his non–science fiction output. Frederik Pohl complained about my "phoney inside stuff." Though I'd stated that I'd never written a science fiction novel, Donald Wollheim wondered why he hadn't seen anything submitted from me. The letter without a name thought I was too vindictive. John Baxter thought I was too petty. But until one of these people *directly* disagrees with this statement—*science fiction is neither an artistic nor a commercial field*—they haven't said a damn thing.

FOUR TEN MOST WANTED

Ten Favorite Mystery Books

Originally published in *The Armchair Detective Book of Lists* (1995), edited by Kate Stine, in the section titled "Famous Authors' Favorites." Careful readers will notice that Westlake only offers nine favorites—I trust the tenth is safe and sound in Andy Kelp's apartment.—Ed.

What you ask is, of course, impossible. I could give you my Top Three or my Top Twenty-five, but once you go past three there's no way to stop at ten; partly because, in only doing ten, I wouldn't feel right listing one author more than once (which is why *A Coffin for Dimitrios* isn't here).

So I've cheated; two of my selections are series, the complete series. And I've done the list in alphabetical order: *my* alphabetical order.

The Hoke Mosely series by Charles Willeford
The Red Right Hand by Joel Townsley Rogers
Kill the Boss Goodbye by Peter Rabe
The Gravedigger/Coffin Ed series by Chester Himes
The Maltese Falcon by Dashiell Hammett
Interface by Joe Gores
The Eighth Circle by Stanley Ellin
Sleep and His Brother by Peter Dickinson
The Light of Day by Eric Ambler

FIVE RETURNING TO THE SCENE OF THE CRIME

On His Own Work

INTRODUCTION TO *LEVINE*

Westlake wrote this introduction to a collected edition of the five stories he'd written over the years about a New York police detective named Abe Levine. For the collection, which was published in 1984 by Grand Central Publishing, he also wrote a new, final Levine story.—Ed.

In some ways, 1959 was for me a very good year. The preceding fall I'd moved to New York and gotten a job as reader for a literary agent and settled myself down at last to the task of figuring out how to (a) become a writer and (b) make a living at it. In 1959, fired with youth and freshness and enthusiasm, I churned out more work than in any other year of my life, and most of it found a market. When the dust had settled, it turned out I had produced over half a million published words that year (we say nothing of the unpublished words) and had become a freelance writer. In April, with blind optimism, no money, and an extremely pregnant wife, I had quit my literary agency job, and since that date I have never once, I am happy to say, earned an honest dollar in wages.

Among that year's output were forty-six short stories and novelettes, of which twenty-seven were published. (That's about a third of all the short stories I've written over my entire life so far.) One of those pieces, written early in March, was a novelette entitled "Intellectual Motivation" (I hadn't yet completely cracked the problem of titles— still haven't, come to think of it), which was published in the December 1959 issue of *Alfred Hitchcock's Mystery Magazine* under the not-much-better title "The Best-Friend Murder." The story contained clear analogies to my own current situation, and when I look back on it from a vantage point (if that's the phrase I want) of twenty-four years I see it contains more than a little self-analysis and self-criticism. I wasn't really aware of all that at the time, of course, or I would have been too self-conscious to write the story. (We do write what we know, whether we know it or not.) What attracted me then—and what I still think is the story's major excuse for existence—was the attitude of the detective toward the idea of death.

In any mystery story, one element is inevitably the detective's attitude toward death, his reaction to the *concept* of death. The amateur detectives, for instance, the whimsical Wimseys and quaint Queens, view death in the shallowest possible way, as a *solvable puzzle*, which is in any event one of the subliminal comforts of the mystery form. Death is stripped of its grief, horror, loss, irrevocability; we are not helpless, there is something we can do. We can *solve* death.

Similarly, it has become the convention that policemen, professional detectives, are *hardened* to death, *immune* to life untimely nipped. "All I want is the facts, ma'am," Jack Webb used to say in his Sergeant Friday persona on *Dragnet*; nothing would make him scream, or cry, or— o'ercome—turn aside his head. (Although they broke with that just once, when the actor who played Friday's partner died. They wrote it in, and on camera Jack Webb—somehow no longer the cop—did cry, was human, faced death squarely.)

But is the policeman not flesh? Doth he not bleed? Hasn't he in his own lifetime buried grandparents, parents? Isn't he aware of his *own* mortality? It was the idea of a cop, a police detective, who was so tensely aware of his own inevitable death that he wound up hating people who took the idea of death frivolously that led me to Abe Levine and "The Best-Friend Murder" (*nee* "Intellectual Motivation").

Which doesn't mean I saw a series in it. The other twenty-six published 1959 stories produced no sequels, nor did I ever expect to see Detective Levine again once he'd finished his gavotte with Larry Perkins. But for some reason he stayed in my mind, a worrying painstaking fretful unheroic man, a fifty-three-year-old who seemed to me at the age of twenty-five to be almost a doddering ancient, but who from my present position I realize is in the absolute prime of life. Levine had not entirely explained himself in that first novelette, nor had his relationship with death been completely explored. From time to time I thought about him, and slowly another story idea took rough shape in my mind, but I didn't get around to writing it.

Then a different story took shape instead, a further exploration of Abe Levine and the idea of death. What if he were faced with a potential suicide, someone who wanted to throw away that which Levine found most precious? Would Levine reject him, hate him, turn away from him? Or would he try, desperately, compulsively, to convert the suicide to Levine's own point of view? And if the latter, what would it mean? It was in June of 1960, fifteen months after Levine's birth, that I put him together with that man on the ledge, in a story I titled (sensibly enough, I thought) "Man on a Ledge," but which *Alfred Hitchcock's Mystery Magazine* published in October of 1960 as (and here I think they were wrong) "Come Back, Come Back."

A sequel does not necessarily a series make. Having used Levine twice, it would have been possible then to go directly to that other story I'd thought of, work out the plot details, and have a true series on my hands—if a short one—but still I hesitated, and then six months later, in December of that year, with Christmas coming on, another permutation in the ongoing story of Levine and death occurred to me, and I wrote "The Feel of the Trigger."

There are several things to say about "The Feel of the Trigger." First, at last *Alfred Hitchcock's Mystery Magazine*, which published the story in October of 1961, agreed with me on a title; it was published as "The

Feel of the Trigger." Second, this story probably shows at its peak the influence of Evan Hunter on my development as a writer. He had run down these same alleys just a few years before me, had worked for the same literary agency, published in the same or similar magazines. His 87th Precinct novels, as by Ed McBain, had started being published just around the time I was first seriously trying to figure out how to be a self-supporting writer. Naturally I read them. They were that rarity, that near-impossibility, something new under the sun, and naturally I was impressed by and influenced by them. I would not for a moment blame Evan Hunter for "The Feel of the Trigger"; I would only say that a kind of specificity of description and a particular method of entering the protagonist's mind did not exist in my stories before I read Evan Hunter

Sometimes poetic justice is comic; maybe we should call it doggerel justice. At the time "The Feel of the Trigger" was published, an 87th Precinct series was on television; the only story of mine ever bought to be the basis of an episode in a television series was "The Feel of the Trigger." It ran as an 87th Precinct story on February 2, 1962, with Meyer Meyer the character who was worried about his heart condition. Unfortunately, I couldn't be home that night, but a friend offered to tape the program for me. Remember, we're talking about 1962, not 1982, and the tape he was talking about was *sound*. He did record the program, and some time later I heard it, and my memory of it is a lot of footsteps and several doors being opened. Someday I'd like to see that show.

After three stories, there was no longer any question in my mind that I had a series on my hands, but at that time I had no idea what one did with a series. A story—any story—is *about* several different things, at different levels. It is about its plot, for instance, but only in the worst and most simplistic writers do specific plots repeat themselves often enough to be termed a series. The repetition of characters makes a series, but if the characters in the original story are tied to a theme or a concern or a view of life that colors them and helps to create them, can they live in stories that are irrelevant to that extra element? I don't think so, and I think over the years there have been several series characters who have been less than they might have been because their later adventures never touched upon those thematic elements which had created the character in the first place.

So if I was going to write another story about Abe Levine, it would have to tie in with his relationship with death, his attitude toward death, his virtual romance with death. Death fascinated Levine, it summoned him and yet repelled him; how could I write a story about Abe Levine without that element?

I couldn't. The series might have died aborning right then, three stories in. I still didn't want to write the one for which I'd had that rough idea, and no other story that included both the character and the theme came to the surface of my brain. Goodbye, Abe.

It was, in fact, not quite a year before another story came along that suited the character and the theme; and had the potential as well to broaden both. It marked a real change in the stories, since for the first time Levine was attacked directly in the area of his weakness. He had been attacked before, as any policeman is liable to be attacked, but in "The Sound of Murder" (my title, left unchanged, hallelujah) Levine is attacked in a way specific to Levine, particular to the character *and* particular to the theme. The generational element became more obvious, though it had been there in some way since the first story. "The Sound of Murder" took Abe Levine farther down the same road, and when I finished it I wondered if I hadn't gone too far, if this most recent experience might not have changed Levine too much, and made him someone no longer relevant to his theme? An odd finish for a character, if true. (That did happen, as a matter of fact, a decade later, to the hero of a series of mystery novels I'd written under the name of Tucker Coe.)

That story, "The Sound of Murder," was written during a strangely sporadic period of my writing life. I had written two mystery novels, *The Mercenaries* and *Killing Time*, published by Random House, and in the summer of 1961 had started a third which I already knew would be called *361*, which is the numerical classification in *Roget's Thesaurus* for "Murder, violent death." Random House did eventually publish the book under that title, with a note in front explaining what the title meant, but they didn't do what I'd wanted, which was to run, in the form of a frontispiece quote, the entire 361 listing from the *Thesaurus*. Read it for yourself some time, and you'll see why I found it striking and wanted to use it.

In any event, *361* was the coldest book I'd tried to write up to that time, a book in which the first-person narrator would never once *state* his emotions, but in which the emotions would have to be implied by the character's physical actions. It was an easy mood to get into, but a hard book to write, and in the middle of it I stopped and switched to another book entirely, one I'd been thinking about for a while, a paperback-style tough guy novel in which the entire world would be like my *361* hero; a world of unstated emotion and hard surfaces. That book was finished in September of 1961, and was published in February of 1963 as *The Hunter* (my title!) by Pocket Books, under the pen name Richard Stark, a name I'd already used for a few of that spate of short stories from 1959.

Having finished *The Hunter*, I should have gone back to finish *361*, but I think I wasn't ready for two emotionless heroes in a row, and that's when the idea for "The Sound of Murder" came bubbling to the surface. Levine is emotional, the Lord knows, and I notice that in this story he even makes a *point* of his being emotional. It was written in October of 1961 and published in *Alfred Hitchcock's Mystery Magazine* in December of 1962. "The Sound of Murder" restored some juice to my brain, some humanity, and made it possible for me to go on and finish *361*.

Another idea for a Levine story had emerged at the same time, fed by the same impulses, another permutation on Levine's reaction to violent death, but that other story had seemed much more of a problem and I'd chosen to ignore it. Not that it would have been a problem to write, but that it might be a problem to publish. The first four Levine stories had all appeared in *Alfred Hitchcock's Mystery Magazine*, but the story I had in mind seemed inappropriate for that market. Unfortunately, I couldn't think of another publication more likely to find it useful, so I turned my back on it, for as long as I could.

Which turned out to be seven months. After four novelettes, nearly forty thousand words, I had grown to know and to like Abe Levine. The story I had in mind, which I was calling "The Death of a Bum," was somehow the inevitable next step in Levine's narrowing relationship with death. It was not, in the normal sense of the word, a "mystery" story, which was why I knew *Hitchcock's* would have trouble with it. Remove Levine from it and it wasn't a story at all; I had written myself into a terrible corner, the one in which the character himself has become the world in which the story is set. (A simpler and sillier example of this is *Batman*. Somewhere around 1955, the evil activity most pursued by the criminals in *Batman* became the *uncovering of Batman's identity!* If Batman didn't exist, they wouldn't be criminals. In self-referential fiction, I can think of no peer to *Batman*.)

Nevertheless, for seven months I turned my attention to other things, and it wasn't until May of 1962 that I finally gave in to the inevitable and wrote "The Death of a Bum." It was one of the easiest writing tasks I've ever had; I knew the character somewhat better than I knew myself; I had known the story for more than half a year; I had already decided it was uncommercial, so there was no point trying to please any particular editor or audience. Sometimes writers say this or that story "wrote itself," which is never true, but "The Death of a Bum" required a lot less midwifing than usual.

As I'd expected, *Alfred Hitchcock's Mystery Magazine* couldn't use the story, though the editor wrote a very nice and sincere letter—not of apology, but of regret, since he too had grown to like Levine. I wrote back explaining that I'd been prepared for the rejection and was neither surprised nor hurt. I then left it to my agent to do what he could.

It took nearly three years, and I don't know how many submissions, but at last "The Death of a Bum" was published, in *Mike Shayne's Mystery Magazine*, in June of 1965. And there the series ended.

It ended for a variety of reasons. One of them, naturally, was the three-year span between the writing of "The Death of a Bum" and its publication; I felt I couldn't write a new story about Abe Levine before the previous story had found a home. This may seem an unnecessary self-restriction, but in my mind the stories had evolved in such a clear step-by-step way, each one leading to the next, that a story written *after* "The Death of a Bum" but published before it or instead of it would at least for me have destroyed the organic reality of the character and his life.

Another reason for the series ending was a change that had taken place in my own career, which had become schizophrenic in the nicest possible way. The tough guy novel I had written under the name of Richard Stark—*The Hunter*—had been liked and bought by an editor at Pocket Books named Bucklin Moon, a fine man of whom I cannot say too much (but one thing of whom I must say is that I wish he were still with us), who had liked the lead character in that book, Parker, and asked me, "Do you think you could give us two or three books a year about him?" I thought I could. For several years, I did.

At the same time, the writing I was doing under my own name had taken a completely unexpected (by me) turn. Comedy had come in.

Let me make one thing perfectly clear. I was never a comic. All through my life, in grammar school, in high school, in college, I was never the funniest kid in class. I was always, invariably, the funniest kid's best friend. Out of college and in New York and beginning to make my career as a writer, I got to know a couple of funny writers and I was their best audience. I wasn't the guy with the quick line; I was the guy who *loved* the quick line.

Comic elements started creeping into my stories in surprising and sometimes alarming ways. Even in "The Sound of Murder," look at how many comic references, comic elements there are in a story which is in no way comic. Undoubtedly that was an unconscious part of my reaction to the coldness and humorlessness of both *The Hunter* and *361*.

It was two and a half years after "The Sound of Murder" before the comic side was at last given its head. In the early spring of 1964 I started a mystery novel, intended to be published under my own name by Random House, about a young man who runs a bar in Brooklyn which is owned by the Mafia. They use it as a tax loss and to launder money, they occasionally use it as a package drop, and the young man has the job of running it because his uncle is connected with the Mob. At the beginning of the story, two Mob hitmen enter the bar as the young man is about to close for the night, try to kill him, and miss.

This was intended to be an ordinary innocent-on-the-run story, in which the innocent can't go to the police because of his uncle's Mob connection. The schnook-on-the-run story, as in *The 39 Steps* or Alfred Hitchcock's movie *Saboteur* (in which Robert Cummings played the schnook, and not to be confused with Hitchcock's *Sabotage*, in which Sylvia Sidney played the schnook), has certain comic elements built into it, but it needn't be a comic story, nor did I initially see my Mob-nephew tale as a comic story.

But something went wrong. The conventions of the form prostrated themselves before me. Something manic glowed in the air, like St. Elmo's Fire. Instead of the comic's best friend—*Shazam!*—I became the comic!

I finished that book in May of 1964 and called it *The Dead Nephew*. My editor at Random House—Lee Wright, the best editor I have ever known, though two others come close—hated that title, and I hated every alternative she suggested, and she hated every other title I offered, and finally, exhausted, we leaned on our lances and gasped and agreed to call the thing *The Fugitive Pigeon*. It became the first of a run of comic novels which, so far as I know, has not yet come to an end.

Well, *The Fugitive Pigeon* was published in March of 1965 and "The Death of a Bum" appeared three months later, and by then I was deeply into being a comic novelist. And in those periods when I came to the surface for air I would turn into a coldly emotionless novelist named Richard Stark who wrote about a sumbitch named Parker. And Levine receded.

But he never entirely faded from view. From almost the beginning I had had that rough idea for a Levine story which I'd never written, and which I now realized was the logical story to follow "The Death of a Bum," but the silence had lasted too long, my concentration was elsewhere, and in any event I had just about given up writing short stories and had *certainly* stopped writing novelettes. From that high of forty-six short stories and novelettes in 1959, by 1966 I was down to zero novelettes and only one short story (which was never published). Between 1967 and 1980 I wrote no novelettes at all and only seven short stories, most of which had been commissioned.

Some of Abe Levine's sensibility, if nothing else, came out in a group of five novels I wrote in the late sixties and early seventies, using the pen name Tucker Coe, about an ex-cop named Mitch Tobin. But Tobin was not Levine, and death was not Tobin's primary topic.

Abe Levine's saga remained incomplete, and I knew it, and it gnawed at me from time to time. Once, in the late seventies, I tried to rework the stories into a novel, intending to plot out the final unwritten story as the last section of the book. (At that time, I thought it was a story about a burglar.) But, although I see an organic connection among the stories, they are certainly not a novel, nor could they be. They are separate self-contained stories, and putting them in novel drag only makes them look embarrassed and foolish. That novelizing project failed of its own futility, and I stopped work on it long before I got to the new material; so the final story remained unwritten.

It might have remained unwritten forever except for Otto Penzler, proprietor of the Mysterious Press. In the spring of 1982 he and I were talking about another project I don't seem to be working on, which is a book about Dickens's *The Mystery of Edwin Drood* (Jasper didn't do it). I told Otto about Levine, about the five stories I'd written and the one I hadn't written, and he asked to read them. Having done so, he then said he would like to publish them as a collection, but they weren't long enough to fill a book. "You'll just have to write the other story," he said.

Well, of course I didn't *have* to write the other story. But the truth was, I wanted to write that story, it had been itching at me for a long time, but I had never had the right impetus at the right moment before. Did I have it now? Obviously, since you are holding the book in your hands, I did.

The last story.

CHAPTER FIVE

I might be able to write just one more story about Levine, but I knew from the beginning that that would be it. I couldn't possibly resurrect the character, dust him off, and run him through an endless series of novelettes, not now. But one story; yes.

There were problems, though, and the very first problem was *time*. The first five stories were all over twenty years old. The final story could not take place twenty years later in Levine's life, even though it was doing so in his author's. Should I rewrite the earlier stories, updating them, moving them through experiences they had never known; Vietnam, Watergate, the Kennedy assassinations, the changing public perceptions of policemen, all the rest of it? Should I rather attempt to write historical fiction, to write the final story as though it were being written in November of 1962 instead of November of 1982?

I've thought about the problem of updating before this, and generally speaking I'm against it. I believe that television has made a deep change in our perception of time—at least of recent time—and that in some way all of the last fifty years exists simultaneously in our heads, some parts in better focus than others. Because of television and its reliance on old movies to fill the unrelenting hours, we all know Alan Ladd better than we would have otherwise. We all understand men in hats and women in shoulder pads, we comprehend both the miniskirt and the new look, automobiles of almost any era are familiar to us, and we are comfortable with the idea of a man making a nickel phone call. Train travel is not foreign to us, even though most Americans today have never in their lives ridden a train. Without our much realizing it—and without the academics yet having discovered it as a thesis topic—we have grown accustomed to adapting ourselves to the *time* of a story's creation as well as to its characters and plot and themes.

Besides which, updating is hardly ever really successful. The assumptions of the moment run deep; removing them from a generation-old story isn't a simple matter of taking the hero out of a Thunderbird and putting him into a Honda. It's root-canal work; the moment of composition runs its traces through the very sentence structure, like gold ore through a mountain.

And if it isn't possible to bring twenty-year-old stories blinking and peering into the light of today as though they were newborn infants, it is equally unlikely for me to *erase* the last twenty years from my own mind and write as though it were 1962 in this room, I am twenty-nine, and most of my children aren't alive yet. If I write a story now, this moment will exist in it, no matter what I try to do.

I have written that final story, called "After I'm Gone." I have as much as possible tried to make it a story without obvious temporal references, neither *then* nor *now*. I have tried to make it a story that could be read in a magazine in 1983 without the reader thinking, "This must be a reprint," and at the same time I've tried to make it flow naturally from the Levine stories that preceded it. No one could succeed completely straddling such a pair of stools, certainly not me. But if I have at least muted my failure and made it not too clamorous, I'll be content.

As for Abe Levine, we are old friends. He's been there all along, inside my head, waiting for the next call. I had no trouble getting to know him again, and it's my fond belief that he is clearly the same person in the last story that he was in the first, however much time may or may not have gone by. I would like to introduce him to you now, and I hope you like him.

In Westlake's files I found a copy of a letter he sent to Evan Hunter a few years before Hunter's death in 2005 in which he mentioned that a fan had recently sent him a video cassette of the episode of *87th Precinct* he discusses in this piece—so, decades later, he'd finally gotten to see it. As for the book about Edwin Drood . . . well, there's always the chance it will see the light of day eventually.—Ed.

TANGLED WEBS FOR SALE: BEST OFFER

This essay was written as a contribution to *I, Witness: Personal Encounters with Crime by Members of the Mystery Writers of America*, which was edited by Westlake's friend and sometime collaborator Brian Garfield and published in 1978.—Ed.

At the kind of literary cocktail party where the only food available is seven or eight trendy variants on potato chips, I sometimes limit my drinking to dry vermouth on the rocks, as a self-protective gesture. That's what I was carrying, while roaming with less and less hope in search of at least one small bowl of peanuts, when the short lady with the lace at her wrists said, "May I ask you a question?"

"You haven't seen any cashews, have you? Possibly a bowl of fruit?"

"Sorry, no. *May* I ask you a question?"

Near to hand was a bowl of trendy potato chips; they had a rippled surface, like my stomach lining. "Yes, of course," I said.

"Tell me," she said. "Where *do* you get your ideas?"

"I am a Crime Novelist, madam," I said. "I steal them."

She laughed, but didn't go away. "Surely not," she said.

"Surely so," I insisted. The rippled chip was very dry and very salty. I sipped vermouth and said, "Tom Lehrer defined it for all." And, in my loud, tone-deaf voice, I sang, "Plagiarize! That's why the Good Lord made your eyes!"

"But not *you*," she said. Nothing would deter her, and my singing—which normally can empty a room—had attracted two or three passersby.

"Everyone," I told her, and them, "everyone steals, whether only a line, a situation, a character quirk, a setting, perhaps a murder method, a complete plot, possibly even an entire thematic substructure, a whole view of life. As we stand here gorging ourselves on potato chips, college students all over the country are writing themes in which every sentence ends with three dots, thanks to their recent exposure to Celine. And why not?" I demanded, noticing that one or two fiction writers had joined the group. "Plagiarism is merely imitation, and imitation is said to be a form of flattery. One of the better forms of flattery. I have in my time," I continued, "both flattered others and been myself flattered by those bastards treading on my heels."

"Sorry," said the short gent behind me. He picked up the chip bowl and moved around front.

"Not you. And in any case there's no point getting upset about people stealing ideas from one another. I'm finally coming to understand that no matter how hard I hustle or how lazily I dawdle we'll all get to Tuesday at the same time."

"What have *you* stolen?" demanded a fellow I recognized as a moderately known novelist reputed to be very handy with a lawsuit.

"I won't tell you what I've stolen personally," I answered, "but I will tell you of a time when I became a receiver of stolen goods, even to the point of filing off the serial numbers and reselling the stuff."

"Who'd you steal from?"

"I didn't steal. I received stolen goods."

"Who from?"

"A Hollywood movie producer."

The entire group shifted from one foot to the other. Hearing that Hollywood movie producers might be found with stolen goods about their persons was not interesting news.

The litigious novelist, however, pursued the point: "Who'd *he* steal from?"

"A gang of professional criminals in France. And they had started the process by stealing from Lionel White."

The lady with the lace at her wrists said, "Who is Lionel White?"

"A very good crime novelist," I told her. "I doubt he himself knows how many of his books have been made into movies. There was *The Money Trap* with Glenn Ford, and an early Stanley Kubrick movie called *The Killing*, and—"

"Get to the point," suggested the novelist.

"I suppose I will, eventually," I said, pausing to sip vermouth. "But mentioning *The Killing* reminds me of another example of how ideas travel. That movie was based on a novel called *Clean Break*. A while later, there was a novel called *League of Gentlemen*, written by John Boland, and made into a movie—"

"—starring Jack Hawkins, with a screenplay by Bryan Forbes," suggested the short gent. He was eating all the chips out of the bowl, one after the other, like a metronome: dip-chip, dip-chip, dip-chip.

"That's right," I agreed. "In that movie, which was a comic treat-

ment of the kind of caper story at which Lionel White has always specialized—the tough gang of professional crooks pulling off a robbery of
some sort—Jack Hawkins assembles his gang by sending each man half
of a five-pound note and—"

"Ten-pound note," corrected the short gent.

"Are you sure? Anyway, half a note and a paperback crime novel.
He wants them to read the novel to see how professionals do it, and
the novel he sends them is *Clean Break*, by Lionel White. So the notion of using Lionel White's ideas to trigger other people's ideas already
exists."

The novelist said, "What does all this have to do with you and receiving stolen goods?"

"Now we've come to that," I assured him. "Among Lionel White's
other books was one called *The Snatch*, which was a kidnapping novel,
featuring his usual breed of hard-bitten professionals. As with many
American crime novels, this was translated into French and published
by Gallimard in their Serie Noir. A minor French criminal read the
book, decided it was a blueprint for a practical crime, and induced a
few of his criminal friends to read it."

"Wait a minute," said the short gent, putting down the empty chip
bowl. "That's what Jack Hawkins did in *League of Gentlemen*."

"Except," I pointed out, "that Hawkins and his gang used the *manner* of *Clean Break* while making up their own crime. Otherwise, John
Boland and Bryan Forbes might very well have found themselves being
sued by Lionel White."

My novelist friend growled low in his throat. He was drinking something as colorless as water, with a bit of lemon rind in it. Such drinkers
are dangerous.

"To return to France," I said, "these criminals—"

"I love France," said the lady with the lace at her wrists. Her drink
was a dark maroon in color, and it coated the glass. Had oil spill become a popular beverage?

"France is all right," I answered, "but if you—"

"Lionel White," insisted the novelist.

"Those French criminals," urged the short gent.

"What happened next?" demanded two or three fringe members of the group. (They were, had they but known it, exemplifying not only the human need for narrative which creates jobs for storytellers like me, but also the professional need which at times drives writers to seek the answer to that question in other writers' books.)

"Well," I said, "the French criminals weren't planning to write any novels, so they didn't have to be careful not to get too close to the original story. They decided to follow White's blueprint *exactly*, doing everything precisely as described in the book." I sipped vermouth. "The book," I went on, "told them how and where to find their victim, so they did that part and it worked. It told them how to engineer the actual kidnapping, and they did *that* part and it worked. It told them how and where to keep their victim, how to make contact with the parents, and how to collect the ransom without getting caught, and everything it told them to do they did, and it all worked."

The novelist, sounding suspicious, said, "This is a true story?"

"It is. The book told them to choose an infant, because an infant wouldn't be able to identify them later, and the infant they chose was the grandson of the automaker, Peugeot. The Peugeot kidnapping became the crime of the decade in France; brilliant, audacious, professional in every way."

The lady with the lace at her wrists said, "What happened to the child?"

"Fortunately," I told her, "the book had emphasized the point that the child should not be harmed in any way. If the child were returned safely at the end of the exercise, the crime would eventually be forgotten and the police would concern themselves with other more recent outrages. But if they were to kill the child, the police—and the wealthy Peugeot family—would *never* give up, until the criminals were found. So, once they got their ransom money, the gang returned the child—in the manner described in the novel—and that was the end of it."

"What happened next?" asked two or three recent additions to the group.

"They ran out of book."

"What did they do?"

"They were left with nothing to rely on but their own teeny brains. They threw their money around in neighborhoods where they were known. They got drunk in bistros and hinted at secret knowledge in the Peugeot kidnapping. Within two weeks they were all under arrest and most of the money had been found and returned to the family."

Smiling—his chin was very salty—the short gent said, "They should have used some of the money to hire Lionel White to write a sequel."

"If he'd put that thought into the book, they would have."

The disputatious novelist said, "Where do *you* come into all this?"

"Rather later," I told him. "Let me make the point here that factual events cannot be copyrighted. It would be clean against the law to steal the plot or characters of Lionel White's *Clean Break*, but it is not against the law to borrow for one's own literary use the true story of a group of criminals imitating a novel. This was the suggestion brought back to me in the late sixties by a producer named Eddie Montaigne. A very nice, pleasant man, Montaigne had been the producer of the Phil Silvers TV series *Sergeant Bilko* and of a long line of movie comedies including the Don Knotts pictures. Universal Studios had offered to finance him for a major-budget comedy, and his idea was to do a movie based on the Peugeot kidnapping. Not that he insisted on a kidnapping, and he certainly didn't want a French background. What he wanted was a story about criminals copying a book. He asked me if I'd like to do this story, and I said I would, and in our final meeting I made my principal contribution to the project, by suggesting that a *movie* about these criminals should have them imitating not a book but a movie."

"Of course," said the novelist.

I sipped vermouth. "We had a step deal," I said, throwing in a little shoptalk to please the novelist (pleasing one's audience is *much* more important than having an opinion about one's audience), "which began with my writing a ten-thousand-word story treatment. Initially I felt I'd rather stay away from kidnapping because if for no other reason it was too close to the truth, and after thinking about felonies for a while

I came up with the substitute of counterfeiting. It seemed to me that Dennis O'Keefe had starred in any number of movies in which he was a Treasury Agent disguised as a crook so he could infiltrate a counterfeiting gang, and I thought it might be fun to cobble up a nonexistent movie out of bits and pieces of those Dennis O'Keefe epics, and make *that* the movie my own crooks would be imitating. The problem was—and it was frequently also a problem in the Dennis O'Keefe movies—there's very little that's either dramatic *or* comic in counterfeiting."

The short gent had wandered away—it's hard to keep an audience interested—but now he came back with a new bowl of potato chips and said, "Why didn't you have them rob a bank?"

"The problem with robbery, and with most other crimes," I told him, "is that they aren't *serial*. They happen and they're over with. There's no reason for the criminals to keep going back to the book—or the movie—to see what to do next. Counterfeiting is at least a serial crime, in a dull way, but finally I had to go back to the original. Kidnapping is, more than any other, a crime that takes place step by step."

"So you did the story treatment about a kidnapping," said the novelist.

I withdrew, from the short gent's new bowl, a potato chip. All the chips in this bowl were identical—medium tan, shaped like a moray eel, with a consistency suspiciously like fiberboard—as though they were all clones from some original proto-chip.

"I did two story treatments," I said, as the tasteless chip passed through my mouth, chased by vermouth. "The counterfeiting treatment was generally agreed to be a mistake, so *then* I did the kidnapping treatment, and that was generally agreed to be okay. Until, unfortunately, it got to Lew Wasserman, head of Universal, who had to approve the project before it could be slated for production."

The novelist said, "Don't tell me Lew Wasserman objected to plagiarism."

"I doubt he approves of it," I said, "at least not in its actionable forms, but that wasn't the problem in this case. The problem was, Lew Wasserman had just become a grandfather. Now, I'd altered from a true-life story—and from *Clean Break* as well—by making the victim a bright self-sufficient ten-year-old boy rather than a baby, since fearing for a baby's safety is inimical to comedy, but it wasn't change enough for Grandfather Lew. 'You can't make a comedy about a kidnapping,' he said, apparently never having heard of O. Henry's 'The Ransom of Red Chief.' In any event, that killed the movie deal."

"Is that it?" demanded the novelist. "That's the whole story?"

"Well, not exactly. In stealing ideas, the professional novelist's richest hunting ground is himself. One's own earlier work is full of potentially useful material. A quick paint job, rearrange the furniture, and *voila!*"

"I do love France," said the lady with the lace at her wrists.

"But if you're going to Europe," I said, "you should certainly—"

"You stole from yourself," suggested the novelist.

"Granted. I would have sued me, but I settled out of court."

The short gent, dip-chipping his way through the pseudo-chips, said, "What did you steal?"

"The whole idea, lock, stock, and barrel. I'd already written two comic novels about a gang of professional criminals who are more unlucky than inept, led by a gloomy fellow named Dortmunder. At the suggestion of my very good friend Abby Adams, I borrowed back the kidnapping story and turned it into the third Dortmunder novel, called *Jimmy the Kid*. Since what I was writing was a book, I changed the original from a movie back to a novel, and included excerpts from that novel, which was called *Child Heist*, written by a tough crime novelist called Richard Stark, who works the same general territory as Lionel White."

The novelist gave me an unfriendly look. "If *I* were Richard Stark," he said, "I'd sue."

"Well, the fact is," I told him, "*I'm* Richard Stark. I've written any number of novels under that name about a tough professional thief called Parker, but *Child Heist* isn't among them. It is an invented novel from a pseudonymous author appearing in a real novel by the same author based on a producer's idea to use a real-life case in which actual criminals performed a crime based on *The Snatch*, by Lionel White." I drank vermouth.

The short gent said, "So the *Child Heist* excerpts in *Jimmy the Kid* are all of the book that was written? The rest doesn't exist?"

"Right."

"Will you ever write the rest?"

"Somehow I doubt it. In the first place, I think I'd get cross-eyed by now, and in the second place, wouldn't it somehow complete the circle? Wouldn't I—or Richard Stark—simply wind up writing *The Snatch*?"

"*Then* Lionel White would sue you," the novelist told me, with some satisfaction.

"He might. On the other hand, having been at both ends of that kind of thievery, I know it takes a lot of provocation to make a plagiarism suit seem worthwhile."

"Oh, no it doesn't," said the polemical novelist.

"It does with most of us. And we *all* borrow, all storytellers do, whether we know it or not. The books we've read, the movies we've seen, they still float in the bilge of our brains, along with our own experiences and prejudices and hopes, and sooner or later something comes out of us that we originally got from somebody else. For instance," I said, backing away from the company, "this entire conversation is non-existent and borrowed from Tom Wolfe."

"Which one?" cried the short gent, as I moved away.

"Both of them!" I told him, and headed for the bar. "A very tall bourbon," I told the chap in the white coat. "And you might as well add an ice cube."

INTRODUCTION TO *KAHAWA*

This was written for a new edition of *Kahawa* published in 1995.—Ed.

I was in Los Angeles, meeting with some other people on some other business entirely, and when I got back to the hotel, there was a message from Les Alexander, in New York. I had known Les as a friend for some years, and while we had talked about working together on something or other, it had never happened. At that time he was a book packager and sometime television producer; he is now a film producer. I was and am a novelist with a minor in screenwriting.

When I returned Les's call, he was boyishly excited. He had a true story, he said, that would make the basis for a great novel. I told him, as I tell everyone in such circumstances, "I'll listen, but I won't give you an answer today. I'll call you tomorrow. I don't want to make a mistake and be locked into something I don't really want to do, or locked out of something it turns out I *did* want to do."

"Fair enough," he said. "A group of white mercenaries, in Uganda, while it was under Idi Amin, stole a railroad train a mile long, full of coffee, and made it disappear."

"Forget the twenty-four hours," I said. "I'll do it."

So it began as a caper. I've written capers, before and since, both serious and comic, so I feel I know a bit about the form. (It probably says something discreditable about me that I put the serious work under a pseudonym and the comic under my own name.)

One thing I know about the caper is that it helps if the job is outrageous in one way or another. Once, for instance, before the government started paying by check, Parker stole the entire payroll from a United States Air Force Base. Dortmunder, not to be outdone, has made off with an entire bank, temporarily housed in a mobile home.

And what could be more outrageous than to steal a mile-long train from the dread Idi Amin, and *make it disappear*?

This is going to be fun, I thought.

Then I started the research. Please permit me at this point to say a strong word against research. I hate it. My feeling is, the whole point of going into the fiction racket was so I could make it all up. We get enough facts in real life; that's the way I see it.

Unfortunately that's not the way anybody else sees it. If you get a fact wrong in a novel, people will write you letters full of the most grating kinds of sarcasm and superiority. Of course, not all facts are equally holy among readers. Should you get a detail about a gun or a car wrong, the weight of mail will drive the postman into the sidewalk, but if you get the population of Altoona, PA, wrong, you probably won't hear from many people at all; three or four. So if I were to write a novel set in Uganda during the reign of Idi Amin Dada, and if I cared about the health of my mailperson, I had to do some research.

And here's the other thing I hate about research. Once I actually start it, I get lost in it. Research is my own personal Sargasso Sea. It's exactly like entering one of our civilization's mental attics, a quotation book or thesaurus or large dictionary, looking for just *one* thing, and being found in there three days later by search parties, seated on the dusty floor, intently reading.

That's what happened this time. I had current events to research (Idi Amin, and how he got where he got, and what it meant) as well as history (the European exploration/invasion of Central Africa, and what followed), so there was much to get lost in. The end was reached when I found myself halfway through a one-thousand-two-hundred-page book called *The Permanent Way*, by M. F. Hill, which was the official history of the building of the railroad on which my coffee train would travel half a century later. "That's it," I said. "This is ridiculous. As soon as I finish the other six hundred pages of this book, I'm going to work."

The Permanent Way, and other books, were interesting and useful, but one book, called *Uganda Holocaust*, by Dan Wooding and Ray Barnett, published by Zondervan, changed both me and the novel I was going to write; for the better, I think.

It seems that some Christian evangelical sects set great store by "giving witness," which is to say, speaking about and airing and publicizing great works of charity or martyrdom or goodness, done in Christ's name. It also seems that Idi Amin's primary goal during his years in power was to eliminate Christianity from Uganda, a large if unworthy task, since Uganda's sixteen million people were seventy-five percent Christian. Amin's onslaught resulted in over five hundred thousand Christian martyrs, people who went to their deaths not because they were political or rebellious or dangerous, but only because they were professed Christians. This was the largest and most extensive Christian martyrdom since Rome before Constantine. How's that for distinction?

The instant Amin was driven from Uganda, Wooding and Barnett flew in with tape recorders to take witness from the survivors, and published the results in *Uganda Holocaust,* a book that not only made me horribly familiar with the workings of the State Research Bureau, but also changed the character of the story I would tell. As I told my wife at the time, "I can't dance on all those graves."

So it was still a caper, but now it was something else as well, something more, and, I think, deeper. My own emotions of pity and rage and contempt were entwined with the story, though I knew better than to let them take over. But they were there, spicing the stew.

And altering the book in more ways than one. As you know, in our country "sexandviolence" is one word, and piously we recoil from its depiction; sure. In *Kahawa,* though, both sex and violence had to play a stronger part than usual in my novels, because the material demanded it. I would never throw in what is called *gratuitous* sexandviolence, because I have too much respect for story. If a word, one single word, distracts the reader from the story I'm trying to tell, out with it. Since both sex and violence can be distracting, I usually depict them sparingly, trying mostly to get my effects by allusion and implication. Not so in *Kahawa;* the book demanded a stronger approach.

Of course, when it was published, I got complaining letters, and their general tenor was, "I've always liked your books, and so has my teenage son/daughter, but how can I show him/her this book with all this graphic sex in it?" Five hundred thousand dead; bodies hacked and mutilated and debased and destroyed; corridors running with blood; and nobody complained about the violence. They complained about the sex. Ah, such wee, sleekit, cow'rin, tim'rous beasties.

My research was not limited to books; my wife and I also went to Kenya, and to London, to see some of the locations and talk with some of the people. (We did not go into Uganda, merely looked at it across Lake Victoria, since this was 1980, Amin was barely three years out of power, and Uganda was still in a state of anarchy. Trips to Uganda at that time were mostly one way.)

Accompanying us on the trip was the person who had originally told Les Alexander the story, which he had knowledge of because of his connections with the pilots who were supposed to fly the coffee shipment from Entebbe. This person has been in many interesting places at interesting times, and was an education in himself, though not quite perhaps as solid as an education from books. Later, when he learned that I was writing an introductory note of gratitude to those who had helped me put the book together, he phoned to ask a favor: Would I mind thanking him under a pseudonym? (He mentioned the name he would prefer.) He didn't want his own name in print, but he did like the idea of being thanked for his part in the enterprise.

So I thanked one person under an alias; is that the strangest part of the story? Maybe.

About that title. *Kahawa*. It is the word for coffee in Swahili. It leads to the slang word for coffee in some parts of Europe: "kawa." (In Polish, "kawa" is the regular word for coffee.) The original is the Arabic "qahwa," or the Hebrew "kavah," and really it's all the same word, virtually around the world. A *c* or *k* or *q* at the beginning, a *w* or *v* or *f* in the middle. Kahawa is coffee. Unfortunately, it's a little obscure to be a title.

The problem was the change in my book as I got into the research. Originally, I was going to call it *Coffee to Go*; a fun title for a fun caper. After a while, that title just slunk off in embarrassment. Then I found myself toying with pomposities like *The Time of the Hero*, but my feeling is, if the title is too boring to read all the way through, it might keep readers from trying the novel. So *Kahawa* it is.

The original publisher of *Kahawa*, in 1982, was in the midst of an upheaval. My original editor was let go before publication, to be replaced with an oil painting of an editor; pleasant, even comforting to look at, but not much help in the trenches. The publisher moved by fits and starts—more fits than starts, actually—and though the book received good reviews, no one at the publishing house seemed able to figure out how to suggest that anybody might enjoy reading it. So it didn't do well.

My current publisher is not suffering upheavals, my current editor is lively and professional, and when it was suggested that *Kahawa* might be given a second chance of life, I was both astonished and very pleased. I've made minor changes in the text, nothing substantive, and agreed to write this introduction, and here we are, by golly, airborne again.

By coincidence, I ran into that oil painting at a party a few months ago. He said, "Are you writing any more African adventure novels?"

"No," I said, "but Warner is going to put out *Kahawa* again, in hardcover."

His jaw dropped. "*Why?*" he asked. (This is what we have to put up with, sometimes.)

"I think they like it," I said.

I hope you do, too.

LIGHT

This was found in typescript in Westlake's files, but it was never published. It seems to have been written sometime in 1998 or 1999, between the publication of *The Ax* and *The Hook.*—Ed.

In 1960 I published my first novel, a crime mystery called *The Mercenaries*. Since then, I have published forty novels, one non-fiction book and one juvenile under my own name, plus twenty-one under the pseudonym Richard Stark, five under the pseudonym Tucker Coe, and a few others. I have never had a major success, but I write fast, and well enough, and so I have made my living with my pen now for thirty-eight years.

In June of 1997, my fortieth novel was published, called *The Ax*. It was in some ways a departure from the general run of my books, but then again, I've made departures before. Most of my books have been comic to one extent or another, though I have written international adventure, and fantasy, and psychological suspense, and straight crime novels.

Starting in 1970, with a book called *The Hot Rock*, I have also written about a series character, named John Dortmunder, a capable and work-manlike professional criminal who lives under a black cloud (me), and to date I have put the poor man through nine novels and six short stories. However, in the same period, I also wrote some twenty novels that were *not* about John Dortmunder, so I've managed to avoid the trap of being shackled to a series character, one of the many traps lying in wait for the unwary writer. (We do remember Conan Doyle's failed attempt to knock off Sherlock Holmes.)

In fact, I've managed to avoid all the traps. Since I was never a best-seller, no one's expectations about my work were very high, but since I was prolific, I could turn out enough wordage to make a living.

Also, the movie industry helped. From time to time, movie rights to one of my books would be sold (or optioned), and from time to time I'd be hired to write a screenplay about something or other. The movie industry needs writers, but ignores writers as a matter of principle; it is the perfect place for a writer who doesn't want to be noticed.

And I didn't want to be noticed. I wanted to write whatever came into my head, and not worry about it. So that's what I did.

But then, in June of 1997, *The Ax* was published. It did not become a best-seller either, except for two weeks on the *Los Angeles Times* list, but it did exceed everybody's expectations. It got excellent reviews. It sold better than my previous books. It got attention. It caught my publisher's attention.

I am published by the Mysterious Press label within Warner Books, and my publisher is an excellent one; knowledgeable and supportive. When *The Ax* "took off," they noticed, and supported, and even took out a full-page ad in the daily *New York Times*. I was very pleased.

At the same time, I had returned to my Richard Stark pen name for the first time in twenty-three years, and in October of 1997 *Comeback* by Mr. Stark was published, again to more than the usual notice, including an extended write-up in *Time* magazine. Again, I was pleased.

In the meantime, I had of course started another book. It was not a departure, like *The Ax*, nor was it exactly like the several books I'd earlier published in the nineties. It was a little comic insurance fraud novel, closest in spirit to books I'd written in the seventies. I finished it, and gave it to my editor and my agent, and the gloom could be heard to descend. (It sounds like a grounded blimp losing air.)

Gently I was told that this could not possibly be the book that would follow *The Ax*, nor could it be the book that followed the return of Richard Stark. I did see that.

Unfortunately, I did. I saw what they meant, and I had to agree. I had a certain responsibility now. The book I published after *The Ax* and Stark redux could not be just any book. I had newer readers now, who would come to that next book with a certain level of expectation. They wouldn't necessarily need *The Ax* again, they could certainly understand that I also had my comic moments, but there was a level of emotional truth that really should be present in whatever book I published next. Later, in the future, I might return sometimes to my more frivolous ways.

I had to agree. I do agree. The only problem is, I don't know what that book might be. As I told my agent, "It's a little late for me to have second-novel problems, but that's what this is." My rhythms have been thrown off, and all because I've lost my precious anonymity (except, of course, in Hollywood, which doesn't matter).

I've seen this happen to friends, other writers, and it makes their lives very stressful. Not only are their incomes dependent upon their producing another egg like the last egg, but so are their reputations dependent upon that process, so are their business and social relationships, and so is their self-esteem. I have commiserated with my friends at those rare moments when the stress bursts forward into uncensored complaint, while at the same time I've hidden my glee that it was never going to happen to me.

It has happened to me. The book I just finished, which would have been perfectly acceptable before *The Ax*—a minor entry in the canon, but not a disgrace—is now not acceptable.

What is worse, for the first time since 1970 it has become inappropriate for me to write about John Dortmunder. It has *always* been appropriate for me to write about John Dortmunder. He has been my bastion and my relief, the easiest and most enjoyable part of my working life. I've even had to ration myself not to write *too* often about him. And now I'm not supposed to write about him at all.

I have no idea what my next book will be. I don't expect this to be the beginning of a long and echoing silence, since I think I don't carry the gene for writer's block, but just at this moment I'm bewildered. The lights have gone on. I've been noticed. The jig is up. I stand paralyzed, in all this light.

HOOKED

Like the preceding piece, I found this previously unpublished essay in typescript in Westlake's files. It seems to have been written around 2000, possibly with an eye toward being included in a paperback edition of *The Hook*. The plot of *The Hook* concerns a writer who has written a great book but is having trouble selling it because of his declining sales record, as tracked by the publishers' and bookstores' computers. He convinces another writer to publish it under his own name . . . which doesn't go smoothly. (Westlake later acknowledged that he got the idea from his friend Justin Scott, a thriller writer who once adopted a new pen name for that very reason.)—Ed.

Visualize a football quarterback on his day off, at the supermarket. When he comes out, I imagine he automatically looks out over the parking lot and has in his mind exactly the force and angle required to heave the bag of groceries in his arm onto the hood of that red Toyota over there.

All intense careers are like that. On your day off, you're still involved in the skills and details of your craft, whether you want to be or not. It's just there, it's part of your day, it's part of who you are.

Following the quarterback out of the supermarket is a novelist, who immediately notices a woman in sunglasses in the back seat of that black Audi over there. Why is she just sitting in the car? Why in the back seat? Why isn't she looking around, or reading, or doing something other than just sitting there behind her sunglasses? Halfway across the parking lot, the novelist has worked out a scenario for her that answers those questions. Ninety-nine times out of a hundred the novelist won't ever make use of that story, or even remember it five minutes later, but he merely automatically flexed the story muscles, there in the parking lot, just as the quarterback automatically flexed his tossing muscles.

What happens to quarterbacks eventually is time; they change. What happens to popular novelists is public taste; it changes. The tools of the craft are still there, but the exercise is now only idle.

Naturally I've brooded about this from time to time, and watched the careers of others in my racket, and wondered what it's like to know you're over the hill. A writer can go on writing, of course, so long as the story pieces keep floating in his or her head, but what if nobody anymore wants to publish any of it? Then what's the point? We're not *hobbyists*, goddam it, that isn't a stamp collection on the shelf.

To add to the normal destructive flow of time and taste in the novelist's career, there has been over the last generation a steady contraction of publishing markets, and a weeding out, sometimes ruthless, of writers. And the introduction of the marketeer's computer has removed the last shred of human emotion, human contact and human reasonableness from the world of publishing. Try to argue with a computer.

Nobody can argue, but a few people have decided to escape, at least for a while, the computer's gaze. They know they're good, and they want this latest novel to be judged on its own terms, as a novel, as a read, but they also know that not one person who really matters at the publishing house will read the novel first, if at all. What is read is the sales figures from that writer's previous novels. The self-fulfilling prophecy is the only business strategy known to these MBA geniuses, who were never fired for the novels they didn't publish.

What this desperate few has done to evade the computer is re-create the self, become a new guy, or a new gal, with *no* track record, nothing to read at all but the goddam book. This can be an effective strategy, if security is maintained, but for how long? B. Traven and Thomas Pynchon and a few others have managed to succeed while never showing up in person, but most careers require a public side.

The catalyst for my writing *The Hook* was one such person. I know about this person because, a few years ago, we discussed the novel, then in its early planning stages, and when, a long time later, I asked, "What's happening with the book?" I was sworn to secrecy and told the truth.

Not everybody has the personality to live in deep cover, to live as it were as a spy without a country. I think my friend does, but I don't know yet how successful the strategy will be, nor for how long.

Like the quarterback hefting his groceries, I hefted this particular plot hook, being the little anomaly that gets a story going, until I thought about the fact that hefting plot hooks is what writers *do*. I've known novelists, for instance, who have treated serious dangerous extended hospital stays as research. It all becomes fiction, or at least material to become fiction.

What happens when a couple of novelists try to take their skills out of the workplace and into the world? What happens when the quarterback throws a hand grenade? Can he be sure he's got *this* game under control?

LETTER TO HOWARD B. GOTLIEB, BOSTON UNIVERSITY LIBRARIES

In March of 1965, Westlake received a letter from Howard B. Gotlieb, chief of special collections at the Boston University Libraries, asking if he would be willing to donate his papers to the university's library. Receiving no reply, Gotlieb followed with a letter on June 30; below is Westlake's response.—Ed.

July 16, 1965
Dear Mr. Gotlieb:

Please excuse my not having replied to your first letter in March, and accept this reply to your letter of June 30 in its stead. It was astonishment that kept me silent the first time, and it is astonishment that makes me break my silence now.

In my own mind, I make a distinction between the words 'writer' and 'author' for which I have no dictionary justification, but which I find at times useful. Since this looks like such a time, let me pass my private definitions along to you as a lead-in to the explanation of my various astonishments. A writer, in my personal lexicon, is a commercial wordsmith, an active professional, a (if the word can be stripped of overtones) hack. An author, on the other hand, is an institution, a brand name, a reputation. John D. MacDonald is a writer. Saul Bellow began as a writer but has become an institution, an author. Arthur Miller has never been anything but an author. John Steinbeck, having resisted authordom, is a writer with an honorary author's membership card.

It has seemed to me a natural state of affairs that authors should be collected, annotated, and assembled, but that writers should be left to do their doodling on sand. (When Erle Stanley Gardner or some other such has himself 'librarianized'—forgive the coinage, but this is ad lib—I always feel a little embarrassed for him. About the only non-author writer I can think of who wouldn't look silly standing nobly in a niche is Georges Simenon.)

When I got your first letter, I was so astonished I put the whole thing completely out of my mind. First, I'm a writer, with only the teeniest and most secret and ephemeral urgings toward authorhood. Second, I'm barely known on my block and have absolutely no national reputation at all. (Nor a category reputation; I've had a few books published, to a smattering and a spectrum of reviews. In the area of my first several books, the 'names' in the field among current workers are Ross Macdonald, John D. MacDonald, Charles Williams and a few others. My most recent books—one out, two more finished—are comedic mysteries, and there I have no reputation at all.) Third, all of the book-length writing I've done under my own name has been exclusively in a category of strictly entertainment writing, in which higher aspirations, even if they existed, are irrelevant.

Please believe me that I am not subjecting you to an effusion of false modesty. I'm not just scuffing my foot in the sand, in hopes of being patted on the head and told, "Shucks, fella, you're more important than you know." I think I do know, and what I think I know collides head-on with the implications of your two letters to me.

The first of these, as I said, astonished me to the extent that I simply didn't think about it. But the second letter, re-emphasizing the first, makes me think you really mean it. So now I'm astonished all over again, since I'm sure my personal evaluation—of place, not potential—is at least close to accurate.

Therefore, this response. Let's simply accept that I'm generally correct in my self-evaluation, and now, with me being the me I know me to be, what is it you want of me?

By the way, I hope it goes without saying that my astonishment both times was more than a little tinged with pleasure. You have made me a very happy kid.

Sincerely (if confusedly),
Donald Westlake

That fall, Westlake demurred once more: "No matter how many books I write, how many are published, how many people I meet who have read something I've written, it has always been possible for me to avoid self-consciousness while actually writing the stuff, by simply believing there isn't anybody out there at all. I do what I do because that's what I do—and because I enjoy it—and nothing else is relevant. . . . What you offer, in essence, is a shot at immortality. Nowhere near a guarantee, of course, no one can offer that, but a shot at it. But at the moment I relish my innocence more." Eventually, however, Westlake was convinced, and his papers are now held by the special collections department of the Boston University Libraries.—Ed.

SIX LUNCH BREAK

May's Famous Tuna Casserole

This recipe was Westlake's contribution to a 1999 collection of recipes by mystery writers, *A Taste of Murder*. The University of Chicago Press has neither attempted to follow nor eaten the results of this recipe and thus disclaims any responsibility for the result should you attempt it. We've seen what happens when even the best-laid plans come into contact with John Dortmunder.—Ed.

I have among my published novels a recidivist character named John Dortmunder, whose joys are few and travails many. Whenever life becomes more than usually difficult for John, his faithful companion, May, lightens his spirits by presenting him with his favorite dinner, May's Famous Tuna Casserole. Over the years, the public demand for the recipe for May's Famous Tuna Casserole has been scant and relenting, and so, some years ago, I felt compelled to offer it to the world at large in *Lit a la Carte*, compiled by Rex Beckham.

Since then, the clamor has continued unheard, which makes me delighted to promulgate the recipe for May's Famous Tuna Casserole (concocted, I must admit, with some exceedingly reluctant help—99 percent—from my wife, the writer and otherwise gourmet, Abby Adams) to an even wider audience.

Just so you know, John's other favorite meal is cornflakes with milk and sugar, in the proportion of 1:1:1.

2 cups milk

3 tablespoons butter

2 tablespoons flour

Salt

Pepper

Nutmeg

Cayenne pepper

12-ounce package egg noodles

2 10-ounce packages frozen, chopped spinach

2 large cans white tuna fish

Grated Parmesan cheese

Bread crumbs

Preheat the oven to 375 degrees.

White sauce: Warm the milk in a small saucepan (do not let boil). In a thick-bottomed saucepan, melt 2 tablespoons of butter and stir in the flour. Cook, whisking continuously, for 4 minutes; add the warm milk gradually and cook while stirring until smooth and thick. Season to taste with salt, pepper, nutmeg, and a pinch of cayenne. Use the other tablespoon of butter to grease a 3-quart casserole.

Meanwhile, cook the noodles until barely done in plenty of boiling water. Drain, and immediately toss in the buttered casserole with 2 tablespoons of the white sauce. Defrost the frozen spinach in boiling water; drain and spread on top of the noodles. Drain the tuna and break up chunks. Spread it on top of the spinach.

Pour the remaining sauce over the top of the casserole. Sprinkle with grated cheese and bread crumbs. Bake for 25 minutes or until bubbling and brown.

Serves 6 for lunch or supper.

SEVEN THE OTHER GUYS IN THE STRING

Peers, Favorites, and Influences

LAWRENCE BLOCK: FIRST SIGHTING

Westlake wrote this appreciation of one of his oldest friends for a special issue of *Mystery Scene* focused on Lawrence Block that was published in 1990.—Ed.

I first saw Larry Block in November of 1958. I was working as a fee reader for the Scott Meredith Literary Agency, reading amateur manuscripts for which the amateurs paid Scott, who paid me one-fifth. This was not the part of the agency that was mail fraud. Another part, even more legitimate than my fee reading, was the actual representation of actual professional writers, like Arthur C. Clarke and Evan Hunter and P. G. Wodehouse, and, a little later, Norman Mailer. One of this select, if eclectic, crew was Larry Block.

In the six months while I was, in the words of the science fiction writer Damon Knight (who'd been in that job before me, as in fact so had Larry), "chained to an oar at a fee agency," I saw a number of writers for the first time, all framed in the speakeasy-style window, the panel of which the English receptionist would slide open in response to an irritating buzz. One of those was Larry.

That particular day, he had a beard. I've noticed over the intervening years that sometimes Larry has a beard and sometimes he has a moustache. Similarly, sometimes he has hair on his head and sometimes he does not. Sometimes he dresses respectably and sometimes he dresses like a biker and sometimes he dresses like a person who's lost his luggage, but at no time, either haired, partially haired nor unhaired, however he may wish to dress, does he look reputable.

So this disreputable person, at that moment bearded, appeared in the wall opening, greeted the receptionist, then, smiling, called over her head to Henry Morrison, at another desk in the room (it was a crowded room), "Is it too late to change the dedication on that book?"

Henry, who worked exclusively with the professional writers and who looked upon us fee readers as though prepared to hear our confession, gave Larry an exasperated look and said, "Yes. Why?"

"I'm not going with that girl anymore," Larry said.

"Well, it's too late," Henry said.

Larry kept smiling. He shrugged, said, "Well . . ." and went away. The receptionist closed the panel on the echo of his smile.

Think of the series of emotional batterings Larry had then just recently undergone, of which I had been present at the finale. He had met a girl. He had found himself so twinned with her that he had dedicated a book to her. Then he had lost this person who had so recently been of such importance to him. And now he had learned that it was too late to keep from having the entire arc of a once-tender relationship permanently recorded in a paperback to be published under a pen name. And yet, he went on smiling. (Over the years, mostly, he has continued to go on smiling.)

I had been, around that time, feeling the need for one or more cheerful persons in my life. I better get to know that guy, I told myself.

ON PETER RABE

Letter to Peter Rabe

The ellipsis in this letter indicates my excision of a section of detailed questions about Rabe's work that were subsequently developed in the essay that follows the letter.—Ed.

December 10, 1986

Dear Mr. Rabe,

I am a writer, under a number of names. Under one of them, Richard Stark, I wrote for a time books that were stylistically very influenced by your Gold Medal work between *Stop This Man* and *The Box*. I've acknowledged that influence in print or public several times, and now that chicken has come home to roost in an odd way.

I have received a letter from an (presumably) academic named Jon L. Breen, who says that he and an indefatigable anthologist named Martin Greenberg are editing "a series of original essay collections on various aspects of mystery and detective fiction," to be published by Scarecrow Press. He goes on to say, "This project is essentially a 'labor of love' and is not expected to prove financially lucrative for either editors or contributors." As my agent, Knox Burger, who I think you knew in an earlier persona, told me, that's the kind of offer I don't seem able to refuse.

Anyway, Breen goes on, "One of our collections will concern the great paperback original writers, and among the subjects we want to cover is Peter Rabe. I know . . . you're a fan of his work . . ." and so on.

So, I went upstairs and brought back down my Peter Rabe books, which include all Gold Medals from *Stop This Man* to *Code Name Gadget*, plus *Anatomy of a Killer* in both Abelard-Schuman and Berkeley, plus "Hard Case Redhead" from *Mystery Tales*. (Don't worry; it just means you're drowning.)

However, God damn it, I must have loaned *Kill the Boss Goodbye* to somebody, that being my favorite of your books, and I can't remember who. I've put in an order for another copy from Otto Penzler at Mysterious Press—no, Mysterious Bookshop, he has all these entities—but God knows if he'll ever find one.

I'll be going through the books again. So far, I've only skimmed a bit, to find out if yesterday's enthusiasm had died (an awful thing that sometimes happens), and was relieved to see it had not. The coolness is there, the smooth surface that never directly refers to the emotions squirming away underneath. Okay. There's nothing in it for you either, but I'll do the goddam piece, as a minor payment for having drained so much of your blood in years past. A small article in an obscure volume in an unimportant series from a nothing publisher: hot damn!

Would you help me a bit in this children's crusade? I can dope out background. Sicily was mentioned, a PhD in psychology. Max Gartenberg (who gave me your address) said you subsequently taught something or other in the California state college system. My wife, who spent a part of her youth in San Francisco when most of her friends were criminally insane, tells me Atascadero was the place they were always either going into or coming out of; am I inventing a pattern? . . .

Obviously, if you felt like helping me on some of all that, it would beat me making it up. Also, there are dumb little questions like: Was "Hard Case Redhead" your only published short story? Have you written nonfiction? Have you written non-crime? Have you written under pen names? Did you come up with all those rotten titles, or did your publisher? (Several of *my* rotten titles are mine, but some are the publishers'!)

If you don't want anything done, tell me, and I won't do anything. If you don't care what I do, but want no part in it yourself, ignore this letter, and eventually I'll get the idea. If you're willing to give me a few minutes of your time—or a lot of minutes of your time, don't feel constrained here—I will be very grateful.

I'm already very grateful for your books, of course, and that's the important part.

Donald E. Westlake

Peter Rabe

Rabe did reply to Westlake's letter, in generous, detailed fashion, and you'll see that Westlake draws on some of Rabe's answers in the subsequent essay, which was published in *Murder Off the Rack: Critical Studies of Ten Paperback Masters* in 1989.—Ed.

Peter Rabe wrote the best books with the worst titles of anybody I can think of. *Murder Me for Nickels. Kill the Boss Goodbye.* Why would anybody ever want to read a book called *Kill the Boss Goodbye*? And yet, *Kill the Boss Goodbye* is one of the most purely *interesting* crime novels ever written.

Here's the setup: Tom Fell runs the gambling in San Pietro, a California town of three hundred thousand people. He's been away on "vacation" for a while, and an assistant, Pander, is scheming to take over. The big bosses in Los Angeles have decided to let nature take its course; if Pander's good enough to beat Fell, the territory is his. Only Fell's trusted assistant, Cripp (for "cripple"), knows the truth, that Fell is in a sanitorium recovering from a nervous breakdown. Cripp warns Fell that he must come back or lose everything. The psychiatrist, Dr. Emilson, tells him he isn't ready to return to his normal life. Fell suffers from a manic neurosis, and if he allows himself to become overly emotional, he could snap into true psychosis. But Fell has no choice; he goes back to San Pietro to fight Pander.

This is a wonderful variant on a story as old as the Bible: Fell gains the world, and loses his mind. And Rabe follows through on his basic idea; the tension in the story just builds and builds, and we're not even surprised to find ourselves worried about, scared for, empathizing with, a gangster. The story of Fell's gradually deepening psychosis is beautifully done. The entire book is spare and clean and amazingly unornamented. Here, for instance, is the moment when Pander, having challenged Fell to a fistfight, first senses the true extent of his danger:

> Pander leaned up on the balls of his feet, arms swinging free, face mean, but nothing followed. He stared at Fell and all he saw were his eyes, mild

lashes and the lids without movement, and what happened to them. He suddenly saw the hardest, craziest eyes he had ever seen.

Pander lost the moment and then Fell smiled. He said so long and walked out the door.

Kill the Boss Goodbye was published by Gold Medal in August of 1956. It was the fifth Peter Rabe novel they'd published, the first having come out in May of 1955, just fifteen months before. That's a heck of a pace, and Rabe didn't stop there. In the five years between May 1955 and May 1960, he published sixteen novels with Gold Medal and two elsewhere.

Eighteen novels in five years would be a lot for even a cookie-cutter hack doing essentially the same story and characters over and over again, which was never true of Rabe. He wrote in third person and in first; he wrote emotionless hardboiled prose and tongue-in-cheek comedy, gangster stories, exotic adventure stories set in Europe and Mexico and North Africa, psychological studies. No two consecutive books used the same voice or setting. In fact, the weakest Peter Rabe books are the ones written in his two different attempts to create a series character.

What sustains a writer at the beginning of his career is the enjoyment of the work itself, the fun of putting the words through hoops, inventing the worlds, peopling them with fresh-minted characters. That enjoyment in the *doing* of the job is very evident in Rabe's best work. But it can't sustain a career forever; the writing history of Peter Rabe is a not entirely happy one. He spent his active writing career working for a sausage factory. What he wrote was often pate, but it was packed as sausage—those titles!—and soon, I think, his own attitude toward his work lowered to match that of the people—agent, editors—most closely associated with the reception and publishing of the work. Rabe, whose first work had a quote on the cover from Erskine Caldwell ("I couldn't put this book down!"), whose fourth book had a quote on the cover from Mickey Spillane ("This guy is *good*."), whose books were consistently and lavishly praised by Anthony Boucher in the *New York*

Times ("harsh objectivity" and "powerful understatement" and "tight and nerve-straining"), was soon churning novels out in as little as ten days, writing carelessly and sloppily, mutilating his talent.

The result is, some of Rabe's books are quite bad, awkwardly plotted and with poorly developed characters. Others are like the curate's egg: parts of them are wonderful. But when he was on track, with his own distinctive style, his own cold clear eye unblinking, there wasn't another writer in the world of the paperbacks who could touch him. Of those first eighteen novels, a full seven are first-rate, another three are excellent at least in part, and eight are ordinary mushy paperbacks that could have been turned out by any junky hack with a typewriter.

The first novel, *Stop This Man*, showed only glimpses of what Rabe would become. It begins as a nice variant on the Typhoid Mary story; the disease carrier who leaves a trail of illness in his wake. The story is that Otto Schumacher learns of an ingot of gold loaned to an atomic research facility at a university in Detroit. He and his slatternly girlfriend, Selma, meet with his old friend Catell, just out of prison, and arrange for Catell to steal the gold. But they don't know that the gold is irradiated, and will make people sick who are near it. The police nearly catch Catell early on, but he escapes, Schumacher dying. Catell goes to Los Angeles to find Smith, the man who might buy the gold ingot.

Once Catell hides the ingot near Los Angeles, the Typhoid Mary story stops, to be replaced by a variant on *High Sierra*. Catell now becomes a burglar-for-hire, employed by Smith, beginning with the robbery of a loan office. There's a double-cross, the police arrive, Catell escapes. The next job is absolutely *High Sierra*, involving a gambling resort up in the mountains, but just before the job Selma (Schumacher's girlfriend) reappears and precipitates the finish. With the police hot on his trail, Catell retrieves the gold and drives aimlessly around the Imperial Valley, becoming increasingly sick with radiation disease. Eventually he dies in a ditch, hugging his gold.

The elements of *Stop This Man* just don't mesh. There are odd little scenes of attempted humor that don't really come off and are vaguely reminiscent of Thorne Smith, possibly because one character is called Smith and one Topper. A character called the Turtle does tiresome malapropisms. Very pulp-level violence and sex are stuck onto the story like lumps of clay onto an already finished statue. Lily, the girl Catell picks up along the way only to make some pulp sex scenes possible, is no character at all, hasn't a shred of believability. Selma, the harridan drunk who pesters Catell, is on the other hand real and believable and just about runs away with the book.

An inability to stay with the story he started to tell plagued Rabe from time to time, and showed up again in his second book, *Benny Muscles In*, which begins as though it's going to be a rise-of-the-punk history, a *Little Caesar*, but then becomes a much more narrowly focused story. Benny Tapkow works for a businesslike new-style mob boss named Pendleton. When Pendleton demotes Benny back to chauffeur, Benny switches allegiance to Big Al Alverato, an old-style Capone type, for whom Benny plans to kidnap Pendleton's college-age daughter, Pat. She knows Benny as her father's chauffeur, and so will leave school with him unsuspectingly. However, with one of Rabe's odd bits of off-the-wall humor (this one works), Pat brings along a thirtyish woman named Nancy Driscoll, who works at the college and is a flirty spinster. At the pre-arranged kidnap spot, Pat unexpectedly gets out of the car with Benny, so it's Nancy who's spirited away to Alverato's yacht, where she seduces Alverato, and for much of the book Nancy and Alverato are off cruising the Caribbean together.

The foreground story, however, remains Benny and the problem he has with Pat. Benny doesn't know Pat well, and doesn't know she's experimented with heroin and just recently stopped taking it because she was getting hooked. To keep Pat tractable, Benny feeds her heroin in her drinks. The movement of the story is that Benny gradually falls in love with Pat and gradually (unknowingly) addicts her to heroin. The characters of Benny and Pat are fully developed and very touchingly real. The hopeless love story never becomes mawkish, and the gradual drugged deterioration of Pat is beautifully and tensely handled (as Fell's deterioration will be in *Kill the Boss Goodbye*). The leap forward from

Stop This Man is doubly astonishing when we consider they were published four months apart.

One month later, *A Shroud for Jesso* was published, in the second half of which Rabe finally came fully into his own. That book begins in a New York underworld similar to that in *Benny Muscles In*, with similar characters and relationships and even a similar symbolic job demotion for the title character, but soon the mobster Jesso becomes involved with international intrigue, is nearly murdered on a tramp steamer on the North Atlantic, and eventually makes his way to a strange household in Hannover, Germany, the home of Johannes Kator, an arrogant bastard and spy. In the house also are Kator's sister, Renette, and her husband, a homosexual baron named Helmut. Helmut provides the social cover, Kator provides the money. Renette has no choice but to live with her overpowering brother and her nominal husband.

Jesso changes all that. He and Renette run off together, and the cold precise Rabe style reaches its maturity:

> They had a compartment, and when the chauffeur was gone they locked the door, pushed the suitcases out of the way, and sat down. When the train was moving they looked out of the window. At first the landscape looked flat, industrial; even the small fields had a square mechanical look. Later the fields rolled and there were more trees. Renette sat close, with her legs tucked under her. She had the rest of her twisted around so that she leaned against him. They smoked and didn't talk. There was nothing to talk about. They looked almost indifferent, but their indifference was the certainty of knowing what they had.

The characters in *A Shroud for Jesso* are rich and subtle, their relationships ambiguous, their story endlessly fascinating. When Jesso has to return for a while to New York, Renette prefigures the ending in the manner of her refusal to go with him:

> Over here, Jesso, I know you, I want you, we are what I know now. You and I. But over there you must be somebody else. I've never known you

over there and your life is perhaps quite different. Perhaps not, Jesso, but I don't know. I want you now, here, and not later and somewhere else. You must not start to think of me as something you own, keep around wherever you happen to be. It would not be the same. What we have between us is just the opposite of that. It is the very thing you have given me, Jesso, and it is freedom.

And this opposition between love and freedom is what then goes on to give the novel its fine but bitter finish.

Rabe kept a European setting for his next book, *A House in Naples*, a story about two American Army deserters who've been black market operators in Italy in the ten years since the end of World War II. Charlie, the hero, is a drifter, romantic and adventurous. Joe Lenken, his partner, is a sullen but shrewd pig, and when police trouble looms, Joe's the one with solid papers and a clear identity, while Charlie's the one who has to flee to Rome to try (and fail) to find adequate forged papers. In a bar he meets a useless old expatriate American drunk who then wanders off, gets into a brawl, and is knifed to death. Charlie steals the dead man's ID for himself, puts the body into the Tiber under a bridge, then looks up and sees a girl looking down. How much did she see?

In essence, *A House in Naples* is a love story in which the love is poisoned at the very beginning by doubt. The girl, Martha, is simple and clear, but her clarity looks like ambiguity to Charlie. Since he can never be sure of her, he can never be sure of himself. Once he brings Martha back to Naples and the vicious Joe is added to the equation, the story can be nothing but a slow and hard unraveling. The writing is cold and limpid and alive with understated emotion, from first sentence ("The warm palm of land cupped the water to make a bay, and that's where Naples was") to last ("He went to the place where he had seen her last").

A House in Naples was followed by *Kill the Boss Goodbye*, and that was the peak of Rabe's first period, five books, each one better than the one before. In those books, Rabe combined bits and pieces of his own history and education with the necessary stock elements of the form to make books in which tension and obsession and an inevitable downward slide toward disaster all combine with a style of increasing cold objectivity not only to make the scenes seem brand new but even to make the (rarely stated) emotions glitter with an unfamiliar sheen.

Born in Germany in 1921, Rabe already spoke English when he arrived in America at seventeen. With a PhD in psychology, he taught for a while at Western Reserve University and did research at Jackson Laboratory, where he wrote several papers on frustration. (No surprise.) Becoming a writer, he moved to various parts of America and lived a while in Germany, Sicily and Spain. His first published work he has described as "a funny pregnancy story (with drawings) to *McCall's*." The second was *Stop This Man*. In the next four books, he made the paperback world his own.

But then he seemed not to know what to do with it. Was it bad advice? Was it living too far away from the publishers and the action? Was it simply the speed at which he worked? For whatever reason, Rabe's next six books were nearly as bad—except for the middle of one—as the first five had been good.

This began Rabe's first effort to develop a series character, beginning with a book called *Dig My Grave Deep*, which is merely a second-rate gloss of Hammett's *The Glass Key*, without Hammett's psychological accuracy and without Rabe's own precision and clarity. The book flounders and drifts and postures. The writing is tired and portentous, the characters thinner versions of Hammett's. The Ned Beaumont character is called Daniel Port, and at the end he leaves town in a final paragraph that demonstrates just how sloppy Rabe could get when he wasn't paying attention: "Port picked up his suitcases and went the other way. By the time it was full dawn he had exchanged his New York ticket for one that went the other way."

That awkwardly repeated "other way" led directly into Rabe's next book, *The Out Is Death*, in which Port is now just a hero with a criminal background. The story is the one about the sick old ex-con forced to pull one last job by the sadistic young punk. Abe Dalton, the ex-con, is a well-realized character, a better version of Catell from *Stop This Man*, but Port, as Dalton's pal trying to help the old man out of trouble, is vague and uninteresting and never as tough as Rabe seems to think he is. Port, having started sub-Hammett, now becomes sub–W. R. Burnett.

After this second outing, Rabe left Port alone long enough to write *Agreement to Kill*, an odd book with a hokey beginning and not much finish at all but a fascinating long middle section. The book begins with Jake Spinner, a dirt farmer near St. Louis, coming out of jail after doing three years for assault. Rabe sets up Spinner as a victim in a land scheme being set up by the town's most important man, Dixon, but suddenly switches gears. A professional hitman from the St. Louis mob kills Dixon. Spinner is blamed, but escapes and finds the killer stuck in his car, mired in a torn-up section of road. The killer convinces Spinner he'll never get justice in that town, so Spinner helps him get away and leaves with him. (The killer, with broken leg, can't drive.)

This killer is named Loma, and comes from Graham Greene's *This Gun for Hire*; Greene called him Raven. Loma is small, gray, clubfooted, quiet, ghostly, unemotional. A similar character, making a brief appearance in *Kill the Boss Goodbye*, was called Mound, and of course *loma* means "hill." The idea of Loma as a kind of mounded grave himself, silent and dead as a low hill, works well against the idea of Spinner endlessly spinning, flailing around, trying to save himself and always making things worse. Rabe's names are usually strange and frequently evocative, never more so than here.

The long middle section of *Agreement to Kill* is Rabe back in form at last, writing material that clearly interests him. Spinner, having decided he'll never make it in the straight world, has decided his only hope is to convince Loma to introduce him to the mob world, where maybe he'll be able to survive. Loma has no intention of introducing Spinner to anybody, but needs Spinner's help and thus strings him along.

Spinner, wanting to "change sides," to become an outlaw, tries to model himself on Loma's emotional emptiness. He has shoulder pains, that increase and become more and more crippling the more he suppresses his emotions. He meets a girl, Ann, the first true pulp non-entity female in Rabe's work since Lily in *Stop This Man*, and keeps pushing her away in his efforts to become emotionless.

Spinner does eventually meet a mob boss, and is given a job . . . to kill Loma. He welcomes this as a chance to show his progress toward coldness, and when Ann arrives just as he's planning to shoot Loma he feels he has to drive her away to demonstrate to himself his icy proficiency. At first, though she's hurt by what he says, she won't leave, and then:

> And then he knew she was crying even though there was no sound, and before it tore him open again—he thought about this very clearly—he lifted his hand and hit her in the face.
>
> A big star of pain exploded in his shoulder, making him tremble. It kept bursting, next to him, it kept shining all the time he could hear her feet running away and the way she breathed, running away down the road through the trees. He had reached such perfection in this that he walked to her car to make sure where she was.

"He had reached such perfection in this. . . ." I can't think of another writer who would have used that phrase. Nor who would have written this of Spinner's next thoughts, on his way to kill Loma:

> Now for the business. It was a very small, surprisingly small matter to do this job now. That's the advantage of this new technique. Turn himself off and do a million things. Of course, one at a time, and each one—by comparison—very small, even unimportant. He walked to the cabin.

But the pain in Spinner's shoulder keeps him from aiming his gun at Loma; finally he drops it on the floor, makes up with Ann, and they drive off together.

Loma turns Spinner in to the police for Dixon's murder. There's a trial, and Spinner's about to be convicted when Loma sends to the court his specially made boot for his club foot, which proves he was the murderer. This is all perfunctory, Rabe's interest clearly having been in the Spinner-Loma relationship. The man who spins all the time, alive but failing, and the man who is a silent cold hill, a mound, a filled-in grave.

After this semi-return to his powerful best, Rabe dropped right down again, with a third Daniel Port novel, *It's My Funeral*. Port seemed to be Rabe's (unconscious?) vehicle for derivative books imitating famous practitioners in the field. This time it's Leslie Charteris and the Saint, with Port involved in a tired story about the blackmailing of a movie star with the porno film she did years ago. Partway through, it switches to the equally tired story about the hotel with the hidden camera behind the two-way mirror. (That particular wheeze got another airing in the fine 1986 film *Mona Lisa*, showing that nothing is ever too old to be used again.)

Doing a fairly good imitation of Leslie Charteris's tongue-in-cheek comedy, Rabe has a subplot about a singer named Tess Dolphin that Port's trying to get into bed with; every time they near the sack, the story starts again, such as it is. The principal trouble here, apart from the slackness of the material, is that Port is not *involved*. Having no motivation for the central figure robs Rabe of his principal strength, which is the delineation of obsessed characters.

Rabe left Port again after this but remained in trouble for his next two books, both of which are flat and derivative and sloppily plotted. *Journey into Terror* combines the artificiality of plot of Cornell Woolrich at his worst with the overwrought emotions of James M. Cain at his worst, plus a dollop of David Goodis when the hero becomes a down-and-out drunk for a while. *Mission for Vengeance* keeps trying to be a John D. MacDonald novel, keeps almost making it, and keeps falling on its face. The villain, Farret, is rather like the villain in MacDonald's *Cape Fear*, except that Farret keeps making threats and not following through. *Mission for Vengeance* is also odd for its use of first-person narration. It was Rabe's initial use of the first person, and it appears only sporadically, most of the book being in third person. The jolts back and forth are irritating, and don't accomplish much because the narrator-hero, John Miner (indeed!), doesn't have much of a distinctive voice.

With his twelfth book, *Blood on the Desert*, Rabe gets his second wind, goes for a complete change of pace, and produces his first fully satisfying work since *Kill the Boss Goodbye*. It's a foreign intrigue tale set in the Tunisian desert, spy versus spy in a story filled with psychological nuance. The characters are alive and subtle, the story exciting, the setting very clearly realized.

And damn me, if it isn't followed by another Daniel Port! In Rabe's own words, in a recent letter to me, *Bring Me Another Corpse* is "a plot without tension and some good writing thrown away in disinterest." The best writing is at the very beginning:

When the road flattened out toward Albany, Daniel Port started to drive faster. For a short while this distracted him, but there was an unpleasant stiffness down his back, and his hands were too tight on the wheel. At moments the fast driving was like running away, though Port didn't know what he was running from.

When the light was almost gone it started to rain. The rain was thin and cold, but it put a veil over the late-fall landscape.

Dan Port slowed a little and lit a cigarette. The rain produced a feeling of shelter inside the car. This feeling grew as it got darker, and when he reached the outskirts of Albany Port felt easy enough to think of stopping and stretching his legs. He slowed for the next gas station and rolled up to the pumps. Then he got out.

The pumps sat in a big orb of light through which the rain showed like driving mist. The rain felt cold and wakeful and Port stood by the hood of the car while the station man let the gas hum into the tank. It was very quiet under the rain. The orb of light over the pumps illuminated a small area only, leaving the highway dark. A few cars passed there, each with two eyes of light and their tires writing signatures on the wet black asphalt.

The next car was just a murmur and a wet sound, because it went by so slowly. For a moment the gas station man thought the car meant to turn into the station, so he looked up. He saw his customer standing by the hood, smoking, hunching a little because of the rain—and then he saw the cigarette spray up in the air. There was a sound like a whipcrack or a sharp rap with a stick on a wooden box, and the man spun suddenly, trying not to fall.

But Port began to bleed almost immediately. He dropped on the cement with a hard slam, which he didn't feel at all.

I quote so extensively the beginning of an otherwise undistinguished book because Peter Rabe is right; that *is* awfully good writing to be "thrown away in disinterest." A physical scene and an emotional ambience are sketched in with very deft strokes.

And what follows? At the end of Daniel Port's first novel, he'd protected himself from the mob bosses by leaving evidence to be given the police should he be killed. In *Bring Me Another Corpse*—what shriveled gnome thought *up* those titles?—someone who wants to make trouble for those bosses has realized the simplest way to do so is to kill Dan Port. Not a bad idea, but nothing *happens* in the book; just a lot of backing and filling.

Rabe followed this with *Time Enough to Die*, the last of the Daniel Port novels—whew!—and the only good one. The setting is the Mexican Pacific coast, mostly a small fishing village where a colony of immigrant Japanese fishermen live in their own separate neighborhood. There's a lot of local color, ocean and islands and jungle, all well done and well described. The plot is tricky without being artificial, and for once Rabe has surrounded Port with strong and interesting characters. *Time Enough to Die* is the last of the Port novels and the first of Rabe's final cluster of five excellent books.

The second of these, *My Lovely Executioner*, is another total change of pace, and a fine absorbing novel. Rabe's first book told completely in the first person, it is also his first true *mystery*, a story in which the hero is being manipulated and has no idea why.

The hero-narrator, Jimmy Gallivan, is a glum fellow in jail, with three weeks to go on a seven-year term for attempted murder (wife's boyfriend, shot but didn't kill) when he's caught up in a massive jailbreak. He doesn't want to leave, but another con, a tough professional criminal named Rand, forces him to come along, and then he can't get back. Gallivan gradually realizes the whole jailbreak was meant to get *him* out, but he doesn't know why. Why him? Why couldn't they wait three weeks until he'd be released anyway? The mystery is a fine one, the explanation is believable and fair, the action along the way is credible and exciting, and the Jim Thompsonesque gloom of the narration is wonderfully maintained.

And next, published in May of 1960, Rabe's sixteenth Gold Medal novel in exactly five years, was *Murder Me for Nickels*, yet another change of pace, absolutely unlike anything that he had done before. Told in first person by Jack St. Louis, right-hand man of Walter Lippit, the local jukebox king, *Murder Me for Nickels* is as sprightly and glib as *My Lovely Executioner* was depressed and glum. It has a lovely opening sentence, "Walter Lippit makes music all over town," and is chipper and funny all the way through. At one point, for instance, St. Louis is drunk when he suddenly has to defend himself in a fight: "I whipped the bottle at him so he stunk from liquor. I kicked out my foot and missed. I swung out with the glass club and missed. I stepped out of the way and missed. When you're drunk everything is sure and nothing works."

Nineteen-sixty was also when a penny-ante outfit called Abelard-Schuman published in hardcover *Anatomy of a Killer*, a novel Gold Medal had rejected, I can't think why. It's third person, as cold and as clean as a knife, and this time the ghostly unemotional killer, Loma and Mound, is brought center stage and made the focus of the story. This time he's called Jordan (as in the river?) and Rabe stays in very tight on him. The book begins,

When he was done in the room he stepped away quickly because the other man was falling his way. He moved fast and well and when he was out in the corridor he pulled the door shut behind him. Sam Jordan's speed had nothing to do with haste but came from perfection.

The door went so far and then held back with a slight give. It did not close. On the floor, between the door and the frame, was the arm.

. . . He looked down at the arm, but then did nothing else. He stood with his hand on the door knob and did nothing.

He stood still and looked down at the fingernails and thought they were changing color. And the sleeve was too long at the wrist. He was not worried about the job being done, because it was done and he knew it. He felt the muscles around the mouth and then the rest of the face, stiff like bone. He did not want to touch the arm.

. . . After he had not looked at the arm for a while, he kicked at it and it flayed out of the way. He closed the door without slamming it and walked away. A few hours later he got on the night train for the nine-hour trip back to New York.

. . . But the tedium of the long ride did not come. He felt the thick odor of clothes and felt the dim light in the carriage like a film over everything, but the nine-hour dullness he wanted did not come. I've got to unwind, he thought, this is like the shakes. After all this time with all the habits always more sure and perfect, this.

He sat still, so that nothing showed, but the irritation was eating at him. Everything should get better, doing it time after time, and not worse. Then it struck him that he had never before had to touch a man when the job was done. Naturally. Here was a good reason. He now knew this in his head but nothing else changed. The hook wasn't out and the night-ride dullness did not come.

It is from that small beginning, having to touch a victim for the first time, that Rabe methodically and tautly describes the slow unraveling of Jordan. It's a terrific book.

There was another novel from this period, a Daniel Port which was rejected by Gold Medal and published as half of an Ace double-book in 1958, under the title *The Cut of the Whip*. Which brings to eighteen the books published between 1955 and 1960. Eighteen books, five years, and they add up to almost the complete story of Peter Rabe's career as a fine and innovative writer.

Almost. There was one more, in December of 1962, called *The Box* (the only Rabe novel published with a Rabe title). *The Box* may be

Rabe's finest work, a novel of character and of place, and in it Rabe managed to use and integrate more of his skills and techniques than anywhere else. "This is a pink and gray town," it begins, "which sits very small on the north edge of Africa. The coast is bone white and the sirocco comes through any time it wants to blow through. The town is dry with heat and sand."

A tramp steamer is at the pier. In the hold is a large wooden box, a corner of which was crushed in an accident. A bad smell is coming out. The bill of lading very oddly shows that the box was taken aboard in New York and is to be delivered to New York. Contents: "PERISHABLES. NOTE: IMPERATIVE, KEEP VENTILATED." The captain asks the English clerk of the company that owns the pier permission to unload and open the box. The box is swung out and onto the pier.

They stood a moment longer while the captain said again that he had to be out of here by this night, but mostly there was the silence of heat everywhere on the pier. And whatever spoiled in the box spoiled a bit more.

"Open it!" said the captain.

They open it, and look in.

"Shoes?" said the clerk after a moment. "You see the shoes?" as if nothing on earth could be more puzzling.

"Why shoes on?" said the captain, sounding stupid.

What was spoiling there spoiled for one moment more, shrunk together in all that rottenness, and then must have hit bottom.

The box shook with the scramble inside, with the cramp muscled pain, with the white sun like steel hitting into the eyes there so they screwed up like sphincters, and then the man inside screamed himself out of the box.

The man is Quinn, a smartass New York mob lawyer who is being given a mob punishment: shipped around the world inside a box, with nothing in there but barely enough food and water to let him survive the trip. What happens to him in Okar, and what happens to Okar as a result of Quinn, live up to the promise of that beginning.

But for Rabe, it was effectively the end. It was another three years before he published another book, and then it was a flippant James Bond imitation called *Girl in a Big Brass Bed*, introducing Manny de-Witt, an arch and cutesy narrator who does arch and cutesy dirty work for an international industrialist named Hans Lobbe. Manny deWitt appeared twice more, in *The Spy Who Was 3 Feet Tall* (1966) and *Code Name Gadget* (1967), to no effect, all for Gold Medal. And Gold Medal published Rabe's last two books as well: *War of the Dons* (1972) and *Black Mafia* (1974).

Except for those who hit it big early, the only writers who tend to stay with writing over the long haul are those who can't find a viable alternative. Speaking personally, three times in my career the wolf has been so slaveringly at the door that I tried to find an alternative livelihood, but lacking college degrees, craft training or any kind of useful work history I was forced to go on writing instead, hoping the wolf would grow tired and slink away. The livelihood of writing is iffy at best, which is why so many writing careers simply stop when they hit a lean time. Peter Rabe had a doctorate in psychology; when things went to hell on the writing front, it was possible for him to take what he calls a bread-and-butter job teaching undergraduate psychology in the University of California.

It is never either entirely right or entirely wrong to identify a writer with his or her heroes. The people who carry our stories may be us, or our fears about ourselves, or our dreams about ourselves. The typical Peter Rabe hero is a smart outsider, working out his destiny in a hostile world. Unlike Elmore Leonard's scruffy heroes, for instance, who are always ironically aware that they're better than their milieu, Rabe's heroes are better than their milieu and are never entirely confident of that. They're as tough and grubby as their circumstances make necessary, but they are also capable from time to time of the grand gesture.

Several of Peter Rabe's novels, despite the ill-fitting wino garb of their titles, are very grand gestures indeed.

PLAYING POLITICS WITH A MASTER OF DIALOGUE: ON GEORGE V. HIGGINS

This review originally appeared in the *Los Angeles Times* on December 2, 1990.—Ed.

Probably the worst thing that ever happened to George V. Higgins was success. When *The Friends of Eddie Coyle* was published in 1972, it was that rarest of things under the sun, something new, and readers gobbled it up like the fresh taste it was.

Unfortunately, however, Higgins wound up praised and remembered for the wrong accomplishment. What people saw was an ex-prosecutor who had listened to and was reporting on criminal speech in an excitingly different and realistic way. This elliptical rump-sprung dialogue, overheard by the reader but not directed at him, full of half-revealed mysteries and unexpected depths of duplicity, seemed like the real thing at last, and catapulted Higgins to fame.

If that were the whole story, if Higgins were merely another guy with a stylistic stunt, like Jeffrey Farnol or Damon Runyon, there would soon have been little reason left to read him. Once you know the stunt, once you can hear the music in your head even before you open the book, why open the book? And other guys—Elmore Leonard, most noticeably—were using similarly bumpy dialogue rhythms for reasons of their own.

But that wasn't the whole story. Higgins was never trying to be merely a hard-boiled crime novelist, one step to the right of the private-eye people; what he was trying to do was write novels. And what linked the characters of his various books was not the world of the criminal but a love of talk.

Higgins's characters wallow in narration and description and mere jazzing around. Stuck together in a car on a long drive across New England, they tell one another stories, recounting in detail the dialogue from those previous adventures. Faced with a decision, they talk it out together, reminding one another of possibly useful parallel situations from the past, worrying the issue with a flood of words.

Since it wasn't really crime stories Higgins was trying to write, his interest from the beginning was never in the caper itself. His interest was a novelistic one: What do his characters want? What are they willing to do to one another to get what they want? How do they manipulate, struggle, excuse? Why do they want what they want, and what happens inside them when they either do or do not get it?

As Higgins, in later novels, moved away from the world of Eddie Coyle, following his true interests into the lives of other characters in other settings, critics and readers alike were annoyed and disappointed. Where were the wonderful romantic losers? Where were the great bouquets of overheard dialogue in grimy smoky bars, the cheap betrayals glancingly alluded to, the flop sweat sheening on those sallow, doomed faces? From his sudden initial burst of success, Higgins soon ebbed into a middle range of unexcited acceptance, publishing roughly one book a year, all of them rewarding but none frantically anticipated.

It may be time to reassess Higgins, and *Victories*, his twenty-second book in twenty-two years, just may be the proper vehicle for it. Beginning with the title. Anyone with even the slightest acquaintanceship with the Higgins world will know that within it there are no total victories, that it would be impossible for Higgins to refer to victory without an ironic edge. And his whole career has been an ironic victory, has it not?

Henry Briggs, the reluctant hero of *Victories*, is a retired ballplayer, a onetime relief pitcher, a star but never a superstar, now sharing a small-town New Hampshire home with a shrewish wife. He's semi-estranged from his grown son and daughter, and through a local politico has taken a job as game warden, which he treats seriously and fairly. Now is 1967, with anti-Vietnam feeling just beginning to show its political muscle, and the local Democratic pols persuade Henry to run for Congress against the entrenched Republican officeholder. Henry doesn't know it, but the pols fully expect him to lose. He's merely the sacrificial lamb, put out there to protect the regulars from the growing power of anti-war radicals within the Democratic party.

There have been any number of political novels written in this politics-besotted nation, but rarely if ever one with the particular angle of view of *Victories*. On a narrow canvas—the struggle over one minor House seat in New Hampshire—and using a limited palette of dialogue and reflection and simple action—no big-league chicanery, no smoking guns of any kind—Higgins lays out as clearly as anyone ever has just how this hopeful hopeless buoyant ridiculous self-governing scheme of ours operates. It probably would be a good idea for the Russians en masse to read this book, to learn before it's too late just what sort of new game they've decided to learn to play.

If Higgins has a major flaw, and he does, it is in his portrayal of women. Apparently he has never been in the presence of an actual woman; how else explain the clumsy failures of this normally brilliant observer? Women are more than a mystery to him, they are blank spaces with names.

One of the most telling ironies of *Victories* is surely an unconscious one: The female character who grates the least is mute. This from a master of dialogue. And the most awful character is a New York woman, a political fund raiser, who marches on for one scene of dreadful monologue—thudding bricks of prose, no cross-pollination of chat from the other characters at all—and then marches away again, dragging a whole lot of the novel's credibility with her.

In order to keep his hero from seeming too good to be true, Higgins assures us he's a womanizer, but not once do we see what that means. Not once does Henry interact with a woman as though he has any interest in her at all. Far from being the womanizer Higgins claims, his Henry is clearly sexless, a nice guy who's polite to the ladies, operates on equal terms with men, and tries to behave decently.

For a writer whose goals are high and honorable, it must be a tragedy to be so totally unable to cope with half the human race. It has to harm every serious attempt he ever makes, and suggests he's best off after all in those smoky male-only bars.

Which is a pity; what he sees, he sees with wonderful clarity. For a nitty-gritty study of politics at ground level, you will not find a better novel anywhere than *Victories*.

ON REX STOUT

Letter to Rex Stout's Biographer, John J. McAleer

November 13, 1973
Dear Mr. McAleer,

Rex Stout has done something very rare in his novels. He has created an on-going mini-world, a sealed-off chamber as distinct from our world as Middle Earth. When I pick up the latest Ross Macdonald I expect *his* character in *our* California, but when I pick up the latest Rex Stout I know I will enter once more into that same alternate universe, in which Archie Goodwin will drive a Heron through the streets of some city called New York. The only other writer I know of currently working in that sort of separate continuum (not counting fantasists like Tolkien) is Anthony Powell, with his *Dance to the Music of Time* series; which is where that comparison ends, since Powell's purposes and methods are very different from Stout's.

A closer comparison is Sherlock Holmes, which of course I'm not the first to notice, and to my taste Nero Wolfe wins that one hands down. To begin with, Stout is a far better writing craftsman than Doyle, and a much more scrupulously fair *mystery* writer. Beyond that, the Holmes-Watson world was rather smaller and rather fuzzier at the fringes than the Wolfe-Goodwin world; I almost think, for instance, that I would recognize Orrie Cather on the street, and of what secondary Holmes character could one have the same feeling?

But the best thing about the Nero Wolfe novels, in my opinion, is

Stout's audacity. Having his own mirror universe to play with, godlike, gives him a confidence and a field of action the rest of us can only envy from a distance, and I love the way he uses it. Only rarely is he noticeably outrageous, as in the finish of *The Doorbell Rang*, but in almost every book he is quietly outrageous. Looking for the murderer of a prize bull; assembling groups of suspects as though that sort of meeting were easy to arrange; giving literary criticism through whether or not Nero Wolfe dog-ears the page.

What Stout has done, finally, beggars comparison. He has arranged a series of novels in such a way that when we open one we are not only meeting again an old friend, but a whole company of friends. And we are not inviting them into our home, they are inviting us into theirs. They are good companions, interesting and clever and humorous, and their surroundings are familiar and comfortable and well-appointed, and sitting among us all, quiet but friendly, is the master of the house himself.

I met Rex Stout for the first time a few years ago, but I'd already *met* him and spent many evenings with him for a long time before that. The rest of us tell anecdotes, one at a time; he has built a house by the side of West 35th Street and has become a friend to man.

And that's what I have to say about Rex Stout. I know it all sounds like a PR man's puff, but it's the way I feel. On the critical side I think the plotting in the Nero Wolfe novels is sometimes loose and often skimpy, but I don't go there for the plots. I go there to see my old friends and watch Archie be archly secretive about his sex life and hear Wolfe say, "Pfui."

Yours,
Don Westlake

Introduction to Rex Stout's *The Father Hunt*

This was published in 1995 as the introduction to a mass market paperback edition of *The Father Hunt* in Bantam's Rex Stout Library series.—Ed.

Some years ago I read an introduction to something or other by some-body or other, in which the introducer presented the idea—as fact—that all writers of fiction have completed their significant work by the age of forty-five. I was, I think, still in my early thirties at the time and so remained calm at this news. Somewhat later the suggestion did return to my mind, however, this time with teeth in it; and I admit I fretted, to the extent that I finally mentioned the gloomy fact to a friend who, taking pity on me, said, "Let me mention two novelists who *began* to write at age forty-five. They are Joseph Conrad and Rex Stout." After which I stopped worrying about introductions.

Rex Stout may have started late, after several other successful careers, but he hit the ground running. Nero Wolfe sprang full-grown from Stout's forehead in that first book, and though in later years he would write non-Wolfe novels and even try his hand at another series character—from Wolfe to Fox should have been easy, after all—his doom was sealed (a melodramatic phrase that Mr. Stout would never have employed) right from *Fer-de-Lance*.

Nero Wolfe has become one of those rare creations—like Sherlock Holmes, Tarzan, Horatio Hornblower, and Jeeves—who both overshadow and outlive their authors; and I remember when I first met Mr. Stout, around 1965, being disappointed that he wasn't Wolfe. (He was, instead, charming, open, witty, and wonderfully generous to a young writer.) Had Stout ever chosen to terminate one of Wolfe's rare journeys to the outside world in the trusty old Heron by dropping him off at (or in) the Reichenbach Falls, no one could have blamed him, but I believe Stout submitted with good grace (a cliche he would never have employed) to Wolfe's dominance, and they lived comfortably together for forty-three years.

That would be a long time for any association to last, and is even more remarkable since one of the associates was forty-five years old at the beginning; but what's more interesting, at least to me, is that Nero Wolfe is not a very nice person. He's self-absorbed, selfish, and self-satisfied. He's arrogant and uncivil and socially a fright. He's prissy and misogynistic. He orders people around and gets away with it; in one book he even orders J. Edgar Hoover around and gets away with it. How on earth did Rex Stout put up with the fellow all that time?

Maybe more important, why do *we* put up with him? Why did all the Nero Wolfe novels sell so very well, and go on selling in edition after edition? Why, seventeen years after Rex Stout's death, is his creation still alive in this freshly printed book you hold in your hands? Are we wrong to enjoy Nero Wolfe so much?

No. We are right to enjoy Rex Stout's presentation of Nero Wolfe so much, through the brilliant prism of Archie Goodwin. Archie is ingratiation itself, an easy raconteur, an amiable chap who is bright without arrogance, knowledgeable without pretension, and quick-witted without brusqueness. If Nero Wolfe is the pill—and he is—Archie is the sugar coating.

What makes Wolfe palatable is that Archie finds him palatable. What makes him a monster we can enjoy rather than flee from is that Archie stands between us and him. We like Archie, and Archie likes (tolerates, is amused by, is ironic toward, but serves) Nero Wolfe. It's a wonderful conception, strong enough to build a massive readership upon, yet flexible enough for Rex Stout to use over and over for decades, in story after story.

Not that *story* is the primary issue here. One doesn't drop in at the house on Thirty-fifth Street for the plot line but for the house itself and its denizens—lovingly described, familiar, comfortable, though with Nero Wolfe in charge and Archie as Virgil never so comfortable as to bore.

That Wolfe isn't really that clever a detective hardly matters. (In the present book Archie even has fun over the fact that he and Wolfe can't tell one cigar ash from another, a nicely ironic reference to Sherlock Holmes, another infuriating madman made palatable by his ingratiating interpreter.) That most Nero Wolfe novels—not including *The Father Hunt*, be assured—depend on at least one thundering coincidence matters not at all. Even the occasional minor glitch, as though Stout had an affinity with those Indian tribes who deliberately include a flaw in their designs so as not to compete with the perfection of the gods, doesn't matter. (This time the glitch is extremely unimportant and occurs in Chapter 12, where Archie assures a young lady that a certain man's name would mean nothing to her even though Archie and the young lady had met the man together in Chapter 8; no matter, no matter.)

Stout had fun with Nero Wolfe. Well, he had fun with life. Having some years earlier written a Wolfe novel called *The Mother Hunt*, it was probably more than he could resist not to write one called *The Father Hunt*. It was written when he was seventy-nine, and it all still works. As time goes by, I increasingly find that another comforting thought.

INTRODUCTION TO JACK RITCHIE'S *A NEW LEAF* AND OTHER STORIES

This was written as the introduction to a 1971 paperback collection of Jack Ritchie's short stories.—Ed.

In July of 1969 I wrote a letter to Jack Ritchie, whom I'd never met. It said, in part:

> Ten, eleven years ago, while trying to learn how to sell stories to *Alfred Hitchcock's Mystery Magazine*, I bought every back issue of the thing and read them all in one extended chug-a-lug, emerging at last with a permanently stunted mind but also with the pleasure of having read two consistently first-rate writers, of whom Jack Ritchie was both the more prolific and the more first-rate. In the years since, I have used you twice with friends who wanted to write short stories, handing them leaning towers of *AHMM* and telling them to read all Ritchie. . . .
>
> Now the suggestion has come from Dell that I write an introduction to your collection, and it seems to me you're the man to decide about that. I've been thinking to myself, what if out of the blue some guy were to suddenly shoulder his way into *my* book, what would my reaction be? I decided I'd get irritated.
>
> If you too would get irritated, please tell me so and I will understand. If you wouldn't get irritated, I'd be delighted to ramble on about you in print.

Jack's response was gracious and to the point: "By all means I'd like you to write an introduction for the collection of stories and don't hesitate a moment about rambling on and on."

So that's what *I'm* doing here. As to what Jack Ritchie is doing here, he is a quiet, unassuming worker out there in the vineyard who has perhaps finally come into his own. First, of course, with the publication of this book, for although his stories have spread like Smiths through most of the anthologies published in the past decade, this is the first volume devoted entirely to Jack Ritchie stories. And second, more indirectly, through films. The first major movie effort of Elaine May, the treble half of Nichols-May (she wrote the screenplay, served as director, and co-starred with Walter Matthau), is based on the title story from this collection.

Jack Ritchie happens to be a brilliant man in the wrong pew, a miniaturist in an age of elephantiasis. He knows, maybe better than anybody else currently at work in the area, that a short story needs emphasis on both words—it should be a *story*, full and round and plotted and peopled and with a satisfactory finish, and it should also be *short*.

The late Anthony Boucher, mystery-story reviewer for the *New York Times* and compiler of the Best Detective Story annuals, summed Ritchie up this way: "Jack Ritchie is consistently one of the most original writers (and possibly the most economic) in the crime-fiction magazines." Jack's stories feed you information like a computer, fast, efficient, precise, and painless.

In the musical *Top Banana*, the comedian complains to his writer about a skit that takes two pages in a doctor's office before the comedian comes on. When the writer says he needs the two pages to set the scene, the comedian says to a crony, "Get me into the doctor's office." The crony turns to the audience and says, "Here we are in the doctor's office." If I ever meet Jack Ritchie, I'll be terribly disappointed if he doesn't look like that crony.

There are a number of different talents we're trying to describe here. A writing talent of the first rank, to begin with. A quiet, deadpan humor that always seems to know precisely how far to go. An imagination that has produced in the last dozen years so many short stories that the eighteen in this volume barely scratch the surface. A skill at economy that just can't be described economically. (Look at the first paragraph of the first story herein, "Package Deal." I know writers who would be two chapters into a novel by the end of that paragraph. And if you went to look, it's seven-to-two you didn't come back to this introduction till you finished reading the story. Good, wasn't it? Required no introduction, did it?)

What do you do with a man who persists in being a brilliant miniaturist in a society that equates literary excellence in terms of poundage, a world that determines how good a book is by how much grass it kills if you leave it under the hammock? One thing you can do is try to tell people how good he is, as I am trying to do now. Or as Anthony Boucher frequently did. Let me offer another statement of his:

> What I like most about Jack Ritchie's work is its exemplary neatness. No word is wasted, and many words serve more than one purpose. Exposition disappears; all needed facts are deftly inserted as the narrative flows forward. Ritchie can write a long short story that is virtually the equivalent of a full suspense novel; and his very short stories sparkle as lapidary art.

Finally, though, Jack Ritchie himself offers (inadvertently) the best and most economical (of course) description of Jack Ritchie. In a story of his called "Piggy Bank Killer," not included in this collection, the narrator says of another character in the story, "I had the feeling the boy could have written *War and Peace* on the back of a postcard."

Exactly.

FOREWORD TO *THURBER ON CRIME*

Westlake contributed this introduction to a 1991 collection of James Thurber's writings and cartoons. When Westlake notes that Thurber made use of confusion and bewilderment, it calls to mind Westlake's own website: in the last years of his life, it opened with a screen that showed nothing but the words "I believe my subject is bewilderment." Bewildered, the visitor waited a few seconds, then the screen changed to read, "But I could be wrong."—Ed.

Gentle comedy is the hardest to make work. The fellow who slips on the banana peel, catches the cream pie smack in the kisser, gets his necktie set on fire—all of those are guaranteed yocks. To laugh at the cartoon character who has already taken three steps into midair before noticing he's gone beyond land's edge, and who has now just time to give us one unbelieving look before the plummet; easy as falling off a cliff. But gentle comedy, comedy in which the disaster is either subtly referential or nonexistent, that's tough. What's funny about a guy who *doesn't* spill the soup in his lap?

In the early days of the *New Yorker*, before that magazine settled into its middle-aged task of being our premier viewer with alarm, it had a much deeper commitment to verbal humor (happily, it retains its commitment to visual humor), and among the slash-and-burn practitioners led by S. J. Perelman (who never saw a window he didn't want to throw a rock through), there were two fellows who time after time made you laugh without having to staunch anybody's wounds later. They were Robert Benchley and James Thurber, and between them they taught me, at the impressionable age at which I first came across them, that it was possible to get where you wanted to go in comedy without running anybody down.

Whatever it was that Robert Benchley did, nobody before or since ever did it so well; or possibly at all. *Sui generis*, he stood, or slumped, alone. Whatever it was he did—and even while reading and enjoying him, you could rarely entirely figure out what he was doing—it was what he did every single time. He had dug himself a narrow literary trench, gracefully curved, and he marched in that trench his whole life long.

Thurber was something else. He wrote short stories, he wrote for the Broadway theater, he wrote oddball little fairy tales with even odder morals attached, he wrote reportage, he wrote articles on all kinds of subjects both comic and serious, he wrote parodies, he even occasionally wrote things kind of like whatever it was Robert Benchley was doing. ("How the Kooks Crumble," in which the writer keeps forgetting he's not to complain about radio, shows some of that quality, here and there . . . in part.) And when he paused in all that writing, Thurber drew cartoons.

About those cartoons. When someone once criticized Harold Ross, the New Yorker's first editor, for keeping on the staff "a fifth-rate artist like Thurber," Ross replied, "You're wrong: Thurber is a third-rate artist." I don't know about that; Ross was a kindly man. In fact, anybody who can't draw better than James Thurber probably has trouble tying his own shoelaces.

But so what? Cartoons are not about their form, they're about their substance. The wonderful weirdness of Thurber's mind is probably best apprehended in these agonizingly amateurish little squiggles. With no technique and hardly any skill, Thurber nevertheless managed to communicate an entire skewed worldview with just a few lines on paper. (My own favorite in the present collection is the one with the kangaroo; I never see it without laughing all over again, surprised all over again.)

It had never occurred to me before Thurber on Crime dropped on my head, how often the skewed Thurber view of the world and all its works contained some element of the criminous. After all, if gentle comedy is hard, gentle crime must be even harder. But Thurber makes it look easy.

For instance. We have in these pages a story concerning a rather clever scheme for a perfect murder, in which the murder doesn't manage to take place but the scheme works perfectly anyway. And when another Thurber character actually does resort to murder, the reason is so arcane that the police reject it at once: "Take more'n [such a reason] to cause a mess like that," says the trooper at the crime scene.

Thurber's interest in the world of crime seems to have been that of the timid man testing his resolve against his fears. He shows himself capable of straight reportage on the famous Hall-Mills murder case, and again on the strange case of the fellow at the New Yorker who'd embezzled from Ross for years without being at all suspected. Or he can turn his attention to a real-life kidnapping with absurd elements and raise that absurdity to hilarious art by telling the story as a Horatio Alger tale; the best Alger parody I've ever read.

Thurber's fictional characters usually live in a fog of bewilderment, but get where they're going anyway. His old friend at the *New Yorker*, Wolcott Gibbs, once said, "Thurber has a firm grasp on confusion," and this confusion may, in fact, be his characters' best defensive weapon; they overcome danger by failing to recognize it, as with the title character in "The Man Who Knew Too Little."

Thurber's interest in crime also led him quite naturally to an interest in, or at least a consideration of, the detective story, and the detective story does not at all emerge unscathed. The woman who reads *Macbeth* as though it were just another traditional detective story does, unfortunately, represent all too well the mindset of the Jessica Fletcher school of crime solving. There are also nice parodies of Cain and spy novels among others, and a surprising little comment about Dashiell Hammett; surprising and, I'm sure, accurate.

Thurber's gentleness and mild air of bewilderment no doubt come at least in part from an accident in his childhood. When he was six, one of his brothers accidentally shot him with an arrow, causing the loss of his left eye. His right eye, never particularly strong, failed when he was forty, and he spent the last quarter-century of his life blind.

The blind cartoonist; is that a Thurber joke? Well, Thurber himself once said he planned to title his autobiography *Long Time No See*.

He didn't, in fact. The entire body of his work is his autobiography, really, a solid portion of it collected in this volume. Thurber was Mr. Bruhl and Mr. Preble and all of them. In other precincts, he was Walter Mitty, whose secret life was both a famous short story and a vastly popular movie starring Danny Kaye. And certainly he was *The Male Animal*, a Broadway play that was a theater success twice (in 1940 and revived in 1957), as well as one of Henry Fonda's better movies. He is the man whose lifelong love of bloodhounds is herein chronicled, but whose constant drawings of bloodhounds invariably show animals who, while they could surely track you down, would then be too polite to point.

Thurber on crime. There's nothing in the world quite like it.

INTRODUCTION TO CHARLES WILLEFORD'S
THE WAY WE DIE NOW

This essay was written for a new edition of Charles Willeford's *The Way We Die Now* that was published in 1996.—Ed.

Charles Willeford wrote very good books for a very long time without anybody noticing. In 1974 one of his novels was made into the film *Cockfighter*, starring Warren Oates, and nobody noticed. In that film, Willeford himself played the professional trainer of the fighting cocks, and was just as laconic an actor as he was a writer, and *still* nobody noticed.

And then along came Hoke Moseley.

From where? After all Willeford's years in the wilderness, writing good books that nobody noticed, why did Hoke Moseley come along to change it all, to force Willeford to come back to him for story after story, and to make readers suddenly *notice* this quirky, oddball, invigorating voice that had been in their midst unheard for so long?

I think I know where Hoke came from. I knew Willeford some in the last years of his life, and found him gentle and knowledgeable and absolutely secure in his persona, which on the surface makes him much different from that final creation of his. Hoke Moseley is anything but secure, has come nowhere near fighting his way to the calm plateau Willeford had reached. So where did he come from?

Out of the wilderness. I think Hoke came out of that same wilderness in which Willeford had labored for so long. Charles Willeford was never a failure, in the sense that his books are very good books, carefully wrought. His career might stutter along in obscurity, but the books were solid. And I think the only way he could go on doing that, year after year, without either giving up or turning bitter, was that he trained himself to know that the work was very important but at the same time it didn't matter at all. And the extension from that was that all of life was very important but at the same time it didn't matter at all. I believe that particular self-induced schizophrenia got Willeford through the lean years and let him keep writing, and I believe it ultimately produced Hoke Moseley, who doesn't so much share that worldview as live it.

Hoke is a good cop, or at least he tries to be a good cop, but in his Miami, one good cop is about as useful as one good paper towel in a hurricane. Hoke is constantly bested by people tougher and meaner than he is, he's constantly lied to and betrayed, he's constantly faced with the futility of what he's doing, and yet he keeps moving doggedly forward, and among the greater hopelessness he does bring off some modest—and very satisfying—successes.

I don't mean that Hoke Moseley was Charles Willeford's alter ego. I mean that Willeford's experience of his life had led him to a certain attitude toward the world and his place in it, and this attitude, ironic without meanness, comic but deeply caring, informed every book he ever wrote, from his two volumes of autobiography through all the unnoticed novels, and that finally Hoke Moseley embodied this attitude more completely than anything else he'd ever done.

To use a musical analogy, Charles Willeford had finally found the key in which he could really sing. These last songs of his are wonderful: human, patient, funny, knowing, cool, and forgiving. I wish he were still singing.

ON STEPHEN FREARS

Westlake wrote a screenplay based on Jim Thompson's *The Grifters* for Stephen Frears's acclaimed 1990 film adaptation, which ended up receiving four Academy Award nominations, including one for Best Screenplay. This essay was published in *Writers on Directors* in 1999.—Ed.

Here are two things Stephen Frears said to me. The first was several months before *The Grifters* was made and, in fact, before either of us had signed on to do the project. We had just recently met, brought together by the production company that had sent us to California to look at the place. Driving back from La Jolla toward L.A., me at the wheel of the rented car, Stephen in the seat beside me musing on life, he broke a longish silence to say, "You know, there's nothing more loathsome than actually making a film, and it's beginning to look as though I'll have to make this one." The second was the night of the same film's New York premiere, at the post-opening party, when he leaned close to me in the noisy room and murmured, "Well we got away with it."

I think what attracted me to Stephen in the first place is that, in a world of manic enthusiasm, here at last I'd met a fellow pessimist. Someone who would surely agree with Damon Runyon's assessment: "All of life is six to five against."

Not that he's a defeatist, far from it. For instance, he refused to let me turn down the job of writing *The Grifters*, a thing that never happens. The normal sequence is, a writer is offered a job, thinks it over, says yea or nay, and that's that. Having been offered this job, I read Jim Thompson's novel—or reread, from years before—decided it was too grim, and said nay. That should have been the end of it, but the next thing I knew, Frears was on the phone from France, some Englishman I'd never met in my life, plaintively saying, "Why don't you want to make my film?" I told him my reasons. He told me I was wrong, and proceeded to prove it—"It's Lilly's story, not Roy's," was his insight, not mine—and I finally agreed to a meeting in New York, which was the beginning of the most thoroughly enjoyable experience I've ever had in the world of movies.

Here's another thing Stephen said to me: "I like the writer on the set." This is not common among directors, and I wasn't at all sure what it meant. Did he want a whipping boy? Someone to hide behind? Someone to blame? (You can see that I too am not a manic enthusiast.)

Anyway, no. As it turned out, what he wanted was a collaborator, and what we did was a collaboration. I didn't direct and he didn't write, and between us both we licked the platter clean.

I am not a proponent of the auteur theory. I think it comes out of a basic misunderstanding of the functions of creative versus interpretive arts. But I do believe that on the set and in the postproduction process the director is the captain of the ship. Authority has to reside in one person, and that should most sensibly be the director. So my rare disagreements with Stephen were in private, and we discussed them off-set as equals, and whichever of us prevailed—it was pretty even—the other one shrugged and got on with it.

The result has much of Jim Thompson in it, of course. It has much in it of the talents of its wonderful cast and designer. It has some of me in it. But the look of it, the feel of it, the smell of it, the three-inches-off-the-ground quality of it; that's Stephen.

If we aren't going to enjoy ourselves, why do it? Stephen's right, much of the filmmaking *is* loathsome. Pleasure and satisfaction have to come from the work itself and from one's companions on the journey. *The Grifters* was for me that rarity; everyone in the boat rowing in the same direction. I hadn't had that much fun on the job since I was nineteen, in college, and had a part-time job on a beer truck with a guy named Luke.

JOHN D. MacDONALD: A REMEMBRANCE

Westlake contributed this remembrance to a 1987 issue of *The Mystery Scene Reader* published in honor of John D. MacDonald following MacDonald's death in December of 1986.—Ed.

John D. didn't often let the comic spirit completely loose in his writing, but on those occasions when he did give the little imp free rein—*The Girl, the Gold Watch and Everything* and *Please Write for Details*, for instance—he showed not only what a fine, healthy, hearty comic novelist he could be, but what a fine, healthy, hearty, humorous man he was.

Gold Medal originals, with their yellow spines, were my education in popular fiction. At first I devoured them all indiscriminately, but gradually I began to go past the yellow spine to the brand name, to differentiate Vin Packer from Harry Whittington, Edward S. Aarons from

Peter Rabe, and to accept some new titles more eagerly than others. There were the writers to skip, there were the old reliables, there were the few really good writers with surprises and felicities somewhere within every book, and there was John D. MacDonald. Almost from the beginning, he was in a class by himself, and I think the secret was that he never wrote a scene, not a scene of any kind, as though he were writing for the pulps. There was never overstatement, never sleaze, no wallowing in the mire. He accepted my, the reader's, intelligence as a given, and not many did that.

I never met John D. until many years later, in 1981, when he and I were both elements of the display in a mystery program presented by Dilys Winn on a transatlantic crossing of the Norwegian liner *Vistafjord*. My wife and I had agreed to take part because it meant a free roundtrip to Europe on a means of transportation new to us, and the MacDonalds had agreed because they loved the big passenger ships. We were seventeen days from Port Everglades, Florida, to Genoa, and got to know one another fairly well along the way. The morning we disembarked, we agreed to meet for a farewell dinner that evening. My wife and I spent part of the day at the Cimitero di Staglieno, a world-famous hillside cemetery on the north side of the city, a necropolis filled with ornate statuary and lavish mausoleums and incredible arcades. That evening, at dinner, it turned out John D. had gone there as well, with a hired guide, and had come back absolutely abrim with anecdotes and facts about the place. The cemetery he'd gone to had somehow been more full of *narrative* than ours.

For the last five years, we and the MacDonalds have seen one another from time to time, for lunch or dinner, but not really very often. Our circles never overlapped that much, and we didn't live handy to one another. John D.'s attitude toward New York is best left unexpressed, and so is mine toward Florida. We also exchanged letters from time to time, though not a whole lot. We last saw John D. and Dorothy in May, at lunch in Sarasota, when my own work had led me briefly to the other coast of Florida and we drove across for respite and laughter. John continued amused by life, as always; we had a good time.

John D.'s writing was always clear and purposeful and utilitarian, not loaded with poetic phrases or quotable quotes, but just once I came across a paragraph of his that I found extremely touching in and of itself. It is from a book called *The End of the Night*, published in 1960, and it is a rumination by a condemned prisoner on Death Row shortly before his impending execution. It contained a phrase I thought might be useful as a title, so I copied that paragraph down, and here it is:

> I am very aware of another thing—and I suppose this is a very ordinary thing for all those condemned—and that is a kind of yearning for the things I will never do, a yearning with overtones of nostalgia. It is as though I can remember what it is like to be old and watch moonlight, and to hold children on my lap, and kiss the wife I have never met. It is a sadness in me. I want to apologize to her—I want to explain it to the children. I'm sorry. I'm never coming down the track of time to you. I was stopped along the way.

(The phrase is "the track of time," by the way, and I thought of it first.)

In any event, I feel a variant of that negative nostalgia now, but what I miss, in addition to the years ahead of friendship with John D. that will not happen, is the years behind that never happened. I feel a "yearning with overtones of nostalgia" for those thirty years between meeting John D. MacDonald on the paperback racks and meeting him on the *Vistafjord*. He was a good friend for such a short time: I would it had been longer.

EIGHT COFFEE BREAK

Letter to Ray Broekel

When Ray Broekel was working on his nonfiction book about chocolate candy, *The Chocolate Chronicles*, he wrote to Donald Westlake to ask what candy bar he would want on a desert island. Westlake, never one to pass up the chance to make a joke, responded.—Ed.

March 14, 1983
Dear Mr. Broekel,

My first reaction to your question was to say, If I were stuck alone on a desert isle with just one candy bar, I would like that candy bar to be Candy Barr; but then it occurred to me almost any mature adult would give you that answer, so then I decided that just any Bit O' Honey would do; but that suggested a certain immaturity on *my* part, so finally I decided if I were stuck alone on a desert isle with just one candy bar, I would like it to be a candy bar with a radio transmitter in it.

Sincerely,
Donald E. Westlake

NINE *ANYTHING YOU SAY MAY BE USED AGAINST YOU*

Interviews

AN INSIDE LOOK AT DONALD WESTLAKE,
BY ALBERT NUSSBAUM, 81332-132

Albert Nussbaum (1934–1996) was a bank robber who spent time on the FBI's Most Wanted list in 1962 before being arrested late that year and sentenced to forty years in prison for robbery and the murder of a bank guard. While in prison, he took up writing, and after being paroled in the 1970s, he published a number of mystery stories and also sold scripts to television.

In 1974 he approached Westlake with the suggestion of an interview conducted by mail. Intrigued by the unusual experience of being interviewed by a prisoner, Westlake agreed.—Ed.

NUSSBAUM: Now that you have seen several of your creations transferred to film, do you subscribe to the auteur theory, or are you one of those wise-ass scribblers who refuses to acknowledge the artistic superiority and creative transcendence of the director? (Answer by mentioning two American and two foreign directors, one of whom must be French; and relate their work to the young Orson Welles and the imitative product of Peter Bogdanovich. Use more than one sentence if necessary.)

WESTLAKE: I love your question. Remember the scene in *The Third Man* where Joseph Cotten, the writer of westerns, is posing as a literary-type lecturer? He's asked a question about James Joyce. If you can find a still of Cotten's face when he's reacting to the question, you'll have my answer to *you*, sir. But I might have some additional things to say, so why not start a new paragraph and see?

I subscribe basically to the theory that a movie is not the book it came from, and in almost every case it shouldn't be the book it came from. I have never adapted one of my own novels to the screen. Movies are a different form, they require different solutions. A new head will see the necessary changes a lot faster. I have written three original screenplays, one of which actually became a movie—*Cops and Robbers*—and which in the movie biz is a damn good percentage. After the *Cops and Robbers* screenplay was finished, I filled it out and made a novel out of it, but I have never wanted to go the other way. Screenplays are very confined, limited to the surface of things, limited in a thousand ways. A screenplay is just an outline with dialogue.

The responsibility for a movie is not as easy to define as the responsibility for a novel; I am responsible for the novel *Cops and Robbers* in a way I could never be responsible for the movie version. The auteur theory is simplism for eggheads. There are two kinds of people in the world: the dummies who think the actors make up their own lines and the sophisticates who know the director did it. In *Cops and Robbers* I am responsible for most, but not all, of the storyline; however, I wind up responsible for very, very few of the details along the way.

Let me give you one small example. In one scene in *Cops and Robbers*, two mobsters are being interrogated by cops at typewriters. The emphasis was on one of the mobsters who was being introduced as a major character; however, the other mobster and the cop interviewing him were not ordinary actors, no, sir. The cop was a real honest-to-god New York City plainclothes detective, and the guy playing the mobster was a real-life Cadillac dealer and no stranger to the bent life. They brought a choreography to that scene that I couldn't have invented and the director couldn't have invented, either. And it was somebody else entirely who thought to have the mobster give his occupation as "wholesale meat," so the cop could look at him and say, "A butcher?" And I'm talking here about the secondary characters in the scene; so, in that three-minute segment, who's the auteur?

There are directors who write their own scripts, and who have a total inner vision of the movie form in front plus the strength to make it happen the way they see it. Bergman, Fellini, probably Woody Allen. There are directors who enforce their own craziness, or determination, or whatever on other people's material (and who consistently choose the same type of material) like Hitchcock. But if I told you you were about to see a Richard Fleischer film, what would you expect to see? How about Robert Wise? William Dieterle? Norman Jewison? Tony Richardson?

No one individual is ever totally responsible for a movie. Auteur theory people, frightened by complexity, wind up singing the praises of a lot of traffic cops. The director, because he's there when the thing is being shot and is in charge of filming and editing, has a chance to be responsible to a greater extent than the screenwriter, *if* he has the strength and desire.

NUSSBAUM: How many books have you written? Had published? Do you care whether your pen names are known, or are they simply a device to signal the reader what to expect?

WESTLAKE: I have written about eighty books, seventy-six have been published. I don't mind telling you about fifty: twenty-one Donald E. Westlakes, twenty Richard Starks, five Tucker Coes, an Ace paperback science fiction novel called *Anarchaos* by Curt Clark, a fat political suspenser called *Ex Officio* by Timothy J. Culver (paperback title, *Power Play*), a children's book called *Philip* by D. E. Westlake, and a Hailey-type parody called *Comfort Station* by the vibrant J. Morgan Cunningham. The pen names are simple brand names, used to differentiate the types of books. I don't mind owning up to them.

NUSSBAUM: With all the books you've written, you must really burn up your word machine. What do you consider a good day's output? A bad day's output? Reason to rejoice?

WESTLAKE: I have no sensible way to define my output. *Pity Him Afterwards* was written in eleven days. The last book I did, which really should have been easier, took five months. When I was writing the books about which I will not speak, I had a set schedule of fifteen pages or five thousand words a day for ten days, at which time the book was finished no matter *what* the characters thought. If I work every day from the beginning of a book till the end, my production rate is probably three to five thousand words a day—unless I hit a snag, which can throw me off for a week or two. But if I work every day I don't do anything else, because everything else involves alcohol; and I don't try to work with any drink in me, so in the last few years I've tended to work four or five days a week. But that louses up the production two ways: first in the days I don't work, and second, because I do almost nothing the first day back on the job. This week, for instance, I did one or two pages Monday, five pages Tuesday, five Wednesday, fourteen Thursday, and three so far today.

NUSSBAUM: When do you write?

WESTLAKE: During my second marriage I used to yell, "I'm sick of working one day in a row!" But you can't yell that at a girlfriend. I work afternoons and nights, with no schedule, no set time, no set output, no discipline of any kind. Sometimes it works and sometimes it doesn't. Today it didn't.

NUSSBAUM: Your Westlake books are (except for early work) well-known for their humor, and Richard Stark's Parker series is every bit as violent and kinky as the Bible. Why do you think they're popular?

WESTLAKE: I'll tell you a funny thing. In the early sixties, when the first Parkers came out in paperback, Richard Stark got a bunch of fan mail. (The Westlake books had gotten practically none.) And almost all of that fan mail was from inner-city urban black males. I think what they liked about Parker was that *he* had chosen to reject society, rather than the other way around. He was the prowling outsider, but it hadn't been forced on him. Or maybe not.

CHAPTER NINE

That fan mail trickled out in the late sixties, by the way, and now all I get is sheriff's assistants in Nebraska telling me I got the guns wrong.

NUSSBAUM: I have noticed over the years that you seem to have been playing musical chairs with publishers, jumping from one to another quite frequently. Was this your idea? Your agent's? The publishers'?

WESTLAKE: Everybody's. The first jump was from Pocket Books to oblivion for Richard Stark in 1965. Pocket Books underwent an editorial shift and dropped their entire line of original crime books. Unfortunately, I'd just finished the ninth book in the Parker series and made the book about Grofield, a secondary character, not Parker. Well, I couldn't very well peddle the Parker series elsewhere with a book in which Parker didn't appear, so the Grofield series was born at Macmillan. Parker finally found a home at Fawcett Gold Medal a couple of years later, but none of us were ever happy with one another, and after four books we quit by mutual agreement.

Meanwhile, Richard Stark did three Grofield books for Macmillan, during which time I worked with four editors there. With these three, an anthology with Phil Klass (William Tenn) and *Up Your Banners*, I had five books published with Macmillan, and not one of them ever came out when the editor who'd bought it was still working there. So Grofield's fourth excursion went to World, where there was a pleasant editor named Jim Wade. He is still there, though I haven't done any more Grofields.

Back to Westlake. There came the point when Random House (which had published my first eleven books and was already doing the Tucker Coes) had to decide whether or not to extend a little more for me or not. My agent put them into a competitive position with Simon & Schuster, who promised me the world and the stars and the moon, and Random House dropped out of the bidding, though Coe stayed there and later the Parker series went there. (Parker is still there. Lee Wright, the woman editor at Random House, is the top of the pyramid in the mystery field and has been ever since she started Inner Sanctum at Simon & Schuster back in the thirties.) S&S turned out not to have the moon and the stars, nor much of the world, and after five books we skedaddled (that's not the editorial we, that's my agent and I) to M. Evans, where I'm just so happy I skip and dance and go tra-la-la all day.

Paperback reprint is another matter entirely, over which I have little control.

NUSSBAUM: How many of your books have been made into films?

WESTLAKE: Nine.

1. *The Hunter*, Richard Stark—*Point Blank*, 1967, screenplay by Alexander Jacobs and David and Rafe Newhouse, directed by John Boorman, produced by Judd Bernard and Robert Chartoff (a Judd Bernard-Irwin Winkler production), MGM.

2. *The Outfit*, Richard Stark—*The Outfit*, 1973, screenplay and direction by John Flynn, produced by Carter DeHaven, MGM.

3. *The Score*, Richard Stark—*Mise à sac* (*Pillaged*), 1967, screenplay by Claude Suatet and Alain Cavalier, directed by Cavalier, produced by Georges Dancigers, Georges Laurent, and Alexandre Mnouchkine, UA (never released in the U.S.).

4. *The Jugger*, Richard Stark—*Made in USA*, 1966, screenplay and direction by Jean-Luc Godard, produced by Georges de Beauregard and Clément Steyaert Rome-Paris films (not yet released in the U.S. because I had to sue them intercontinentally).

5. *The Seventh*, Richard Stark—*The Split*, 1968, screenplay by Robert Sabaroff, directed by Gordon Flemyng, produced by Irwin Winkler and Robert Chartoff, MGM.

6. *The Busy Body*, Westlake (at last!)—*The Busy Body*, 1967, screenplay by Ben Starr, directed and produced by William Castle, Paramount.

7. *The Hot Rock*, Westlake—*The Hot Rock*, 1972, screenplay (a damn good one, better than the movie) by William Goldman, directed by Peter Yates, produced by Hal Landers and Bobby Roberts, Twentieth-Century Fox.

8. *Bank Shot*, Westlake—*Bank Shot*, 1974, screenplay by Wendell Mayes (yech!), directed by Gower Champion (yech!), produced by Hal Landers and Bobby Roberts, UA.

9. *Cops and Robbers*, Westlake—*Cops and Robbers*, 1973, screenplay by

Westlake (actually, because it's an original, the credit line reads, "written by"), directed by Aram Avakian, produced by Elliott Kastner, UA.

NUSSBAUM: Who starred in the French films, *Mise à sac* and *Made in USA?*

WESTLAKE: *Mise à sac*—cast list in *Variety*, my only source—Michel Constantin, Daniel Ivernel, Franco Interlenghi, Irene Tunc, Paul Le Persen. Because the characters' names were changed to French names, I don't know who played what.

Made in USA—Parker was played by Anna Karina. A friend of mine, referring to this and Lee Marvin (*Point Blank*) and Jim Brown (*The Split*), said, "So far, Parker has been played by a white man, a black man, and a woman. I think the character lacks definition."

NUSSBAUM: What is your problem with Godard? Don't you feel a little sheepish for causing trouble for an internationally acclaimed cinematic genius? Have you no respect for your betters? Or do you think fingers should be slapped whenever Fate or Justice decrees?

WESTLAKE: My problem with Godard is that he let himself be put in the middle. A French producer named Beauregard wrote my agent asking to buy movie rights to a Richard Stark Parker novel called *The Jugger*, which happens to be the worst book I ever wrote under *any* name. Maybe the French version was different. Anyway, we sold it to him for $16,000, in eight monthly installments of two grand, and one failure to pay would revert the rights to me. Meantime, Beauregard had put all his money into a movie either about a whore becoming a nun or a nun becoming a whore, I'm not sure which, and when he was finished the French government told him he couldn't (a) show it in France, or (b) export it. Which didn't leave much of a market. He didn't say anything to us, ask for extensions or anything; he just disappeared after making three payments.

Time passed. A girl I know who was living in Paris wrote to say she'd seen my movie. What-what? Correspondence ensued, and here was this movie called *Made in USA*, and Godard had said in an interview in a French cinema magazine that it was based on a thriller by

Richard Stark. What had happened, Godard had been making *Two or Three Things I Know About Her*, and to help out his old friend Beauregard, who was financially strapped, Godard took my book—which he thought was Beauregard's property—and in twelve afternoons made *Made in USA*. (If you see it, you'll wonder what he did the last three afternoons.) Godard had changed things around so much that Beauregard may have figured the film could be considered an original, but he didn't tell Godard, who innocently blabbed.

Now comes the lawsuit. An intercontinental lawsuit, taking three and a half years, at which I win, hands down. Absolutely. Because Beauregard is still broke, there's no financial restitution possible, so we hold out for North American distribution rights. (We'd blocked the film's showing in the United States for just that reason.) Fine. The French court awards it to us. However, the film is partly Godard's copyright. The movie can't be shown without my permission, but it can't be shown without *his* permission, either. And he won't sign. He isn't holding out for more money or anything like that; he just doesn't like those fat American capitalists dumping on his sweet friend Beauregard.

NUSSBAUM: Besides *Cops and Robbers*, Elliott Kastner has put together some very successful projects. In discussing the picture, you didn't characterize Kastner. Was this because you fear a slander suit? Love him like a brother and don't want to bandy his name about? Or think you may be able to swindle him again if you keep your cool?

WESTLAKE: Elliott Kastner is a living legend. Seriously. When producers sit around to shoptalk, they tell Elliott Kastner stories. I will tell you about him. I was here one day, at my typewriter, and the phone rang. "Hello, I'm Elliott Kastner, calling you from my office in London. I think the world is ready for another *Rififi*, and I think you're the man to write it. Why don't you send me a letter with an idea or two?"

I had never written anything for the movies, not really, and I had no idea who this nut was. I asked around, and he had produced *Harper*, among other movies, and I know Bill Goldman, who wrote the screenplay for *Harper*. I called Bill and asked him about Kastner, and he said, "Did anybody else call you like that?" "No," I said, "he's the first."

"That's Elliott," Goldman said. "You're about to be hot, and he'll know it before anybody else." Goldman also told me that Elliott was not a movie producer, but that he was a packager, and that his projects got made.

In writing books, of course, what you do is more important than how often you've done it, but in writing screenplays a credit is better than no credit at all. That you've written a piece of shit that got made is one up for you; that you've written three beauties that have not been made is three down for you. If a producer gets his projects made, what more can you want from the man? So I put together a story idea and sent it to Kastner, and he phoned and said no.

Then he said an associate of his, Jerry Bick, was coming to New York, so why didn't we talk? So Jerry Bick and I met, and we talked about how New York looked worse to Bick every time he came back from London, and the idea of *Cops and Robbers* was born.

At first Michael Winner was going to direct—Winner co-produces his films, and thus Kastner wouldn't have to pay him anything in front—but Winner's prior commitments elsewhere got in the way, and Kastner scrounged around and came up with Aram Avakian, who had had a reputation for being difficult just long enough to be hungry enough to not be difficult. (I'll wait for you to work your way through that sentence. Ready? Onward.) So he got Aram on the cheapo, and meanwhile United Artists—whose pocket Elliott was picking this time—had bought *Lenny* for Dustin Hoffman, leaving the Broadway star of *Lenny*, Cliff Gorman, up for grabs. Why not get Gorman, too? Since he wasn't coming with *Lenny*, he, too, was cheap; an Emmy winner cheap. (Do you suppose the pyramids were made this way?) I don't know how Joe Bologna got into it, maybe it was the first time his wife let him out of the house alone. Elliott, having assembled this square-wheeled package, disappeared, returning the night of final shooting to pat everybody's back, smile nervously, and depart again.

I heard this exchange of dialogue between Elliott and another producer at dinner one night: Other producer: "You ever get that tax problem straightened out?" Kastner: "All but a hundred fifty thousand of it." I wish I could write dialogue like that.

Early in our relationship, Kastner said these two sentences to me in a row, very earnestly and seriously: "I've made seventeen pictures in six years. I've never made a picture I didn't care deeply about." St. Francis of Assisi couldn't care about seventeen pictures in six years.

One last thing about Elliott: I like him.

NUSSBAUM: Is there a filmmaker whom you esteem greatly?

WESTLAKE: No. John Huston wrote and directed two of the best movies ever made, *Treasure of the Sierra Madre* and *The Maltese Falcon*, but look what he's done to us lately. His last picture that was any good was *Beat the Devil*, and *there's* a picture to drive auteurs mad: Capote inventing the screenplay on the set. Lorre being told one day there hadn't been time to write his dialogue for the scene, so just go in there and pretend to be somebody who has to stall those people in that room, and so on, and so on. *Beat the Devil* was in 1954.

NUSSBAUM: No one has ever criticized anything about your books except their style and content, so there must be a few things coming up, right?

WESTLAKE: Finished, and due out in the spring, is a nasty comedy called *Two Much*, about a guy who meets twins and pretends to be twins himself so he can score on them both. Then he marries them both, murders them both, inherits their millions and lives happily ever after.

Unlike book agreements, movie deals never get completed. Sorry—finalized. There are, as usual, several of them snuffling around my leg at the moment. I mean deals for me to write something for the movies. Also, more of my books have been sold to the movies than have been made into movies. Like so:

1. *The Fugitive Pigeon*, Westlake—sold to Max Youngstein and Columbia Pictures in 1964, screenplay by Richard Maibaum, no movie.
2. *The Damsel*, by Richard Stark—optioned by John Bennett in '66 or '67, option lapsed
3. *The Spy in the Ointment*, by Westlake—optioned by somebody named Morris in '66 or '67, option lapsed.

4. *Kinds of Love, Kinds of Death*, by Tucker Coe—bought for Robert Mitchum by somebody, that's all I know, no movie.

5. *God Save the Mark*, by Westlake—optioned by Campbell, Silver, Cosby for Bill Cosby in 1967, option renewed, no movie, option lapsed. Also, screenplay done by yours truly with Buddy Hackett in, I think, '69, nothing happened, no movie. (That wasn't really a case of me adapting my own work; it was a case of me organizing Hackett's flights. He's a genius, by the way.)

6 *Murder among Children*, by Tucker Coe—bought by somebody, paid for, no movie.

7. *Who Stole Sassi Manoon*, by Westlake—an early *Cops and Robbers*. I wrote an original screenplay for Palomar, no movie, but I'd retained publication rights and I novelized the screenplay.

8. *Somebody Owes Me Money*, by Westlake—bought by United Artists, 1972, for Elliott Gould. Screenplay by Allan Dennis. In limbo at the moment.

9. *Deadly Edge*, by Richard Stark—bought by Hal Landers and Bobby Roberts, 1972, screenplay by Don Peterson, everybody hates it, probably no movie.

10.*Help, I Am Being Held Prisoner*, bought by Hal Landers and Bobby Roberts, 1973, screenplay by Carl Reiner, hated by everybody, probably no movie. (This and the other four marked with asterisks will now sit on the shelf. No movie, no turnback to me, no chance to do *anything*.)

NUSSBAUM: Okay, you've told what you've done and what is on the horizon, but what do you see for yourself in the long, l-o-n-g view—like next month and beyond. Put simply, what do you want to be remembered for ten years after you're dead that you haven't achieved, yet? Take your time with this one. You have a full minute to answer.

WESTLAKE: Several years ago David Susskind was allegedly going to buy movie rights to one of my books. It didn't work out, but in the course of it he told me he'd checked into my other movie deals, including an option that Bill Cosby had taken on *God Save the Mark*. Susskind had wanted to know why the movie hadn't been made, and when he'd questioned Cosby's business partner the fella said, "Bill decided he only wants to make posterity pictures." Susskind told me this, and we both laughed, and then I said something like, "It's tough enough writing for the people alive right now. I thought Cosby was smarter than that." And Susskind said, "Never expect brains from an actor." I don't know if this answers your question or not, but it's the only paragraph I intend to put here.

NUSSBAUM: All right, what do you think the people alive right now want?

WESTLAKE: I have felt for some time, with growing conviction, that there weren't any stories around to be written. I haven't been able to do a Richard Stark novel in a year and a half, the comedy caper is dead, storylines are drying up like African cattle. Storylines reflect, refer to and attempt to deal with their period of history, and that's why they become old and obsolete and used up. Another reason is that the same story gets done and done and done and done, and suddenly one day nobody wants to read or hear or see that story again. And another reason, come to think of it, is that all of the gold in that vein has been mined, and there's nothing left; for example, the screwball comedy of the thirties, young lovers, one rich, one poor. The rich-poor thing was made obsolete by the end of the Depression, but the gags and situations and potentialities were wrung out of the story by then anyway.

And at this moment, *everything* is used up. Maybe the problem is that the times really *are* changing. None of the stories we now have properly reflect things anymore. Are you going to have a couple in your story? What's their attitude about marriage? Are you going to have a rich hero? What's his attitude about money, about poor people, about other rich people? We don't know what the new myths are going to be because we don't know what the world looks like right now.

The result is a mis-named nostalgia. The movies are frankly set in the past. We can believe in *Chinatown* only because it doesn't claim to be telling about us. That isn't nostalgia, that's re-runs. The book publishers and movie makers and TV factories have to produce *something*, but nothing contemporary feels *right*, so everybody's treading water with Sherlock Holmes and the Orient Express.

What will tomorrow's popular fiction, commercial stories look like? What are the attitudes of today that call for mythologizing? What consummations would we like to see in parable form? What are the next stories going to turn out fifty years later to have *really* been about?

You want to wrap your head around that one?

The wily interviewee turns the tables.

THE WORST HAPPENS: FROM AN INTERVIEW
BY PATRICK McGILLIGAN

This selection draws on an interview conducted by Patrick McGilligan that was originally published in the Autumn 1990 issue of *Sight and Sound*, then later republished in expanded form in *Backstory 4: Interviews with Screenwriters of the 1970s and 1980s*. McGilligan doesn't include his questions, only Westlake's answers. If you're interested in Westlake's film work, it's worth your getting a copy of *Backstory 4* to read the whole interview, but for this collection, I've selected a number of Westlake's detailed analyses of the film adaptations of his books, with an eye toward covering topics, projects, and writers that haven't come up elsewhere. I've included the whole of his commentary on each film I've selected except *The Grifters*, where elisions are indicated with ellipses. All other ellipses are in the original. Bracketed interpolations are McGilligan's.—Ed.

The Hot Rock

Rarely has a screenwriter talked to me about adapting one of my books. The first time was William Goldman [scenarist of *The Hot Rock*], who holds the whole field of screenwriting in contempt. Either in spite of that, or because of that, he is, I think, the best living screenwriter. Nobody on earth could have made a movie out of *All the President's Men* [1976], and he did.

When he took the job of doing *The Hot Rock*, he called me and said, "I want to take you to lunch and I want you to tell me everything you know about those characters that you didn't put in the book." I thought, "What a smart guy this is!" We spent time together. The director [Peter Yates] and producers [Hal Landers and Bobby Roberts] didn't give a damn, but Bill would send me portions of the script and say, "What do you think?" He was very forthcoming.

He took out the only thing I thought of as a movie scene in the whole book, a scene where they have stolen a locomotive from a circus because they have to break into an insane asylum. It's a complicated scene, but that seemed to me like a movie scene. Bill explained why he couldn't use it and he was right. Every once in a great while—I don't think in terms of movies if I'm writing a book and I think anyone who does is crazy—I'll look back at something I've written and say, "*That's* a movie scene . . ." And if the movie rights are sold, that scene is never used.

The Outfit

The Outfit is one movie made from a Stark book that got the feeling right. That movie is done flat, just like the books.

John Flynn was the writer-director, and it was early in his career, and I thought he was going to be a world-beater. He put together an incredible cast, everybody from Robert Duvall and Karen Black and Robert Ryan, to Elisha Cook and Archie Moore and Anita O'Day. He wrote it "period," but then de-emphasized that. He had everybody moving fast. It was efficient but it was also thoughtful. I didn't meet him at the time, but have met him a couple times since and he did not have the career I expected. It takes more than talent. It takes luck, and a genius at making choices. *The Outfit* is about the only thing he's done that shows what he can do.

The Bank Shot

I saw one scene from *The Bank Shot* once, and it looked pretty bad. It was [Gower] Chanpion's only movie [as director]. A friend who saw it said it was a farce in extreme close-up, so whenever somebody stepped on a banana peel all you knew was that they'd left the frame.

The credits on *The Stepfather* are rather weird. I'm the main writer, but the story is credited to Brian Garfield, Carolyn Lefcourt, and me. Carolyn Lefcourt was an editor at a publishing house in New York; Brian had published some books with that house. Carolyn Lefcourt gave Brian a clipping about this guy, John List in New Jersey, who killed his family and disappeared, saying to Brian, "A novel about his next family might be interesting . . ." Brian said, "Yeah, it might," but didn't do anything about it right away. A year or two went by before he told me about the idea, though he had lost the clipping. By then he thought he was a movie producer (it took him several years to realize he wasn't). He said, "I'll never write it as a novel, would you like to do it as a movie? My production company will hire you . . ."

The story did connect with me in a very strange way. At one point during the Depression, my father lost his job and didn't tell my mother that he had lost his job, and spent several weeks leaving the house every day as though going to work—but actually looking for work and not finding any. On Fridays he would take money out of his savings account and bring it home as though it were his salary. One day a woman friend of my mother's blew his cover. My mother and father always had trouble comprehending each other. As far as my mother was concerned, the marriage was a partnership and she had been frozen out.

The guy in the clipping had done the same thing: either quit, or been fired from, his Wall Street job, and then, for the next several weeks, he did the same thing my father did, except in his case it led to murder. I found that a little spooky. I decided not to turn away from that idea, but to take a look at how people have different viewpoints of what their communal experiences are.

Early on [director] Joe [Ruben] and I were talking, and he asked me if I had any images of what the movie should be like. I told him about a movie that Alexander Mackendrick directed called *A Boy Ten Feet Tall* [a.k.a. *Sammy Goes South*, 1963]. Twice in that movie Mackendrick did something that I love: in one scene planes fly over and bomb the kid's house. The kid is playing, he hears the sound and he looks up, and then there is a quick cut to the sky as the plane is leaving. You don't get a chance to think about it . . .

There's another scene where one of the native bearers is standing on one side of a large bush and on the other side is a lion. The guide is aware of the lion, but the lion isn't aware of the guide; yet the guide is afraid to move, he just stands there and calls for the white hunter with the gun, who is played by Edward G. Robinson, to come quick. As the hunter's still running, we cut back to the guide and the lion, and the lion is already in motion, halfway around the bush . . .

I told Joe, "That's what I want for *The Stepfather*—not a long setup for the violence. There shouldn't be a lot of violence, but when violence happens it should happen faster than you could know it." So from the very beginning it was written into the script that when the stepfather hit his wife it would be the second half of a gesture with the phone. It's scary because he can't be reasoned with, and it just happens very quickly. That's not far from comedy, and hitting 'em with a punch line. Comedy is simply another way of hiding and jumping out—you hide and jump out with the punch line. The whole idea of *The Stepfather* is that the punch line would scare you instead of making you laugh.

My deal was with Brian, and since we are both writers we made an absolute sweetheart contract that was quite distressing to Joe Ruben at one point, when he wanted to bring in a friend of his just to do a little polish. Part of the contract said I could not be replaced without my permission. So *The Stepfather* stayed mine, more so than usual, just like *The Grifters* stayed mine, more than usual.

The Grifters

All of a sudden everything of Thompson's that hadn't been made was being put under option. His moment had come. It seems perfectly appropriate to him that his fifteen minutes of fame should have come so many years after his death. That's a Jim Thompson irony. . . .

. . . At first I turned Stephen [Frears] down, however. He asked why.

I said, "The book's too gloomy. These people are just too grim and depressing and I don't want to spend all that time with them." He said, "If you don't think about it from the young man's point of view, then it isn't gloomy and depressing. If you think of the mother as the principal character, then—although it's not a comedy—it's a story of survival. It's a story about someone who is going to survive, no matter what. And a story of survival is a little more upbeat."

It's true: Thompson is hard to take because he isn't upbeat and the best you can hope from him is "We can survive." I had read most of his books, of course. The only book of his I ever had trouble with—which I didn't like—is the one that everybody thinks is the greatest: *The Killer Inside Me*. That one I've never warmed up to, but some of the others are good, and *The Grifters* is very good. There's always quirkiness and surviving against odds and an off-kilter view of life in Thompson's work.

I think Thompson, because of the Depression, because of his personality, because of his drinking, because of his own family and other stuff, he was always writing too fast, slogging away. Still he managed to do, almost exclusively, stuff that came from "within." In *The Grifters* he's really telling a story about the tangled emotions between a mother and a son, but he puts the characters both in the mob. That's for the market, but the story is for him. I think he thought of himself as a seriously intentioned and talented novelist who was in the wrong place at the wrong time. The Depression robbed him of the college education he needed. He came out of Anadarko, Oklahoma, and was in the wrong place to have literary confreres. He was a lost figure out in Oklahoma, which is what his characters are.

He always wrote from his guts—too fast, but from his guts. He was usually doing stuff for too little money in secondary markets. Every one of his books was published at least one draft too soon, so there's lumpy, undigested stuff in them, because he wouldn't have the time or impetus to go back and redo parts, smooth things out, and get it right. In that situation you've got to get it done, send it in, get your $2,000, and pay the rent.

I did some of that in my early days of writing, so I know how it happens. You're going along until you get to a point in the story where you say, "Oh, my gosh, this story isn't going to work unless she was *married* before . . ." You can solve it two ways: you can go back and put the marriage in where you should have put it in the first place, or you can just stick it right in: "She was married before . . ." and keep going. That's what Thompson does. So my first job with *The Grifters* was to untangle all the knots and lay the story out.

The difference between a movie and a novel is that a movie is just the surface of things, and the meanings and emotions can only be implicit. Even if somebody stands on screen and says, "I'm in terrible pain at the moment," you're simply seeing someone who says, "I'm in terrible pain at the moment," whereas a novel can convince you that you're really in the presence of someone feeling terrible pain at this moment. It's a different intensity, a novel. Even a shallow novel is "inside" somewhere.

Since a movie is dealing on the surface of things, it's easiest to start scripts in the instruction manual mode, as if you are doing an instruction manual from which somebody is making a film. Start with basics—like in painting, where you put the colors on a canvas to convince somebody to get an emotional response—that's what a basic script is. You then put on top of that as much meaning and emotion and reality as you can, but what a script really is basically is a set of instructions. I would never do a novel in the same way.

One thing Stephen and I agreed on right away was updating the book. A story shouldn't be done "period" unless it is about the period. There's no problem with updating Thompson because his people only live in a very narrow world, with each other. Their whole interest is the emotional struggle between them. To update it, all you have to do is take their hats off. . . .

Le Jumeau (France, 1984) and *Two Much* (USA-Spain, 1996)

I have never seen either version [of these two films based on the Westlake novel *Two Much*], having been warned away by friends who cared about me. Both versions make the same simpleminded, totally destructive mistake. In both versions, the main character doesn't kill anybody. So what's it about? A guy screws twins? People shouldn't be handed a camera until they reach the age of reason.

Mr. Ripley's Return

Mr. Ripley's Return is one of the odder episodes. Let's see if I can do it justice without meting out justice to the participants.

In 1992, I was hired by an indie prod [indie production company]— one American LA-based, nice guy; one Frenchman, Paris-based, charming guy; one German, never met, I think he was the money guy—to do the second Ripley novel, *Ripley Underground.* I've always loved the deadpanness of [Patricia] Highsmith, and I thought it reached a peak in that book. The guy Ripley is tormenting, in his passive-aggressive way, suddenly turns around, smashes Ripley's head with a shovel, and buries him in Ripley's own garden. Ripley survives, comes up out of the grave later that night, takes a nice hot tub, patches his cut parts, and then what does he do? Call the cops? No. Shoot the guy? No. He haunts the guy for the next one hundred pages of the book, appearing and disappearing in windows, stuff like that.

I was delighted to take a crack at the book, and I didn't mind Highsmith's weirdnesses and repulsivenesses, because I wasn't going to meet her or deal with her; that was the ground rule. I did my first draft, and that attracted Michael Tolkin to direct. He had some lovely ideas, details of menace and suspense for the second draft, which I wrote, and then never heard from them again.

Another constant with the indie prod is, if the movie isn't going to get made, they disappear, owing you money. It's happened to me before, it could happen again. However, if the movie gets made after all, they have to pay before it's released. Three times over the years, the American producer called my LA agent to say that it looked like a go and, "We know we owe Don the money." My agent said, "Don knows you owe him the money, too." This third time, magic time, the movie got made, I got paid. (Little problems such as with health and retirement payments, nothing serious.) However, there was also a potential production bonus, if I had a solo or shared credit. I have no idea what happened to the script over the last eleven years, but there was no point not putting my hand out. I did, and lo and behold, a shared credit! Initially in first place, but the other guy got annoyed and said he'd done far more work on it than me, which must be true. Both shares get the same bonus. Do I want to argue the case and read twelve scripts on the same story, particularly when some of those scripts I am likely to look upon as less than felicitous? I'm happy to be Martha Washington.

Michael Tolkin did not direct. I don't know director [Roger Spottiswoode] or cast or anything. No one has contacted me directly. I am merely that truck-stop waitress in Amarillo they fucked in 1992. That's okay. I think highly of them, too. Someone working on the set of the movie—I think it was shot in France, but don't know for sure—said it wasn't coming out well, which could merely be schadenfreude.

On a happier note, at this moment, in Paris, [Constantin] Costa-Gavras is shooting my book *The Ax* from a screenplay by him and his usual writing partner. I don't have high hopes, I have high expectations.

TEN MIDNIGHT SNACK

Gustatory Notes from All Over

This was first published in 1986 in a collection of pieces by a number of writers on a similar theme titled *Bred Any Good Rooks Lately?* It's more fun if we leave it to you to figure out the theme.—Ed.

A rare delicacy is *sloth à la Dortmunder*. Using the middle part of the great Australian three-toed sloth—the only edible part of that large, furry, indolent creature—the careful chef debones it, pounds it as with veal, and sautees it briefly over a hot flame with shallots, carrot circles, and just a touch of Tabasco. Prepared in this fashion, sloth is an excellent main course, not unlike alligator in texture and taste.

Many people are under the false impression that sloth does not make a good meal, but this is because they've eaten it improperly prepared. It can only be sauteed, *à la Dortmunder*, a fact ill-appreciated in culinary circles. *Too many cooks broil the sloth.*

ELEVEN SIDE JOBS

Prison Breaks, Movie Mobsters, and Radio Comedy

BREAK-OUT

Westlake wrote this for the third issue of *Ed McBain's Mystery Book* in 1961. Westlake would later use this title for the twenty-first Parker novel, and in an interview he explained, "Sometimes the title is almost the only seed needed. *Breakout* came about when I realized that, in all these years, Parker had never been jailed except once before the first book. Get him arrested, and watch how he handled it." To no one's surprise, he handled it better than a lot of the characters Westlake describes below.—Ed.

Alcatraz is probably the toughest and best-known prison in the United States, long considered an impregnable, escape-proof penitentiary. The entire imprisoned population there consists of hard cases transferred from less rugged federal penitentiaries. In the middle of San Francisco Bay, it is surrounded by treacherous currents and is almost always enveloped by thick fog and high winds. A high percentage of the prisoners sent there are men who have already escaped from one or more other prisons and penitentiaries. "Now you are at Alcatraz," they are told. "Alcatraz is escape-proof. You *can't* get away from here."

It was a challenge, and sooner or later someone had to accept it. That someone was a felon named Ted Cole. Cole had already escaped once, from an Oklahoma prison, where he had been assigned duty in the prison laundry. That escape had been made by hiding in a laundry bag. But now Cole was on Alcatraz, and Alcatraz, he was told repeatedly, was escape-proof.

Cole's work assignment was in the prison machine shop, which suited him perfectly. Through an involved code in his infrequent mail, he managed to line up outside assistance from friends in the San Francisco area. While waiting for things to be set up outside, he spent a cautious part of each workday on the machine-shop wall, on the other side of which was the rocky, surf-torn beach of the island.

The day finally came. Leaving right after a head count, so he would have an hour or two anyway before his absence was noticed, Cole went through the machine-shop wall and dove into the water, swimming straight out from the island, the fog so thick around him he could barely see the movement of his own arms as he swam.

This, as far as he was concerned, was the only really dangerous part of the escape. If his friends couldn't find him in the fog, he would simply swim until he drowned from exhaustion or was recaptured by a police patrol from the island.

Finally, a launch came out of the fog ahead, throttling down beside him, and Cole treaded water, staring anxiously, wondering whether this was escape or capture.

It was escape. His friends fished him out of the water, gave him blankets and brandy, and the launch veered away toward shore. Yet again, society's challenge had been accepted, and another "escape-proof" prison had been conquered.

Accepting society's challenge in his own antisocial way is second nature to the habitual criminal. The desire for freedom is strong in most men, and perhaps it is strongest in those who have, by the commission of crime, tried to free themselves from the restraint of society's laws. The much harsher and much more complete restraint of a narrow prison cell and an ordered, repetitive existence within the prison walls, plus the challenge of being told that escape from this prison is impossible, increase this yearning for freedom to the point where no risk seems too great, if only there is the *possibility* of freedom. No matter what the builders of the prison have claimed, the imaginative and determined prisoner can always find somewhere, in a piece of wood or a rusty nail or the manner of the guards' shift change, the slim possibility that just might end in freedom.

This yearning for freedom, of course, doesn't always result in imaginative and ingenious escapes. At times, it prompts instead wholesale riots, with hostages taken and fierce demands expressed and the senseless destruction of both lives and property. Such outbreaks are dreaded by prison officials, but they never result in successful escapes. They are too noisy and too emotional. The successful escapee is silent, and he uses his wits rather than his emotions.

The prisoner who is carefully working out the details of an escape, in fact, dreads the idea of a riot as much as do the prison officials themselves.

The result of a riot is inevitably a complete search and shakedown of the entire prison. And this means the discovery of the potential escapee's tunnel or hacksaw or dummy pistol or specially constructed packing case or rope ladder or forged credentials. And the escapee has to think of some other plan.

He always does. No matter how tight the control, how rigid the security, how frequent the inspections or "impregnable" the prison, the man who desires freedom above all other things always does think of something else.

Take John Carroll, perhaps the only man ever to break both *out* of and *into* prison. In the twenties, Carroll and his wife, Mabel, were known throughout the Midwest as the Millionaire Bandits. Eventually captured and convicted, John Carroll was sentenced to Leavenworth while Mabel was imprisoned at the women's reformatory at Leeds.

At that time, in 1927, Leavenworth was still thought of as being *nearly* escape-proof, and the constant shakedowns and absolutely rigid daily schedule had Carroll stymied for a while. But not forever.

Carroll had been put to work in the machine shop, and he spent months studying the guards, realizing that he would be much more likely to escape if he could get one of them to collaborate with him.

He finally picked the shop foreman himself, a truculent, middle-aged, dissatisfied guard obviously unhappy in his work. Carroll waited in the machine shop one afternoon until everyone else had left and he was alone with the foreman. The foreman wanted to know what he was still doing here. Carroll, making the big leap all at once, said, "How would you like to make thirty-four thousand dollars?"

The foreman showed neither interest nor shock. Instead, he demanded, as though it were a challenge, "How do I do that?"

"I have sixty-eight thousand hidden on the outside," Carroll told him. "Help me get out of here, and half of it is yours."

The foreman shook his head and told Carroll to go on with the others. But the next day, when work was finished, he signaled to Carroll to stay behind again. This time, he wanted to know what Carroll's plans were.

Carroll told him. A part of the work in this shop was devoted to building the packing cases in which the convict-made goods were shipped outside. Carroll and the foreman would construct a special case and when Carroll felt the time was right, the foreman would help him ship himself out of prison and to the foreman's apartment.

The foreman agreed, and they went to work. Carroll was a cautious man, and they worked slowly, nor did Carroll make his escape immediately after the special packing case was completed. Instead, he waited for just the right moment.

A note from his wife, delivered through the prison grapevine, forced Carroll to rush his plans. The note, which he received on February 28, 1927, read: "Your moll has t.b. bad. I'll die if you don't get me out. I'm in Dormitory D at Leeds."

Carroll knew that his wife's greatest terror was of dying in prison, of not dying a free woman. He left Leavenworth that same night, in the packing case. But the case was inadvertently put in the truck upside down, and Carroll spent over an hour in that position, and had fallen unconscious by the time the case was delivered to the foreman's apartment.

Coming to, Carroll broke out of the case and discovered the apartment empty and the new clothes he had asked for waiting for him on a chair. He changed and left before the foreman got home, and the foreman never saw a penny of the thirty-four thousand dollars.

Carroll went straight to Leeds. Posing as an engineer, he became friendly with one of the matrons from the prison, and eventually learned not only the location of Dormitory D within the wall, but even the exact whereabouts of his wife's cell.

It took him five months to get his plan completely worked out. Finally, shortly after dark the night of July 27th, he drove up to the high outer wall of the prison in a second-hand car he'd recently bought. In the car were a ladder, a hacksaw, a length of rope, a bar of naphtha soap and a can of cayenne paper.

Setting the ladder in place, Carroll climbed atop the wall and lay flat, so as not to offer any watchers a clear silhouette. He then shifted the ladder to the other side of the wall, climbed down into the prison yard, and moved quickly across to Dormitory D. He stood against the dormitory wall and whistled, a shrill, high note, a signal he knew his wife would recognize. When she answered, from her barred third-story window, he tossed the rope to her. She caught it on the third try, tied one end inside the cell, and Carroll climbed up to the window.

Mabel then spoke the only words either of them said before the escape was complete. "I knew you'd come."

Carroll handed the tools through to his wife, then, one-handed, tied the rope around his waist, so he'd have both hands free to work. Meanwhile, Mabel had rubbed the hacksaw with soap, to cut down the noise of sawing. They each held an end of the saw and cut through the bars one by one, with frequent rest stops for Carroll to ease the pressure of the rope around his waist.

It was nearly dawn before they had removed the last bar. Carroll helped his wife clamber through the window, and they slid down to the ground, where Carroll covered their trail to the outer wall with cayenne powder, to keep bloodhounds from catching their scent. They went up the ladder and over the wall, and drove away.

Carroll was recaptured over a year later, and returned willingly enough to jail. His wife was dead, had been for five months. But she hadn't died in prison.

Most escapees don't remain on the outside for anywhere near as long as a year. The majority seem to use up all their ingenuity in the process of *getting* out, and none at all in the job of *staying* out. Such men have fantastic courage and daring in the planning and execution of one swiftly completed job, be it a murder or a bank robbery or a prison break, but seem totally incapable of giving the same thought and interest to the day-to-day job of living successfully within society.

Another escape from Leavenworth is a case in point. This escape involved five men, led by a felon named Murdock. Murdock, employed in the prison woodworking shop, was a skilled wood-carver and an observant and imaginative man. On smoke breaks in the prison yard, Murdock had noticed the routine of the main gate. There were two gates, and theoretically they were never open at the same time. When someone was leaving the prison, the inner gate was opened, and the outer gate wasn't supposed to be opened until that inner gate was closed again. But the guards operating the gates had been employed in that job too long, with never a hint of an attempted escape. As a result, Murdock noticed that the button opening the outer gate was often pushed before the inner gate was completely closed, and that once the button was pushed, the gate had to open completely before it could be closed again.

This one fact, plus his wood-carving abilities, was the nucleus of Murdock's escape plan. He discussed his plans with four other convicts, convinced them that it was workable, and they decided to go ahead with it. Murdock, working slowly and cautiously, managed to hide five small pieces of wood in the shop where he worked. Taking months over the job, he carved these pieces of wood into exact replicas of .38-caliber pistols, down to the safety catch and the trigger guard, then distributed them among his confederates.

The day and the time finally came. A delivery truck was leaving the prison while Murdock and the other four were with a group of prisoners on a smoke break in the yard. Murdock saw the outer gate opening before the inner gate was completely closed. He shouted out the prearranged word signal and ran for the gate, the other four with him. They squeezed through just before the inner gate closed all the way and Murdock, brandishing his dummy pistol, warned the guards not to reopen it. The five dashed through the open outer gate and scattered.

This much planning and imagination they had given to the job of *getting* out. How much planning and imagination did they give to the job of *staying* out? Murdock himself, the ringleader, was the first one captured, less than twenty-four hours later. He was found, shivering and miserable, standing waist-deep in water in a culvert. A second was found the following morning, cowering in a barn, and numbers three and four were rounded up before the week was out.

The fifth? He was the exception. It took the authorities nearly twenty years to find him, and when they did, they discovered he had become the mayor of a small town in Canada. His record since his escape from Leavenworth was spotless, and so he was left to live out his new life in peace.

The courage and daring, the ingenuity and imagination, the skill and talent demonstrated in these and similar escapes, if used in the interests of society rather than directed against society, would undoubtedly make such men as these among society's most valuable citizens. But the challenge is given these men, and they accept that challenge. They are not challenged to use their talents to *benefit* society, but to *outwit* society.

In fact, there seems to be a correlation between rigidity of control and attempts to escape. The tighter the control, the stronger and more secure and solid the prison, the more escape plans there will be, the more attempted escapes, and the more successful escapes.

The career of Jack Sheppard, probably the most famous despoiler of "escape-proof" prisons of all time, is a clear-cut demonstration of this. In one five-month period in 1724, Sheppard escaped from Newgate, England's "impregnable" prison, no less than three times! The first time, he had help from inside the prison, which is probably the easiest and most common type of jailbreak. The second time, he had tools and assistance from outside, a little more difficult but obviously not impossible. The *third* time, without tools and absolutely unaided, he successfully completed one of the most daring and complex escapes in history.

Sheppard, born in 1701 and wanted as a highwayman and murderer before he was out of his teens, was first jailed in Newgate in May of 1724. When arrested, he had been with a girlfriend, Bess Lion, who was also wanted by the police. They swore they were married and so, in the manner of that perhaps freer day, they were locked together in the same cell. Bess had managed to smuggle a hacksaw in with her—history doesn't record how—and as soon as the two were alone, they attacked the bars of the window. But it was a twenty-five-foot drop to the prison yard, and the rope ladder they made of their blankets didn't reach far enough. So Bess removed her clothes, which were added to the ladder, and they made their way down to the yard, nude girl first. Bess rolled her clothes into a bundle, and she and Sheppard climbed over a side gate which was no longer in use. Bess put her clothes back on, and the two of them walked away.

He was recaptured almost immediately, returned to Newgate, and this time held long enough to be tried for his crimes and sentenced to be hanged. The day before the scheduled hanging, he was brought, chained and manacled, to the visitors' cell. His visitors were Bess Lion and another girlfriend, Poll Maggott. While Bess "distracted" the guard—history is somewhat vague on this point, too—Poll and Sheppard sawed through the bars separating them, and Poll, described as a "large" woman, picked Sheppard up and carried him bodily out of the prison, since the ankle chains made it difficult for him to walk.

That was July of 1724. Two months later, Sheppard was captured for the third time and once more found himself in Newgate. This time, the authorities were determined not to let him escape. He was allowed no visitors. After a whole kit of escape tools was found hidden in his cell, he was moved to a special room known as The Castle. This room was windowless, in the middle of the prison, and with a securely locked double door. There was no furniture, nothing but a single blanket. Sheppard's wrists were manacled, and his ankles chained, with the ankle chain slipped through an iron bolt embedded in the floor.

Sheppard, at this time, was twenty-three years of age. He was short, weak, sickly, suffering from both a venereal disease and too steady a diet of alcohol. His physical condition, plus the manacles and the placement of his cell, seemed to make escape absolutely impossible.

Sheppard waited until October 14th, when the opening of Sessions Court was guaranteed to keep the prison staff too busy to be thinking about a prisoner as securely confined as himself. On that morning, he made his move.

First, he grasped in his teeth the chain linking the wrist manacles, squeezed and folded his hands to make them as small as possible, and finally succeeded in slipping them through the cuffs, removing some skin in the process. He then grabbed the ankle chain and with a single twisting jerk, managed to break the link holding him to the bolt in the floor.

He now had a tool, the one broken link. Wrapping the ankle chains around his legs, to get them out of the way, he used the broken link to attack one wall, where a former fireplace had obviously been sealed up. He broke through to the fireplace, only to discover an iron bar, a yard long and an inch square, bisecting the flue a few feet up, making a space too small for him to slip by.

Undaunted, he made a second hole in the wall, at the point where he estimated the bar to be, found it and freed it, and now had two tools as well as an escape hatch. He crawled up the flue to the floor above, broke through another wall, and emerged into an empty cell. Finding a rusty nail on the floor—for tool number three—he picked the door lock with it, and found himself in a corridor. At the end of the corridor he came to a door bolted and hinged on the other side. He made a small hole in the wall beside the door, reached through and released the lock.

The third door, leading to the prisoners' pen in the chapel, he popped open with the iron bar. The fourth door got the same treatment, and now he came to a flight of stairs leading upward. He knew his only chance for escape lay in reaching the roof.

This sixth door was fastened with a foot-wide iron-plated bar, attached to door and frame by thick iron hoops, plus a large iron bolt lock, plus a padlock, and the whole affair was crisscrossed with iron bars bolted to the oak on either side of the door.

Sheppard had now been four hours in the escape. He was exhausted, his hands were bleeding, the weight of the leg shackles was draining his energy, and the door in front of him was obviously impassable. Nevertheless, Sheppard went to work on it, succeeding at first only in bending the iron bar he was using for a tool.

It took him two hours, but he finally managed to rip the crossed bars down and snap the bolt lock, making it possible to remove the main bar, and he stepped out onto the prison roof.

So far, the escape had taken six hours. It was now almost sundown. Sheppard crossed the roof and saw the roof of a private house next door, twenty feet below him. He was afraid to risk the jump, not wanting to get this far only to lie down there with a broken ankle and wait for the prison officials to come drag him back. So, regretfully, he turned around, recrossed the roof, went down the stairs and through the chapel, back down the corridor and into the cell above The Castle, down the fireplace flue and *back into his cell*, which was ankle deep in stone and plaster from the crumbled wall. He picked up his blanket, retraced his steps again, and went back to the roof. He had forgotten tool number four, and so he had simply gone back for it!

Atop the prison again, Sheppard ripped the blanket into strips, made a rope ladder, and lowered himself to the roof of the house next door. He waited there until he was sure the occupants had gone to sleep for the night, then he crept down through the house and out to freedom.

In the ordinary manner of escapees, however, Sheppard could never learn to devote as much energy to *staying* out as to *getting* out. He spent the first four days hidden in a cowshed, until finally someone came along who would bring him a hacksaw and help him shed the ankle chains. He then went straight home, where he and his mother celebrated his escape by getting drunk together on brandy. They were still drunk when the authorities showed up, and this time Sheppard stayed in Newgate long enough to meet the hangman.

Here is the core of the problem. The tougher the prison officials made their prison—the more they challenged Sheppard and told him that this time he *couldn't* escape—the more determined and daring and ingenious Sheppard became.

This misdirected genius was never more evident than in the ten-man escape from Walla Walla State Penitentiary in Washington State in 1955. Their escape route was a tunnel under the main wall, but one tunnel wasn't enough for them. They also had tunnel routes between their cells, so they could communicate and pass materials and information back and forth. When they were recaptured—which, in the traditional manner, didn't take very long at all—the full extent of their ingenuity and daring was discovered. Each of the ten carried a briefcase containing a forged draft card, business cards, a driver's license, birth certificate and even credit cards and charge-account cards for stores in Seattle. Beyond all this, they all carried identification cards claiming them as officials of the Washington State prison system, and letters of recommendation from state officials, including the warden of the Walla Walla State Penitentiary. And four of the escapees carried forged state paychecks, in amounts totaling over a thousand dollars. Every bit of the work involved had been done in the prison shops.

Compare this with the record of a jail such as the so-called "model prison" at Chino, California. Escaping from Chino is almost incredibly easy. There is a fence, but no wall, and the fence would be no barrier to a man intent on getting away. The guards are few, the locks fewer, much of the prisoners' work is done outdoors, and the surrounding area is mostly wooded hills. For a man determined to escape, Chino would offer no challenge at all.

And yet, Chino has had practically no escapes at all!

Perhaps the lack of challenge is itself the reason why there are so few escapes from Chino. The cage in which the prisoner must live is not an obvious cage at Chino. He is restricted, but the restrictions are subtle, and he is not surrounded by stone and iron reminders of his shackled condition. At tougher, more security-conscious prisons, the challenge is flung in the convict's face. "You *cannot* escape from here!" Inevitably there are those who accept the challenge.

The challenge at Chino—and at other prisons constructed from much the same philosophy—is far different. "You *should* not escape from here! And when you know *why* society demands that you stay here, you won't need to escape. You will be released."

Both challenges demand of the prisoner that he think, that he use his mind, his wit and his imagination. But whereas the one challenge encourages him to think along lines that will drive him yet further from society, the other challenge encourages him to think along lines that will adjust him to society.

No matter which challenge it is, there will always be men to accept it, as the warden of Walla Walla State Penitentiary—from which the ten convicts escaped with their forged-card-bulging briefcases—inadvertently proved, back in 1952. He gave the prisoners a special dinner one day in that year, in honor of the fact that a full year had gone by without the digging of a single tunnel. Three days later, during a normal shakedown, guards found a tunnel one hundred feet long.

LOVE STUFF, COPS-AND-ROBBERS STYLE

This was first published in the *Los Angeles Times* on May 7, 1972.—Ed.

The gangster is coming back. To the movies, that is; in real life, he never went away. But in the motion picture, after dominating the screen throughout the '30s and into the '40s, the mob departed, muscled out by—something, I forget what. And now at last they're coming back.

But with a difference. The crooks are no longer quite what they used to be. The crime movies way back when were built on the headlines of the time, of course, based on the Dillingers and the Capones of that era, but somehow the people were altered in translation and came out totally unlike anybody who had ever trod this earth. Something Runyonesque occurred, and both the crooks and the society they lived in became jauntier, stronger, better.

You could always trust a deathbed confession, for instance; if Humphrey Bogart said the kid wasn't in on the jailbreak, the warden took his word for it and the kid went free. Edward G. Robinson might try to bump off a tough DA, but it would never occur to him to try to buy him off. And James Cagney might rob banks for a living, but he'd die before he'd turn over secret military information to a foreign power; he was a crook, yes, but he was an American crook.

And like all the rest of the movie crooks of that time, he had a tough line of patter and a fast right hand and a lot of self-reliance, and if he finally had to walk that Last Mile, he did it with his head up and his shoulders back.

But not only the crooks were better than life in those movies; the whole world was. The DA really didn't take bribes. Reporters loved their jobs so much they constantly risked death to bring in the story. Justices of the peace would put on a ratty bathrobe and marry a sweet young couple on the lam at any hour of the night. And when the bank robbers got to the bank there was a parking space out front.

The people in those movies also had a language all their own, never heard anywhere other than a sound stage. All their sentences, for example, began with the word "say," as in, "Say, you can't get away with that." Or, "Say, that's a pretty snazzy heap you got there." Or, at particularly important turns, "Say, don't I know you from someplace?"

Well, all things do come to an end, and sometime around World War II the boys all turned legit. Robinson suddenly showed up as an insurance investigator, Cagney metamorphosed into Yankee Doodle Dandy, and Bogart came twitching back as—an assistant district attorney.

Be that as it may. Wherever they went, and for whatever reason, something broke up that old gang of ours, and the screen was a blander place without them. But now, at long last, they do seem to be coming back.

Though with a difference. Things never do return exactly as they were before. What would Edward G. Robinson's Rico, for instance, think of Warren Beatty's Clyde? Akim Tamiroff once played a syndicate boss named Steve Recka, who played the organ in moments of stress, who lived with his Oriental mistress (Anna May Wong), and whose downfall was caused by his futile love for a girl from the upper classes; the level of romance in Don Corleone is pretty well summed up by his style of overcoat.

The fact is, the romance has gone out of our lives, and we aren't going to believe anybody who claims otherwise. For example, I wrote a comic robbery novel a couple of years ago called *The Hot Rock*, which was recently turned into a movie. At one point in the film the crooks use a helicopter, and director Peter Yates had a grand time showing the helicopter moving among the skyscrapers of Manhattan.

Most of the people who've talked to me about that picture say they loved that sequence, and I think I know why. It's almost the only romantic moment in the whole film, and by the time it comes along the audience already knows these crooks are simply ordinary shmos trying to make a living like anybody else; romance when it does happen is accidental and incidental and a happy surprise, as in life. The audience is pleased for the characters because they've been given a good moment, which is still possible for any of us, and therefore both hopeful and believable.

So although the crooks are coming back, they aren't quite the same breezy glib semi-indestructible crew they were the last time around. Organized crime, whether treated seriously as in *The Godfather* or comically as in *The Gang That Couldn't Shoot Straight*, is simply a business these days, operated by businessmen with business problems to resolve; nothing at all like the Cagney-Bogart business partnership in *The Roaring Twenties*, brought to an end by trouble over a girl singer (a "chantoozie," as the boys used to say).

And the big robbery, too, has changed. Whether done seriously as in *The Split* or comically as in *The Hot Rock*, the boys are no longer anything at all like the tough loner of *High Sierra* who was pulling one last job to get the money for a crippled girl's operation. The thieves, too, are businessmen these days, small independent businessmen trying to survive in the era of the major corporation.

Does the return of the crook to the motion picture mean that America is becoming more crooked than it used to be, or that Americans will start to turn crooked by the thousands after seeing these movies? I think just the reverse is true; we have more laws this year than we had last year, and several thousand more laws are on the books now than existed before World War II. We're so law-abiding we're strangling in all the rules and regulations, and it's a respite and a relief for all of us to see contemporaries of ours who survive somehow outside the law's crushing grip.

So even in a deromanticized world, even as a businessman among businessmen, the crook still has one advantage over most heroes of fiction. Stepping outside society, operating without regard for those proliferating rules that hem in the rest of us, he is in one of the few businesses where romance can still happen. Not as frequently as when gang members were putting their kid brothers through medical school, but sometimes they do get that occasional helicopter ride. And we get to ride along with them.

SEND IN THE GOONS

This essay was first published in the *Washington Post Magazine* on July 18, 1999. Attentive Westlake fans will notice that the opening paragraphs describe an experience that Westlake gave to his protagonist in his 1962 novel *361*.—Ed.

In November 1957 I completed my enlistment in the U.S. Air Force. I had been stationed the last year and a half in Germany, at Ramstein Air Base, and I was very ready to go home. There's a lot good to be said for the military, but from that point on I preferred to say it from a distance.

I left Germany on a cold and sunny day, flying by Military Air Transport Service to McGuire Air Force Base in New Jersey, from where I would be bused to Manhattan Beach Air Force Station at the southern end of Brooklyn (the military at times has trouble getting names right) to receive my discharge papers. I was looking forward to it.

At that time, most planes did not cross the Atlantic in one hop, but stopped somewhere to refuel. It seems to me Goose Bay in Labrador was the most frequent stopover, but in this case we went to the Azores, a rather grim sheaf of volcano tips jutting out of the middle of the ocean and claiming to be part of Portugal, although the rest of Portugal is a thousand miles away.

When we arrived and deplaned—a couple hundred passengers, a mixed bag of officers and enlistees and family members, already a little travel-scuffed, expecting a wait of an hour or so while the plane was being refueled—we were told that a major storm had descended on the east coast of the North American continent and had closed every airport from Florida north. We would have to stay in transit barracks here in the Azores until the storm went somewhere else.

Remember, I was on my way to get my walking papers from the Air Force, an event I was looking forward to and which would happen promptly at journey's end, as soon as the damned journey ended. How long are we going to be stuck here in the Azores? Nobody knew.

I don't suppose anybody on the plane was really happy about this turn of events. There were families aboard with little children. There were staff-level officers who'd always assumed they were more important than weather. There were grunts going home on leave. And there was me, who would become a civilian just as soon as ever I got to Manhattan Beach.

I don't want to say anything bad about an ally, and I presume Portugal is still an ally, but the Azores are never, ever going to be mistaken for Club Med. The weather, probably the leading edge of my friend the storm, was overcast and clammy. The landscape was vertical and dour, darkly jagged, unfit for human occupancy, rather like a Bronte novel without the characters. If there were a Michelin guide to the place, it would consist of one word: Don't.

CHAPTER ELEVEN

We orphans of the storm were restricted to a transit camp under the control of the Portuguese army, which was mostly short wide guys in dark uniforms who looked like they came out of one of those barroom scenes from *Star Wars*. There was nothing to do, nowhere to go, nothing to see, and we single enlistees were housed in the kind of cots-in-rows vast open dormitory usually reserved for winos of a certain age. It was the kind of place where nobody wants to wind up, certainly not at twenty-four. (I'll try not to mention the food.)

Also, none of us had packed for an extended stay. Most of my stuff had been mailed home, and I was traveling light. Socks and underwear I could wash, but I very quickly ran out of anything to read. And now what?

Just sit there, little boy blue, that's what, sit there and count your fingers. And the days. We spent a night, and then we spent another night. The storm, meanwhile, continued to spend all its time on the Eastern Seaboard.

We people of the plane were not a cohesive group. We'd never met before, had nothing in common but irritation, and would have been happy to see one another's backs. So I assure you there were no impromptu softball games, no glee clubs were formed, and not one photo of a wife or girlfriend was passed around. No one suggested reunions. Each of us merely simmered in his or her own private stew.

It was worse than Alcatraz. At least if you were there, you'd be able to see San Francisco out over the water, and there was always that one chance in a million you might actually swim to that city across the bay; I'd take those odds, or I would have then.

But in the Azores, what? You make a break for it and jump in the water and if the ocean doesn't throw you right back onto a volcano, what do you do? The nearest land is a thousand miles away, and that's Portugal. Manhattan Beach Air Force Station is 2,400 miles the other way.

Frustration, impatience, boredom; I would say that this was not one of the high points of my life.

On the afternoon of our third day—I'm supposed to be home by now, in clothing of my own choice—I had found some kind of old magazine somewhere and had sat on my cot to try to find something of interest in it, or at least something bearable, when a guy half a dozen cots away switched on a radio. Oh, now, that's the last straw, I thought. Now I gotta listen to somebody's tinny little radio.

It was AFN he had tuned to, the Armed Forces Network, American radio for the troops overseas, which was being beamed to us, the lost patrol, somewhere at sea. Unwillingly I listened, because when there's a radio on you have no choice but to listen, and I was beginning to think that maybe a good fistfight would clear the air. Bust that radio over that clown's head, mix it up with a couple Air Police, get thrown into a Portuguese brig, duke it out with a few of them for a while, work it all out of my system. Self-destruction therapy: Why not?

But then I was snagged by a bit of dialogue:

"How is her ladyship at the moment?"

"Her lady doesn't have a ship at the moment."

What? Unwillingly, I paid attention.

The show seemed to be British, with an inspector questioning Lady Marks about the disappearance of her son, Fred Nurke, the scene ending as the inspector says, "Just leave everything to me—your furs, jewels, checkbook, ginger glass eye, war bonds, trombones . . ."

What? Next, in a shipping office, the inspector is told that Fred Nurke left for Guatemala on a banana boat, disguised as a banana, but left this banana behind. Seizing on the banana, the inspector triumphantly cries, "Now I know I'm looking for a man who's one banana short!" Great cheers from the studio audience, and a segue to a jazzy version of "You're Driving Me Crazy" from a bouncy combo backing a lead harmonica.

What? This was the most stupid, the most ridiculous, the most asinine thing I'd ever heard in my life. I was too angry and too upset and too thwarted by life to have to put up with nonsense like this.

Back with the story, if that isn't too grand a word for it, the inspector is now in Guatemala, talking with a rebel who intends to search him, because any foreigner found hiding a banana on his person "will be shot by a firing squad and asked to leave the country." The inspector draws his banana and aims it: "You can't fire a banana!" (BANG!) "You swine! It was loaded!"

Oh, please, I shouldn't have had to listen to this. What I should have done, short of mayhem, is gotten out of there, gone outside, looked for a wall to throw stones at.

Somehow, the inspector is in a prison cell where "the only other occupant was another occupant." The two decide to escape by piling chairs one atop another to reach the high window. As we hear them begin, an announcer tells us that fifty to a hundred chairs will have to be piled up before our friends can reach that high window, so in the meantime here's a song by Cyril Cringenut. A terrible version of "Three Coins in the Fountain" follows, interrupted when the announcer tells us the chairs have now all been piled, he interrupted by cries and crashes, followed by another run at "Three Coins in the Fountain."

Oh, why go on? It did go on, like that, as brain-dead as ever, and why was I laughing? I didn't feel like laughing, I felt like being sorry for myself. So why did I no longer want to conk the radio owner on the noggin with his radio? Why couldn't I bring myself to leave here and find someplace private where I could sulk in peace and quiet?

And where are we now? "On the grounds of the British Embassy our heroes are dug in around the lone banana tree, the last symbol of waning British prestige in South America." But not for long. Pretty soon, the inspector is alone, tied to a chair in the remote rebel headquarters deep in the jungle, and the phone rings. The phone rings, all right? And if that isn't enough, deep in the jungle, the tied-up inspector answers it: "This is Fred Nurke, and this is my banana night. In three seconds a time bomb explodes in your room!"

And so, with the roars of explosions and the rasp of the banana tree being sawed down, the fastest and most lunatic half-hour of radio I'd ever heard crashed to a close, to be replaced by something more normal and less interesting. But that was all right; I didn't need any more. Somehow, I felt a whole lot better than I had thirty minutes before. Day Three in the Azores, and I was smiling.

I asked the guy with the radio what that show had been, but he didn't know. He'd just switched the radio on to see what was there. I knew the station was AFN, but the AFN I'd listened to in Germany had never broadcast a program like that. I would have noticed.

Whatever it had been, it had done its job. I was calm, I was patient, I was even cheerful. The storm clouds had cleared from my brow.

And the next day, they cleared from America as well. We all climbed back aboard our plane, I did finally get to Manhattan Beach Air Force Station and out of uniform, and life went on.

But over the years, from time to time, I found myself wondering anew: What in the world was that show? Maybe nothing in the world. Maybe, instead of AFN, that little radio there in the Azores had picked up a broadcast from Mars. That was a better explanation than most.

It was a decade or so before the mystery was solved, when first I heard about *The Goon Show*, the utterly daft (British for "wacko") BBC series from the '50s written by Spike Milligan and starring Milligan with Peter Sellers (that's where he started) and Harry Secombe (that's where he finished). The episode I'd heard was called "The Affair of the Lone Banana," and a few years ago, in London, I found that the BBC had put *The Goon Show*, including "The Affair of the Lone Banana," onto audiocassette.

Obviously, I now own it. You never know when the Azores are going to reenter your life. Every once in a while, medicinally, I listen to it again:

"Headstone, you're a footman."

"Two-foot-six, to be precise."

"How lovely to be tall."

I don't want to get all misty-eyed here about the beneficial effects of humor. I'll leave that to Preston Sturges, who, at the end of his movie *Sullivan's Travels*, had Joel McCrea say, "There's a lot to be said for making people laugh. Did you know that's all some people have? It isn't much, but it's better than nothing in this cockeyed caravan."

Right on. I don't suppose *The Goon Show* has ever been accused of saving anybody's sanity before, but in my case, that's pretty much what happened.

TWELVE SIGNED CONFESSIONS

Letters

Donald Westlake wrote a lot of letters. His files are full of business letters, personal letters, and responses to fans—all typed neatly, and nearly all of them revealing his light-fingered approach to hotel stationery. (The best hotel stationery in the batch? From the Hotel Dead Indian, in Dead Indian, Illinois, birthplace of John Dortmunder. The genius who sent him that gag gift? Tabitha King.)

Westlake almost never failed to get at least one joke into a letter, and I'll admit to including a couple here solely for their humor. The others I've selected because they shed light on his thinking about his work, the work of others, or the writing process.

In some cases I have made excisions rather than reprinting the whole of a letter. The excised portions, marked by ellipses, dealt in detail with uninteresting business matters, referred in a complicated fashion to recent interactions, or are simply inexplicable without reference to the whole of the correspondence. The occasional bracketed interpolations are my own.—Ed.

TO JUDY ?

Judy (last name unknown) was an assistant in Westlake's UK agent's office.—Ed.

February 20, 1999
Judy,

I feel this may not be the last chapter of this story, which is why I'm sending you copies of everything so far, except of course my initial phone call to Lawrence Chance pointing out the problems. (I love it that the guy who deals with residuals and royalties at the Guild is named Lawrence Chance.) (I believe his brother is Fat.)

Don

TO PETER GRUBER

Peter Gruber was professor of English at SUNY-Binghamton.—Ed.

November 17, 1981
Dear Pete,

Enclosed please find my weird play.

We had a grand time last night. Apart from anything else, it was lovely just to make contact with Ellen again, and to marvel at how thoroughly she has not changed in twenty-two years. Jesus!

I read the Creative Writing thingy, and of course it does strangle on its own contradictions; as it must, I suppose. The contradiction stands out most clearly at the top of pages 2 and 3. On page 2, what is called "pop" fiction, also defined as "the widely published" and "money-making," is cast into the outer darkness. On page 3, top paragraph, poor W. Shakespeare is called upon to shlep it back in again. How "art" can "return to the community" without being "widely published" or even (whisper this) making money I know not.

Of course, this isn't one program here, it's two programs—fiction and poetry. In poetry there's no real choice, is there? The poet has a vocation in poetry, but he also has a job somewhere, or a rich family, or a wife with good job-market skills. In fiction, though, the choice is still open; it can be a hobby, or it can be a career. So I guess each person has to decide which way to go, then choose the education or preparation that's appropriate. An honest writing program would say either, "You will learn here how to make a living as a storyteller," or, "You will learn here how to enhance your leisure hours by refining the uniqueness of your storytelling talents."

I like to think of myself as being in a profession, which of course implies that it can be taught. Doctors, lawyers, accountants, journalists, engineers, dentists, even teachers can go to a university and be taught their profession without anybody for a second being embarrassed by the undeniable truth: These kids are going to take this knowledge and try to turn it into money.

Sex, sports and writing are the three fields where it is considered somehow a fall from grace to accept money for doing what you're good at. (At the other extreme, I have a plumber who's happy to take my money, and he isn't even *good* at what he does.) I think writing program people are afraid of being tarnished with that brother image, which also combines with the notion that their field is an *art*, goddammit, and they don't want to have to think of themselves as teaching shop. But are they teaching shop in law school?

And the word "art" gets bandied about a lot, doesn't it? An individual's sensibility is engaged upon a specific subject; a medium (writing, painting, whatever) is selected; a level of craft or technical knowledge or expertise is employed; the result is invariably art. Which doesn't mean it's invariably good. Crappy art is still art. And where in that series of steps is there a role for a teacher? In the individual sensibility? Of course not. In the subject to be chosen, or the medium to be chosen? Only in the most shallow and insubstantial way. In the level of available craft? Ah *hah*!

To suggest, as this brochure does, that "art" can be taught is an absurdity on the face of it, rather as though a medical school offered a course in post-operative recovery.

Is a university an appropriate place to teach a profession? Of course. Is it an appropriate place to teach an avocation?

Maybe what it comes down to is, it's a holding pattern for poets. As the monasteries of the Middle Ages kept alive valuable human learning through the time of darkness, the universities of today shall succor the poets until a better age shall find a use for them. Of course, one couldn't quite say that out loud, particularly when fund-raising or justifying a teaching program's existence, which is why I guess people suddenly find that their tongues are all elbows.

A million bucks does seem a little steep to keep poets from having to knock over liquor stores, but I guess it's okay. Only what does it have to do with *teaching writing*?

How rapidly I have become a curmudgeon. Talk to you soon.

Don

TO JAMES HALE

James Hale was an editor and also served as Westlake's UK agent for a few years.—Ed.

April 20, 1978
Dear James,

Enclosed, if I have my wits about me, is the short-story manuscript called "The Girl of My Dreams," which I am submitting to you for *The 14th Ghost Book*. If it's wrong, or inept, or not-quite, or unsuitable for whatever reason, don't send the thing back to me. Do with it as you would with any fairly soft pieces of waste paper.

My understanding from our phone conversation—we may be going mad, you know—is that I am keeping for myself magazine rights, for one magazine appearance subsequent to the publication of the book.

The real trick, of course, if we're going to deal with the eerie and the supernatural, would be for me to get a story *now* into *The 12th Ghost Book*. And next year into *The 11th Ghost Book*. And the year after that . . . And the year after that . . .

My favorite story from #13, by the way, was "The Uninvited." Charming story, charming idea, charming character.

Drawrof,

Don

TO STEPHEN AND TABITHA KING

The following selection is from a letter sent just over a year after Stephen King, out walking, was nearly killed by an out-of-control driver behind the wheel of a van. (King offers a gripping account of the story of the accident and his recovery in his *On Writing*.)—Ed.

July 23, 2000
Dear Steve and Tabby,

It was wonderful to see you both again. On the other hand, Steve, it affected us all strongly how much you're going through and how powerfully you're dealing with it. Steve Sorman was talking about it in the car afterward. He has been hospitalized for meningitis, getting him in there two hours before death, and a few years later, as a belated result, back in for a heart valve transplant, and what he said was that the guy who already had somebody to be and to do, like you (and like him), has a better chance of true survival than somebody who previously was not much more than a wage earner and a dinner consumer who now has nothing to say beyond gee-look-what-happened-to-me. Steve is a painter and a graphic artist, and I can remember him, a big guy reduced to a beached whale, saying, "All I wanna do is get back in that goddam studio."

As you will recall, the next day after we saw you, Saturday, garden tour day, included a certain amount of rain. Abby and Melissa and Steve squished around seven gardens while I sat in the car and read, so we all had a good time. . . .

Oh, all right, what was I reading. Proust, through no fault of my own. Years ago, Abby and a few women friends started a reading group, going through Dickens and Trollope and so on. (We called them the Trollopes then.) Then they branched into nineteenth-century French, and one evening Abby was flinching and gasping and moaning while reading, and I knew *I* wasn't having anything to do with it, so I asked her what was happening, and she said, "This is the most exciting novel I ever read in my life." *Germinal*, by Zola; down the coal mines, nineteenth century. With that recommendation, I had to read it, and she was right. You will never meet a character as close to rock bottom as the lead of that book on its opening page. And then he gets going.

Anyway, after that, I watched her read, for clues, and when she started laughing a lot I said, "Now what are you reading?" and she said, "Proust," and I said, "*Proust?*"

So she and her four companions romped through Proust, then, this May, they went to France for ten days for a Proustian tour, and now they read everything *about* Proust, and I am once again trailing in their wake. I've done the first volume, Swann and all that, and now the second, the Budding Grove, and once I adapted to the idea that he had no passing gear everything was fine. Some of the stuff is, in fact, very funny.

Your lovely Harry [Potter] review in today's *Times* has convinced me. The next time I'm twelve, I'm going to read those books; the rate I'm going, it won't be long. . . .

Abby will be writing you and sending you a book. As for me, I'm going to get this out in the morning's mail and then do chores. *Tomorrow* I work. Honest to God.

Be well. Be better. Be yourselves. As you said to me the first time I met you, years ago at Tavern on the Green, don't die.

Don

TO BRIAN GARFIELD

November 11, 1985
Dear Brian,

As soon as I turned my back, the people doing *The Stepfather* did the very worst thing you can do to a movie, any movie. (It was, for instance, the worst thing that was done to *Reds*.) They tried to earlier and I fought them back, and I believed I'd won that one, and they patted me on the back, and said, "Terrific, Don, everything's fine, we'll go to Vancouver and shoot the movie now, you just go on to New York and don't worry about a thing." I *thought* I heard them giggling behind my back, but I figured that was just paranoia. What I forgot—briefly—was that paranoia is the clearest view of reality. They did it, you know, they did the worst thing that can possibly be done to a movie.

They added a puppy. . . .

You know, when I started, it was just sit at the typewriter, try to think of stories and dialogue and motivations and all that, then go down to the Post Office from time to time. Who knew? You know what I mean? Who the fuck knew?

For instance. The new Dortmunder being sold through the Nieman-Marcus catalog. A coup, right? Special edition, boxed, five months before regular publication. So I signed a thousand and forty-six—one thousand, plus the alphabet, plus twenty to allow for problems—and they sold ninety-seven the first two days, and then one of the ninety-seven phoned the store and told them Nieman-Marcus was misspelled on the page I'd signed.

Fucking busybody.

Well, Nieman-Marcus did *not* laugh it off, so I have now signed 1,046 big thick *labels* that won't fool anybody, that have to be inserted into the existing books down there in Dallas by a lot of illegal immigrant slave labor that never before in their *lives* have been asked to line up two pieces of paper and make sure they're both right side up.

Kee-rist on a crutch,

Don

TO DAVID RAMUS

This is Westlake's response to the the first part of the manuscript of what would become Ramus's first novel, *On Ice.*—Ed.

September 29, 1998
Dear David,

I finally got to read the ms. I had to go to New York Sunday, coming back Monday, and I read it on the trains, which is where I seem to do most of my reading.

Your primary question is whether or not your hero is believable with the background you gave him, and the answer is yes. I had no trouble accepting that. Who he used to be as an art maven doesn't show.

However. You could improve the portrayal a bit, I think, and you have to beef up one part of his motivation. Before I get to it, let me tell you briefly about my first editor, Lee Wright at Random House, who is still the best editor I ever had. She told me once that she would never say something was wrong in a novel unless she could make a suggestion for an alternate way, not to say "do it this way" but to say "there's more than one way, here's a second, maybe here's a third." So I'm following her dictum, making suggestions for illustration only.

I think you can improve the reader's grasp of Ben Hemmings by having other people say what they think of him. Not a lot, maybe two or three times in the book. But for instance, when Grace, on the boat, tells him he doesn't look like an ex-con, he could *ask* her what do I look like, and she could say something along the lines of "You look like a carnival roughneck, but a nice one, who'd let a poor kid sneak in." But earlier than that, possibly with Grantham, who could tell him how he'd look to a jury.

The other thing is, toward the latter part of what I read, his motivation seemed to be to get the five mil, and if that happens, you lose the reader's sympathy. The motivation is to get out from under. If he gets out with a lot of money, that's nice, but the point is to get out. He could tell us, but not Black, for instance, that if he fails to get the money but still gets out from under, that's okay, too, though he knows that might make Black unhappy.

Next point. If you tell us something twice, it's a plot plant. When Black mentions that FBI men never work alone but Partone is working alone, that's the second time I've been told that, and now I know Partone is a rogue, not doing the government's work but his own.

Now a minor point. We all do clinkers from time to time, and yours is on page 22, eighth line from the bottom. I think what you want to say is "I could count on my fingers the number of times she cried."

Now I also think you need to do a little tweaking of story procedure, how you unfold it for us. Page 52 was way too late to introduce a flashback and then let the flashback wander. You say you're going to tell us about the first time Ben met Dana, and then you tell us a bunch of other stuff for eight pages. I am very impatient during all this. I don't mind leaving prison to go to court, but if I'm leaving court, by this point in the story I want to get back to prison. My suggestion here is, make the flashback a separate chapter, make it chapter 4, then juke the other even-numbered chapters forward until it's realigned. (It wouldn't be quite that easy, of course, it would take some reconstructive surgery, but I do believe it would help.)

I wanted to tell you that the business about the prison phone is just terrific. Terrific.

Now a tiny moment when you nodded. On page 99 Ben looks at the watch he wasn't wearing on 97 when McGee searched him.

Finally, I have one absolute objection. We do not overhear plot points. No no no. He just happens to be standing here when somebody standing over there says the stuff he needed to know. No. But if Ben wanted to know what was going on, and felt it was important, he could put himself at risk to *deliberately* eavesdrop. Almost get caught.

Anyway, it's a lovely devious book, and I'm looking forward to reading the rest of it and seeing it in print. And don't worry about Ben; I'd hire him to build me a barn any day.

Don

In his grateful reply, Ramus wrote, "I had to hold the ms in one hand because I was busy slapping my forehead with the other. I was also muttering, 'Of course . . . Of course. . . '"—Ed.

TO PAM VESEY

Pam Vesey was the copyeditor for M. Evans and Company working on *Brothers Keepers.*—Ed.

February 24, 1975
Dear Pam,

I don't intend to get into a thing here like Brian with his commas, but I do want to rise to say a word or two for the semicolon. It does exist as a tool of punctuation in written English prose, and is just as respectable as any other piece of punctuation you can think of; goes to church on Sundays and all the rest of it.

In fact, my *Random House Dictionary* goes so far as to define it. "The punctuation mark used to indicate a major division in a sentence where a more distinct separation is felt between clauses or items on a list than is indicated by a comma, as between the two clauses of a compound sentence."

I point out in that definition the phrase "is felt," and I suggest that the individual doing the feeling is presumed to be the writer. I point out the phrase "more distinct separation," and I suggest that the purpose of the semicolon is at least in part rhythmic.

My own rhythms tend to be long ones, and I grant you that as a result I tend to over-use the semicolon, but *some* of them are right, and in most instances (in this book and others) the copyeditor's alternative is less correct. Breaking the offending sentence into two sentences is grammatically correct but often rhythmically wrong. Replacing the semicolon with a colon is correct only if a list or a new sentence follows the punctuation, in which case (a) I would probably have used a colon myself, and (b) a double space should follow, as it follows a period. Replacing the colon with a dash is *never* right, since dashes, except in speech—in which they indicate a break in the flow—must always appear in pairs. The function of the dash in ordinary prose is identical to—but less formal than—the function of the parenthesis.

Why does everybody hate the poor semicolon? It's nice; it's useful; it's even rather pretty.

Second topic. I have added a page to the very end of the book. It didn't seem right to end on a downer, so I brought Brother Benedict home and showed him happy. (The new material contains a semicolon; it has orders to call me if anybody gives it any trouble.)

Yours in Strunk,
Don

TO GARY SALT

What follows are selections from Don's correspondence with his West Coast agent, Gary Salt.—Ed.

July 22, 1994
Dear Gary,

Personally, I've always found Sherlock Holmes a self-important, humorless drug addict, a Henry Higgins without redeeming features, and I also believe he was wrong half the time.

Don

March 10, 1995
Dear Gary,

So it's Dawn Powell's fifteen minutes, is it? Well deserved. My favorite quote from her, re her writing method: "I give my characters their heads. They provide their own nooses." We know people who knew her, and I believe Abby met her a few times. So I was delighted when I saw *Locusts* being considered.

Alas, no. There's no good movie in there, though some callow youth might find a bad one; Winona Ryder and Brad Pitt dressing up in their parents' clothes again. The problem is, her books were never plot driven, and they weren't even character driven. They were attitude driven, and nothing staledates faster than attitude (except politics, of course). A mournful pass.

Don

TO HENRY MORRISON

Henry Morrison had been Westlake's agent, but at this point Westlake was unrepresented.—Ed.

March 28, 2005
Dear Henry,

Here I go again, breaking a cardinal rule in the freelance writer's sacred oath: putting a little something on paper for free. Well, at least it's a first draft.

Our lunch was not only very pleasant, but also very useful. I've always enjoyed your skill at changing the subject, and I particularly liked it this time. To rid ourselves quickly of the topic I brought in with me, Richard Dannay agreed I should stay with Tuttle-Mori and let the comic book lie in limbo, at least for now. So I e-mailed here and there in Japan and did nothing about the comic, but will say "not now" if he resurfaces.

Now to the sequel. I had to think longer and harder on that. What is my five-year plan? Is Warner Books a part of it? Are you a part of it? What, at this point, do I want?

You may be right—in fact I'm sure you're right—that opportunities have been missed in forwarding my career, particularly after *The Ax* but also at other nexi—can that be right?—here and there. Do I now try to recapture a moment and take a different fork in the road? Is that possible? Is it worth it?

I am not rich, but I am comfortable, and see no reason for that to change, so economics can't drive me the way it did when I was elbow deep in growing children. Whatever my position may be in the writing world is pretty well fixed, I believe; the reputation and the glory are unlikely to alter much, unless I write a glowing biography of Osama Bin Laden. So, much more than earlier in my life, it's a dealer's choice.

One reason why *The Ax* didn't change things, and *Kahawa* didn't change things, and *Humans* didn't change things, is that I am not consistent. Can you imagine Wodehouse writing any of those three? Can you imagine Jonathan Franzen writing the Dortmunder novels? No publisher can count on me, because I can't help myself; I follow what interests me. And that—new scents to follow—has slowed a bit of late.

I'm still earning in the screen world. I've done one thing this year and have been asked to do a screenplay to a Heinrich Boll novel which I'll do if the deal is right. I want, on the other side, to finish the Stark novel that's been giving me trouble, then do whatever occurs to me to complete the Westlake contract with Warner, then not commit myself at all. Do whatever comes next, make the best deal I can for it, and go on. When the time comes, I'll fire a warning shot across your bow and we'll see if you're interested. Until then, I appreciate the time and the advice. Thank you.

Don

TO JON L. BREEN

Jon L. Breen is editor of *Murder Off the Rack: Critical Studies of Ten Paper-back Masters,* to which Westlake contributed the essay on Peter Rabe.—Ed.

December 10, 1986
Dear Mr. Breen,

A lot of work for no money. As my agent, Knox Burger assures me, this is the kind of offer I seem unable to resist. "Okay," as Joseph Cotten said in *The Third Man*, "I'll be your dumb decoy duck." He was a writer, too.

However, I am a mere grazer on the lower slopes of the lit biz, so you'll have to explain a couple of things to me, such as:

What is MLA format?

What is a Sherlockian-type speculation? "I *think* this is Turkish tobacco." Like that, you mean?

I've started rereading Rabe, and by golly he *was* good, and if I can find out why his career ended so shortly after it began I'll include that in the piece. Critically, of course, not descriptively.

By the way, I mentioned to Coe and Stark that your wife Rita doesn't like their books. Coe cried, but Stark left the house and I haven't seen him since. Maybe you ought to mention this to Rita.

Don

THIRTEEN JOBS
NEVER PULLED

Title Ideas

In his files Westlake kept typed lists of title ideas, divided into crime titles and comic crime titles. Over the years, a few were struck through as they were used; fans will notice that Westlake also struck out one title, *Dead of Night*, that he never used.—Ed.

CRIME TITLES

~~Nobody Runs Forever~~

Death of the Party

Long Shot

The Mannequin

Crossfire

Cry of Alarm

Blind Spot

Clay Pigeon

Cloak and Dagger

Lady in the Mirror

Blind Alley

Checkmate

Fair Warning

Fatal Lady

The Final Night

Dark Angel

Hideout

Dead Wire

Crack Shot

Cross Purposes

Danger Sign

The Bolt from the Blue

Riddle Me This

Slaying Song

The Other Side of the Night

Died in the Wool

Delegate at Large

~~Dead of Night~~

Never Say Die

Night Hawk

Quick Money

The Night Riders

Walk a Crooked Mile

Ride a Crooked Mile

Ready Money

Trouble Ahead

Sudden Money

Wake Up and Die

Whipsaw

The Wrong Road

Dead Cinch

Gun Money

The Long Pursuit

Seven Men and a Bank

Dark Glitter

After Midnight

All the Past Is Here

Beyond the Night

Borrower of the Night

City of Night

Clash by Night

The Dark Backward

Corkscrew

Deadly Night

Here Lies Yesterday

In No Time

Into the Night

Lonely Again

Night Hawk

~~Nobody Runs Forever~~

Old Times

The Other Side of the Night

Out of the Night

Past and Gone

The Road Back

The Story of the Night

Yesterday Is Here

Whirligig

Back to the Wall

Afternoon Women

Cry for the Moon

Fair Dame

Not Yet, But Soon

The Fifth Down

Sudden Laughter

The Maiden All Forlorn

Wit's End

Man Here Says He Has a Gun

The Lady Tries Her Luck

Harlequinade

The Trumpets of Liliput

The Seamster and the Teamtress

~~Comeback~~

All Fools in a Circle

Mouse among the Cats

Hard and Fast

Free and Easy

Escapade

Kaleidoscope

Flying Colors

Road Story

Ill Met by Moonlight

The Road Back

The White Silence

Safety in Numbers

COMIC CRIME TITLES

Kid Stuff

Babes in the Wood

Hammer and Tongs

The Plot Thickens

Smart Alex

The Deuce

Through Thin

Winking Streak

Oops

Off the Hook

Wit's End

Out of the Jaws of Victory

All of Life is 6 to 5 Against

Don't Make Me Laugh

The State of the Art

Another Day, Another Dolor

~~The Scared Stiff~~

The Farmer in the Well

The Crookbook

~~Too Many Crooks~~

League of Rogues

Crook's Tour

A Crooked Smile

The Babbling Crooks

Crook Your Little Finger

A Crooked Stile

The Shepherd's Crook

The Crook of the Month Club

Crook Burning

A Lean and Hungry Crook

Crooked Circle

Crook in the Ice

The Crook of Doom

The Crook on the Hearth

Jiminy Crooked

A Crook in Time

Thick as Thieves

Question Time

Miscreant's Way

False Profits

No Score

On the Bend

Worse Than a Crime

The Soft-Boiled Yegg

Idle Hands

Sticky Fingers

Rough Stuff

Publish, and Be Damned

Black and Blue and Read All Over

Read Me

FOURTEEN DEATH ROW (OR, THE HAPPILY EVER AFTERLIFE)

Letter to Ralph L. Woods

Westlake often received letters from writers assembling anthologies or jour-nalists writing articles that asked his opinion on a specific question—like Ray Broekel's question about chocolate bars found earlier in this book. As they were perfect occasions for joking, he couldn't resist answering. The letter below, to Ralph L. Woods, was written in response to a question about the afterlife.—Ed.

October 7, 1975
Dear Mr. Woods:

The last time I thought deeply I got the bends. If I ran into Socrates, for instance, I'd be likely only to want to ask him what hemlock tastes like; potentially useful information, if people write books in the afterlife. And if they don't write books, what's the point?

Nobody has ever been able to describe for me what the afterlife is beyond *the simple continuation of existence*. Does personality continue? If so, then Heaven can't very well be heavenly. Who am I if I'm not working on a book? The afterlife sounds to me to have much the same quality as a prefrontal lobotomy.

Therefore, if I am to assume life after death, and if I am to further assume that the me over there would still be recognizably me, then I would like to meet O. Henry, Mark Twain, Ambrose Bierce and Dashiell Hammett, sit down with a bottle of beer—I won't be on a diet then—and talk shop for a century or two. After that, I'd like to go off with Robert Benchley and look for girls.

Sincerely yours,
Donald E. Westlake

ACKNOWLEDGMENTS

Thanks to all my colleagues at the University of Chicago Press for making it a place that I feel honored, happy, and grateful to work at every single day. Thanks also to two of my most reliable Westlake informants, Trent Reynolds, whose Violent World of Parker (www .violentworldofparker.com) site is essential, and Nick Jones of Existential Ennui (www.existentialennui.com). Parker would trust those two on a job any day. My early readers, Charles Ardai (whose Hard Case Crime publishing enterprise introduced me to Westlake) and Sarah Weinman, earned great thanks by giving generously of their time and knowledge of Westlake's work and crime fiction in general. And thanks to Lawrence Block, whom I've been reading since an auspicious trip to the Carmi Public Library at sixteen landed me *A Ticket to the Boneyard*, for his fine foreword. Speaking of libraries, I also owe thanks to the Chicago Public Library and the University of Chicago Library and their staffs for help with the research for this book.

Bonus thanks to Ethan Iverson (http://dothemath.typepad.com) for his unparalleled knowledge of Westlake and his indispensable help in going through Westlake's cryptically organized files. And to Ethan's wife, Sarah Deming, for her cooking and her company during our trip to the Westlake house, where Abby Adams Westlake was a gracious, friendly hostess and raconteur. I'll be forever grateful to Abby for trusting her late husband's legacy to me, and to Chicago. I hope we've done him proud.

To my mom, for giving me Agatha Christie, my dad, for giving me John D. MacDonald, and to Stacey Shintani, for happily living with me in a house full of books. And finally, ultimately, to Donald Westlake, for the countless hours of pleasure he gave us all.

CREDITS

"Writers on Writing: A Pseudonym Returns From an Alter-Ego Trip, With New Tales to Tell," originally published in the *New York Times* on January 29, 2001, is reproduced courtesy of the *New York Times*.

"The Hardboiled Dicks," originally published in *The Armchair Detective*, volume 17, issue 1, is reproduced courtesy of Otto Penzler.

"Introduction to *Murderous Schemes*," originally published in *Murderous Schemes: An Anthology of Classic Detective Stories* (Donald E. Westlake and J. Madison Davis, editors), is © 1996, Oxford University Press, and is reproduced by permission of Oxford University Press.

"Ten Most Wanted," originally published in *The Armchair Detective Book of Lists* (Kate Stine, editor), is reproduced courtesy of Otto Penzler.

"Introduction to *Kahawa*," from *Kahawa* by Donald E. Westlake. Copyright © 1994 by Donald E. Westlake. By permission of Grand Central Publishing. All rights reserved.

"Peter Rabe," originally published in *Murder Off the Rack: Critical Studies of Ten Paperback Masters* (Jon L. Breen and Martin Harry Greenberg, editors), is reproduced courtesy of Scarecrow Press / Rowman & Littlefield.

"Foreword to *Thurber on Crime*," from *Thurber on Crime* by James Thurber. Copyright © 1991 by Rosemary A. Thurber. By permission of Grand Central Publishing. All rights reserved.

"The Worst Happens," originally published in *Sight and Sound,* Autumn 1990, and later, in expanded form, in *Backstory 4: Interviews with Screenwriters of the 1970s and 1980s* (Patrick McGilligan, editor), is reproduced courtesy of *Sight and Sound* and the University of California Press.

INDEX OF NAMES AND TITLES

Interlenghi, Franco, 157
Ivernel, Daniel, 157
Iverson, Ethan, 213

Jacobs, Alexander, 156
Jewison, Norman, 153

Karina, Anna, 157
Kastner, 157, 158–60
Kaye, Danny, 141
King, Stephen, 197–99; *On Writing*, 197
King, Tabitha, 193, 197–99
Klass, Phil. *See* Tenn, William
Knight, Damon, 109
Kubrick, Stanley, 88; *The Killing*, 88

Ladd, Alan, 85
Landers, Hal, 156, 161, 164
Laurel, Stan, 23
Laurent, Georges, 156
Lefcourt, Helen, 165
Lehane, Dennis, 62
Lehrer, Tom, 87
Lenny, 159
Leonard, Elmore, 128, 129
Leone, Sergio, 52; *The Good, the Bad, and the Ugly*, 52
Le Person, Paul, 157
Lion, Bess, 180
List, John, 165
Little Caesar, 116
Lord, Sheldon, xii. *See also* Block, Lawrence
Lord Peter Wimsey series (Dorothy L. Sayers), 33, 76
Lorre, Peter, 160
Ludlum, Robert, 19

MacDonald, John D., xviii, 47, 52, 105, 122, 145–47, 214; *Cape Fear*, 122; *The End of the Night*, 147

Macdonald, Ross, 20, 46, 47, 49–50, 52, 105; *Black Money*, 49–50; Lew Archer series, 46, 49–50. *See also* Millar, Kenneth
Mackendrick, Alexander, 165; *A Boy Ten Feet Tall* (a.k.a. *Sammy Goes South*), 165–66
Maggott, Poll, 180
Maibaum, Richard, 160
Mailer, Norman, 10, 109
Manners, William, 72
"Man Who Read John Dickson Carr, The" 53
Marshall, Alan, xi, xii. *See also* Westlake, Donald E.
Marvin, Lee, 28
Matheson, Richard, 64
Matthau, Walter, 137
May, Elaine, 137
Mayes, Wendell, 156
McAleer, John J., 132–33
McBain, Ed, 72, 78; 87th Precinct series, 87. *See also* Hunter, Evan
McCall's, 119
McCarthy, Eugene, 51
McGilligan, Patrick, 163–70
McLuhan, Marshall, 38
McNeely, Thomas H., 62
McRea, Joel, 192
Meredith, Scott, 10, 11, 109
Merrill, Judith, 64
Mike Shayne's Mystery Magazine, 81
Millar, Kenneth, 46. *See also* Macdonald, Ross
Miller, Arthur, 105
Milligan, Spike, 192; *The Goon Show*, 190–92
Mills, Robert P., 68
Mitchum, Robert, 161
Mnouchkine, Alexandre, 156
Mona Lisa, 122
Money Trap, The, 88

Roberts, Bobby, 156, 161, 164
Robinson, Edward G., 166, 185, 186
Rockefeller, Nelson, 25–26
Rogers, Joel Townsley, 73; *The Red Right Hand*, 73
Rosaire, Forrest, 37
Ross, Harold, 140
Ruben, Joe, 165–66; *The Stepfather*, 165–66
Runyon, Damon, 58, 129
Ryan, Robert, 164
Ryder, Winona, 204

Sabaroff, Robert, 156
Salt, Gary, 203–4
Santesson, Hans Stefan, 72
Schaefer, Jack, 40; *Shane*, 40, 52
Scott, Justin, 102
Secombe, Harry, 192
Sellers, Peter, 192
Sergeant Bilko, 91
Shakespeare, William, 13, 196; *The Tempest*, 42
Shaw, Captain Joseph M., 36
Sheckley, Robert, 64
Sheldon, Sidney, 20
Sheppard, Jack, 179–83
Shintani, Stacey, 214
Sidney, Sylvia, 83
Silvers, Phil, 91
Silverstein, Shel, 62
Simenon, Georges, 105
Sinatra, Frank, 51
Smith, Thorne, 19, 116
Socrates, 211
Spillane, Mickey, 17, 46–47, 48–49, 114; *I, the Jury*, 46–47; Mike Hammer series, 15, 17, 36, 46–47, 48–49, 52
Stahl, Levi, xiii
Stark, Richard, 13–22, 23, 24, 26, 27–30, 80, 82, 83, 93–94, 99, 100–101, 153, 154, 155, 156, 157–58, 160, 161, 162, 164, 205, 206; *Backflash*, 29; *Breakout*, 173; *Comeback*, 29; *The Damsel*, 160; *Deadly Edge*, 161; *Firebreak*, 29; Grofield series, 27, 155, 160; *The Hunter*, xvii, 80, 82, 156; *The Jugger*, 156; *The Outfit*, 156, 164; Parker series, xvii, xviii, 14, 15, 26, 27–30, 82, 83, 93, 95, 154, 155, 157–58, 173; *The Score*, 156; *The Seventh* (a.k.a. *The Split*), 156, 186. *See also* Westlake, Donald E.
Starr, Ben, 156
Star Wars, 189
Steinbeck, John, 105
Stine, Kate, 73; *The Armchair Detective Book of Lists*, 73
Stout, Rex, 132–36; *The Doorbell Rang*, 133; *The Father Hunt*, 133–35; *Fer-de-Lance*, 134; *The Mother Hunt*, 136; Nero Wolfe series, 132–36
Sturges, Preston, 192; *Sullivan's Travels*, 192
Suatet, Claude, 156
Susskind, David, 161–62

Tamiroff, Akim, 186
Tenn, William (Phil Klass), 155
Thirty-Nine Steps, The, 83
Thompson, Jim, 27, 143, 144, 145, 166–68; *The Grifters*, 27, 143–45, 163, 166–68; *The Killer Inside Me*, 167
Thurber, James, 138–42; "How the Kooks Crumble," 140; *The Male Animal*, 141; "The Man Who Knew Too Little," 141; *Thurber on Crime*, 138–42
Tolkin, Michael, 169–70
Tony Rome, 51
Top Banana, 137
Trollope, Anthony, 198
Tunc, Irene, 157
Twain, Mark, 61, 212
Tyre, Nedra, 16